WORLD
WAR I

DAVID SHERMER

CHANCELLOR PRESS

Introduction by
A.J.P. Taylor

WORLD
WAR I

CHANCELLOR
PRESS

Cover photograph: Corbis, UK

First published in 1975 by Octopus Books Ltd

This 1998 edition published by Chancellor Press
an imprint of Reed Consumer Books Limited
Michelin House, 81 Fulham Road, London SW3 6RB

ISBN 0 75370 034 4

A CIP catalogue record for this book is available
at the British Library

Printed and bound in China

Produced by Toppan Printing Co., (H.K.) Ltd

Contents

Introduction by A.J.P. Taylor

To contemporaries the war which began in August 1914 and ended with the armistices of autumn 1918 was quite simply the Great War – an experience without parallel, eclipsing all previous wars and, it was hoped, the last war of all time. The combatants were far more numerous than ever before; the dead and mutilated correspondingly numerous also. The material destruction was staggering both on the battlefields and in the general loss of national wealth. All the Great Powers of Europe were involved. The United States of America intervened in European affairs for the first time. The war extended into Asia and Africa. Naval engagements took place in the South Atlantic and the Pacific. The Great War shook monarchs off their thrones, destroyed four great empires, endangered the existing social order and sometimes brought it to the ground. The old landmarks disappeared. General Smuts declared: 'Mankind has struck its tents and is on the march.' Men of the time felt that they were adrift on an uncharted sea, with the old days of security gone for ever.

How does the Great War appear 50 years after, when mankind has experienced a second war, more truly worldwide and even more destructive in its effects? Has the Great War become merely another historical episode, a war much like any other? Certainly it has passed into history. The survivors are now elderly men, nearly all of them living in retirement. President de Valera is one of the few exceptions. The physical wounds of war have all healed without apparently leaving any lasting scar, although the death toll was enormous. The British Empire lost a million dead. France lost a million and a half and Germany a million and three-quarters. Russia lost more than all the other combatants put together. But there has been no permanent effect. No country was diminished for generations as Germany was by the Thirty Years War. No community was obliterated as many were by the barbarian invasions centuries earlier. Germany, Great Britain and France did not fall out of the ranks of the Great Powers, as Sweden and Holland had done after wars in previous centuries. Every country which took part in the Great War has now a larger population than it had in 1914.

The material destruction was also soon overcome. Though great, it was limited in area – northeastern France, parts of Poland and Serbia, a remote corner of Italy. All this was restored within ten years, if not on the highest esthetic standard. The actual loss of economic resources was also temporary. Economists calculate that the combatants 'wasted' ten years of economic effort. By 1924 most European countries had surpassed the level of 1914. Even Russia, devastated also by revolution and famine, reached that level by 1927.

But immediately after the war this recovery seemed to be far in the future. Most men imagined that their countries had come near to ruin. Their most pressing problem was: 'How shall we ever pay for this war?' This was a misleading question. Every country had paid for the war while it was being fought, in the sense that the munitions had been produced and the armies sustained without economic collapse, except in Russia. But the Governments had not paid for the war out of taxation. They had paid for it out of loans. Even the British government only met 28% of the war bill from taxation. War debts seemed crushing in every country. So far as these were internal, owed by governments to their own citizens, they were merely bookkeeping transactions. Governments could pay the full interest on the loans from taxation as happened in Great Britain. They could lessen the burden by depreciating the currency as happened in France. They could repudiate the loans by destroying the currency altogether as the German government did. The real national wealth of capital equipment – factories, railways, houses – was unaffected. Even maintaining the loans in full only meant that the poor paid tribute to the rich for the privilege of having been allowed to fight and die.

Debts from one country to another were a different matter. All the former Allies owed enormous sums to the United States. These war debts caused bitterness for many years until they were virtually repudiated in the early 1930's. The real economic significance of the war came from the fact that European countries, especially Great Britain, had drawn on their overseas investments in order to meet their bills. It was even supposed that Great Britain had ceased to be a creditor country. This was far from the truth. Great Britain still had vast investments overseas and more than replaced those she had lost during the last few years. Her decline as the financial centre of the world came from causes which had little to do with the war. The United States, for example, was already a far greater industrial power than Great Britain, war or no war. Great Britain was saddled with out-of-date industries. Other countries were becoming industrialized and had less need for British goods. The war simply accelerated the process. Here was a problem which is always recurring: the world was changing at a great rate, and men blamed the war for changes which had little to do with it. As often happens, war accelerated the changes. It did not cause them.

This was true also in political affairs. Sociologists make great play nowadays with the 'participation' factor. Men, it is said, were drawn into contact with the state as they had never been before. Politicians had to address a wider audience and to remember that they could not succeed without popular support. This was undoubtedly the case. Millions of men were drafted as soldiers into the service of the state where previously they had hardly been aware of its existence. Whatever the machinery of coercion, they had in the last resort to be persuaded. Hence public opinion became more important. The instruments for affecting it were still crude. Newspapers were virtually the only means of spreading information or propaganda, and most of them did not reach a wide readership. In Great Britain, for example, only the Daily Mail had what would now be called a mass circulation, and that, at something over one million, would seem derisory nowadays. Statesmen could address the public only at political meetings, bellowing their case without the aid of a microphone. Thus, though everyone was affected by the war, only a minority received any direct information of what it was about, either in the newspapers or at public meetings. Political affairs were still decided by the group at the top – members of Parliament, themselves often ill-informed, and above them the closed circle of ministers with a few of them exercising the real power.

The essential difference was that statesmen had now to succeed or at least to give the impression of doing so. It is sometimes said that the war shook men's faith in governments. This is a half-truth. Where governments ran the war badly, their prestige was shaken or destroyed. This happened most obviously in Russia and Austria-Hungary and to some extent in Italy. Where governments appeared to run the war reasonably well, respect for them went up. Great Britain was more stable politically after the war than it had been before it. In 1926 the social order could face the challenge of a general strike without the slightest tremor – an achievement impossible to imagine earlier. The German government also enhanced its standing by the efficiency with which it ran the war, although with defeat this gain was rapidly cancelled. Hence the confusion of German politics later, when governments swung from extreme weakness to excessive power – both the legacies of war.

'Advance to democracy'
Ostensibly the advance to democracy was completed. Universal male suffrage was established after the war in every European country except Hungary and Monaco. Defeat brought ruin politically, though not financially, to many European monarchs. The German Emperor lost his throne, and every lesser German king or grand duke along with him. The Emperor of Austria and the Sultan of Turkey lost their empires as well as their thrones. The Emperor of Russia lost both throne and life. Before the war there were only two republics in Europe, or, if we count the Swiss confederation which did not call itself a republic, three. After the war there were twelve, and even where kings survived they had to operate within democratic constitutions. But only in Russia was the old governing class completely swept away. Elsewhere those who had ruled before continued to do so.

In some parts of Europe there was a more serious social change. Before the war great estates had been the rule in all Europe east of the Elbe. Now many of these estates were broken up.

In Russia the landowners were expropriated without compensation and often lost their lives as well. In Czechoslovakia, Rumania and to a lesser extent Yugoslavia, there was a land reform which got rid of the great estates more painlessly. The aristocracy disappeared. Instead there came peasant politicians who changed the character of politics. Aristocrats survived in Poland, Hungary and even in supposedly democratic Germany. A second world war was needed to get rid of them.

Democracy was one of the catch phrases with which the Allies fought the war. Nationalism or, in the phrase of the time, self-determination was the other. Strictly speaking they were not synonymous. Self-determination might only mean that men should be free to choose the state they lived in, not that every nationality had a right to independence, and this is probably what President Wilson had in mind when he launched the idea. In practice nationalism was supposed to have triumphed in 1918. This was not really true. Only the defeated peoples – Germans, Hungarians, Bulgarians – had national states virtually without minorities. The new states which established themselves as Allies were national conglomerations. The Poles comprised only two-thirds of the population of Poland, and the Rumanians were little better off in Rumania. The Czechs and Serbs were minorities in the two states – Czechoslovakia and Yugoslavia – where they constituted the governing nation.

The real political change produced by the war was that men were now loyal to a nation where previously they had been loyal to a King or Emperor. Monarchy lost much of its prestige even where it survived. Territorially the greatest change, transforming the political map from Switzerland to the Persian Gulf, was the disappearance of the Habsburg and Ottoman empires. The Habsburg Monarchy had existed longer than the Roman Empire in the West. The Ottoman Empire had continued for 450 years the Roman Empire in the East which had existed for a millennium. Now both were dismembered. Vienna and Constantinople dwindled from imperial capitals into relatively provincial towns.

The disappearance of the Ottoman Empire is a reminder that the effects of the Great War were not confined to Europe, were indeed greater outside Europe. The new European states, though nationalistic, continued the political habits of earlier times. The way of life in, say, Prague or Warsaw was not much changed for the ordinary citizen: the same occupations, the same newspapers. In Asia the Great War brought a deeper revolution. Politically there was a vacuum. The Allies tried to fill it in two different ways. Theoretically they gave the benefits of national freedom as they had done in Europe. So-called national states were set up – Syria, Transjordan, Iraq. In fact there was no national feeling, at best a vague pro-Arab sentiment which extended across the new frontiers. The political habits of Europe were superficially adopted just as the Arab leaders wore European clothes. The underlying reality was unchanged.

These states were a facade for the practical Allied policy of transforming the former Ottoman Empire into British and French colonies, thinly disguised as mandates. The French carried off Syria, much to the distaste of its inhabitants. The British took the rest: the Empire stretched from Egypt to the frontiers of India, richly endowed with oil. The British were particularly ingenious in Palestine. They undertook the duty of establishing there a national home for the Jews, thus barring the French from proximity to the Suez Canal. Two legacies followed. The Middle East, as it was now called, became the key point of British imperial strategy for more than a generation and thus shaped the events of the Second World War. Much of Palestine developed, in time, from a Jewish national home into a Jewish national state and thus inserted Israel into the Arab world. All the problems of the Middle East at the present day spring from the settlement of 1919.

The British and, to a lesser extent, the French empires reached their zeniths outside Europe in 1919. In Europe their position was diminished. This was hardly perceived when they stood out as victors, but it became clear in the following years. The European balance of power had not merely shifted against them. It had ceased to exist. Before the war there had been three Great Powers east of the Rhine – Germany, Austria-Hungary and Russia. Now Austria-Hungary had vanished, and Russia had ceased to count. France could no longer find effective allies to set against Germany, though she made a pretence of doing so with the new states. In 1919 the peacemakers tried to solve the problem of German power, or at any rate to postpone it, by imposing strict limits on German armaments. This was a contradictory arrangement. The victors were able to impose disarmament on Germany because they were temporarily the stronger. But they imposed this disarmament because they, particularly the French, recognized that this superiority wouldn't last.

Britannia Overruled

France's position was diminished in Europe. That of Great Britain was diminished in the outer world, although this was perhaps not apparent in 1919. Great Britain had then an army of continental size, which was probably the best fighting force in the world. The Dominions, the colonies and India had all rallied to the British side, and in 1919 it was believed, mistakenly, that the machinery of imperial unity had been permanently strengthened. At the end of the war Great Britain had added new territories to an Empire which was already the greatest the world had ever known. There was one great flaw: Britannia no longer ruled the waves, as she had done for the previous 200 years. This was the consequence of America's entry into the war in 1917.

There were other consequences, of course. Intervention by the United States helped to secure Allied victory in 1918. President Wilson attended the Peace Conference in Paris. It was expected that the United States would play a full part in the League of Nations and so in Europe thereafter. This expectation was belied when the American Senate refused to ratify the Treaty of Versailles. The United States did not join the League of Nations. It is true that they often exercised an indirect influence later in European affairs, particularly in the search for financial stability. American money aided German recovery and helped to make Germany the greatest power in Europe. Essentially the United States did not become permanently involved in European affairs until the Second World War, a generation later.

The American naval challenge, however, was made at once. Until 1914 the Americans had been willing to acquiesce in British naval supremacy, confident that it was a shield for them as much as for the British Dominions. During the war they resented the British blockade, though they participated in it when they became belligerents. After the war they were determined to assert naval equality with the British and were strong enough to do so. The British were in no position to resist. By the Washington naval treaty the British surrendered their sole domination of the seas forever. Between the wars Great Britain maintained naval equality with the United States and in the long run the American navy ruled the waves.

Nor was the United States the only challenger. During the war, Japan, though ostensibly a loyal ally, had established her naval supremacy in the Far East. After the war she refused to relinquish it. On paper she did not receive equality. Her capital ships were nearly a third less than those of either the United States or of Great Britain. But all her ships were in the Far East. British ships were spread over the world. From this moment Great Britain's naval power stopped at Singapore. Her position in the Far East rested solely on Japanese good will. The British Empire had depended on British sea power, and, though no one noticed it in 1919, this was now at an end.

These shifts in world power passed almost unregarded in 1919 when the Allies basked in the afterglow of victory. Men did not think then in terms of power. What they feared was social revolution. The Bolshevik Revolution of November 1917 then stood out as the most dramatic consequence of wartime. In Russia the old order had collapsed. Private property had been abolished. Private profit ceased to be the motive force of society. Instead the workers ruled, or so it was supposed. Socialism had triumphed: the Marxist Utopia had arrived. But Bolshevism in Russia was only the starting point; men feared that it would spread to the defeated countries. Nor were the victors immune. There were great strikes in Great Britain and France. The Red Flag flew over Glasgow Town Hall. In Italy the workers occupied the factories. Class war in its literal sense seemed about to break out.

The peril proved to be less than the men of 1919 feared. Certainly Soviet Russia survived the wars of intervention. The Bolsheviks, or Communists as they now called themselves, established a system of dictatorship in Russia which has lasted to the present day. In 1919 they set up the Third or Communist International in order to spread revolution throughout the world, but the Communists had surprisingly little success. There was a short-lived Soviet Government in Hungary and an even briefer one in Bavaria. Communist parties sprang up in nearly every country, and there were many admirers of Soviet society, but nearly everywhere these Communists and their associates remained an ineffective minority. Despite the upheavals of two world wars, capitalism is still the established economic system in most parts of the world, and private profit the main motive of economic activity.

'No More War'
Immediately after the war, it was universally believed that there had been a great change in the attitude towards war itself. The war had been 'a war to end war'. 'Never Again' and 'No More War' were the slogans of the 1920's, drummed home in nearly every war novel or book of reminiscences. Nor was this merely talk. The peacemakers of 1919 created an institution which, they hoped, would make future wars impossible. This was the League of Nations, President Wilson's most prized achievement. For the first time independent states acknowledged an international body, even if its authority was purely moral. Some people, such as H. G. Wells, hoped that the League of Nations would grow into the United States of the World. Such hopes were disappointed. The League became a useful meeting ground for statesmen. It controlled or attempted to control such anti-social activities as narcotics and the white-slave traffic. In 1928 the Kellogg Pact, renouncing war as an instrument of policy, was signed by every important country in the world. In practice the League was little more than a fifth wheel on the coach of international diplomacy, effective when the nations wished to agree, but impotent otherwise.

No country in fact renounced war, or at any rate preparations for war, whatever the statesmen might say or sign. The French maintained a large army. The British and Americans maintained large navies. All the new states introduced universal military service. The Germans, with their many grievances, numbered denial of their right to arm as the worst. Public opinion might turn against war. The statesmen still regarded war as a habit, though maybe a bad one. Men either drew the moral that all war was wrong or assumed that there was no practical moral to draw. The motives for the Great War or the methods of conducting it were rarely examined as practical questions. Indeed to the present day the Great War is treated as the first of its kind. In retrospect it seems remarkably old-fashioned. There was very little new in the way it was waged except that it was on a larger scale. Millions of men fought where hundreds of thousands fought before. But the equipment of armies was much the same. The artillery was heavier. The small-arms fire was more rapid, particularly when its rapidity was mechanized into the machine gun. But, almost to the end tactics were much the same as those operated by Napoleon a century before. Masses of men were flung against each other after a preliminary bombardment, and the cavalry waited for the breakthrough which never came.

Railways delivered men and supplies to the battlefront more quickly than horse-drawn transport had done. This, too, was not new. Railways had already shaped the strategy of the American Civil War and the Franco-Prussian War. Far from increasing mobility, railways increased the deadlock. The attackers always outran their supplies and lost their momentum. The defenders always fell back into security. Apart from railways, most of the war was fought as though the Industrial Revolution had never happened. Gas was an attempt at modernity and proved more of a handicap than a help. The internal combustion engine was only exploited late in the war. Staff officers used horses, not motor cars. Supplies were brought from railhead to the front by mule, not by truck. No army went over to troop-carrying transport.

The tank was the most remarkable innovation. But, again, it was used tardily and inadequately. Although used successfully by the British at Cambrai in 1917, and thereafter in France by both the British and the French, their armies, even so, moved slowly. The advance could still only move at the speed of the infantry, and the Allies never broke through the German lines. Twenty years after the First World War Marshal Pétain could still declare that the infantry were the Queens who moved at the speed of pawns. Similarly with communications, the armies still relied on runners, occasionally supplemented by the telegraph. Wires were laid everywhere. No army in the First World War communicated by wireless.

Naval strategy had some more modern features. The battleships themselves were machines of great ingenuity. But their purpose remained traditional: to draw out the line of battle against the enemy fleet. This was achieved once only, at the battle of Jutland, and then with no decisive result. There was one new naval weapon: the submarine. The Germans developed submarine warfare later and with inadequate preparation. Even so they nearly brought Great Britain to defeat. The British on their side had to devise impromptu means of defence against a danger which they had not foreseen. They ultimately triumphed by reverting to convoy – a traditional method which most British admirals condemned as unworkable.

The aeroplane was often extolled as a weapon of an entirely new kind which would change the face of war. During the Great War it did not do so. Aeroplanes were sometimes useful as observers. They fought dramatic battles against each other in the skies. Broadly speaking the course of the Great War would have been unchanged if aeroplanes had not existed. Both aeroplanes and tanks were portents for future wars, not instruments for the present one. After the war Liddell Hart in England, and Guderian and others in Germany, thought in terms of a strategy based on tanks. Similarly many authorities – Trenchard, Douhet, Billy Mitchell – foresaw a future war of bombardment from the air. Few of these speculations were based on experience, and not all of them turned out to be accurate. Tanks certainly shaped the Second World War on land. Aerial bombardment proved a false, and disastrous trail.

The politics of war were equally barren and without rational purpose. Governments had the organization of the home front forced on them by events and undertook it more or less successfully. None of them, except that of Communist Russia, drew the moral that measures adopted in wartime for the control of economic and social life could also be organized for peaceful purposes. Economic direction and control were jettisoned everywhere as soon as the war was over. Looking round Europe a few years after the war, one observer remarked that Summer Time – the advancing of the clock by one hour during the summer months – was the only permanent change which the war had brought in social affairs. An Englishman could add the closing of public houses during the afternoon.

What was the war about? How can it be explained to future generations? The ostensible reasons for war were lost sight of once it had started. For instance, Austria-Hungary began the war in order to exact reparation for the assassination of Archduke Franz Ferdinand. This demand was never mentioned during the secret peace negotiation which Austria-Hungary attempted in 1917. Great Britain went to war in order to protect the independence and neutrality of Belgium. Later her statesmen repeatedly declared that a German withdrawal from Belgium would not be an adequate reason for Great Britain to make peace. Both Russia and France went to war in order to defend their national territory. Russia could have had a separate peace on the basis of the status quo in 1915, and France could probably have had one in 1917. Both countries rejected such ideas out of hand. Germany had started the war from the belief that she could not sustain a prolonged war on two fronts and must therefore knock out France within six weeks. Though she failed to knock out France, she sustained a two-front war for four years and achieved considerable victories during the process. Ironically, in fact, she lost the war only when the second, Russian front ceased to exist and Germany was fighting a one-front war.

All the belligerents devised war aims as justification for going on with the war. Few of these aims, perhaps none, were worth the price which the belligerents ultimately had to pay for them. Italy could have had peace at any time, and the Italian-speaking part of Tyrol with it. Instead she got impoverishment and Fascism, all for the sake of German-speaking Tyrol and Istria. Austria-Hungary could have got out of the war by making a few concessions to Italy. By refusing these, she prepared the way for her own disintegration. Russia demanded Constantinople and the Straits, acquisitions which her own statesmen regarded as too burdensome to be worth having. Her reward was social collapse and revolution. It is useless to speculate what the Turks were fighting for. But there is little doubt that they could have had peace at any time if they had merely stopped.

France claimed to be fighting for Alsace-Lorraine, which she could not have on any terms short of Germany's defeat. Even so the destruction of a generation was a high price to pay. The Germans formulated the most ambitious war aims, particularly the economic control of Belgium and north-eastern France. The integration of these areas with the Ruhr was already developing before the First World War and has been achieved, despite the defeat of Germany, after the Second. The British tried to persuade themselves and others that they were fighting in order to acquire German colonies. A celestial chartered accountant, considering the balance sheet of war, would have said at any time during it: 'Cut your losses'.

The war in fact was fought for its own sake. Once the war had begun, the belligerents could see no way of ending it except by the total defeat of the enemy. Germany had to destroy Russia and France in order to be secure in Europe and so free to become a World Power. France and Russia had to defeat Germany if they were to survive as independent Powers. Austria-Hungary had to defeat somebody if she were to survive at all. Great Britain had to destroy the German navy and to secure the independence of France if she were to remain a great imperial power. Previously peace had been a habit. Now war became a habit in much the same way. Only victory, it seemed, would provide the solution.

The statesmen went on with the war in order to protect themselves from revolution – thus often causing the revolution they dreaded. The peoples were equally obstinate. Though soldiers hated the trenches and civilians grumbled against harsh conditions, public opinion in every country applauded the warmakers and condemned those who sought a way out. Statesmen fell from power when they were alleged to be soft or ineffective in waging war – Bethmann in Germany, Asquith in England, the Tsar in Russia. The hard men – Lloyd George, Clemenceau, Ludendorff – triumphed. British soldiers sang this song:

We're here because we're here
Because we're here
Because we're here.

This was the spirit of the First World War. They fought because they fought because they fought because they fought. The war was not a great tribute to human wisdom.

CHAPTER ONE
The Conflagration Begins

Daily

NO. 4,438.

HEIR TO AUSTRIAN THRONE MURDERED.

ARCHDUKE AND HIS WIFE SHOT DEAD IN THE STREET.

DETERMINED PLOT.

BOMB FIRST THROWN AT THEIR CAR.

SECOND ATTEMPT WITHIN AN HOUR.

BOY ASSASSIN.

MURDERED
The Archduke Francis F

the burgomaster and the m
town council, and it was
that he was then in a fu
and bitterly resentful of s
period.
The burgomaster stepp

Above: News of the assassination made headlines, but few grasped the significance of this event. **Opposite, top left:** Sarajevo, 28 June 1914. Archduke Franz Ferdinand and his wife arrive for their triumphal procession. **Top centre:** After the first assassination attempt, the princely pair continued along the parade route. **Top right:** They arrive at the City Hall to be greeted by the Mayor. **Left:** The second attempt was all too successful.

The incident that provoked World War I was the assassination of the heir to the Habsburg throne, Archduke Franz Ferdinand, and his wife, Duchess Sophie. The underlying causes of the war were, of course, more complex and of longer standing. As Sir Basil Liddell Hart wrote, 'Fifty years were spent in the process of making Europe explosive.' Yet on 28 June 1914, the day of the double murder, a crisis began which seemed to lead inexorably to war.

The fact that Habsburg royalty were on that date in Sarajevo, capital of the Austrian province of Bosnia-Herzegovina and neighbour of independent Serbia, was a needless provocation. Serbia's greatest national festival, commemorating St Vitus and the medieval battle of Kosovo, was held on 28 June. But 28 June was also the fourteenth wedding anniversary of the Archduke and his morganatic wife. Franz Ferdinand's visit to Bosnia in his capacity of inspector general of the Austro-Hungarian armed forces gave him the chance to appear in public ceremonially with his beloved Sophie. In Vienna, on the other hand, the Duchess led a socially withdrawn life under the shadow of imperial disapproval of their marriage, since Sophie's rank was considered too low for marriage to the heir to the throne. So, ironically, it was Sophie's wedding anniversary treat that led her to death beside her husband.

Vladimir Dedijer, the leading historian of the Sarajevo incident, has noted that Duchess Sophie had arrived in Bosnia with forebodings of what was to come. She recalled that one of the leaders of the Bosnian assembly or *Sabor* had warned that the visit should be cancelled because of pan-South Slav feeling in the province, provoked by Serbia. Despite this and other warnings, the visit had to take place. Cancellation would have seemed an admission of Austrian nervousness. Yet the police protection of the imperial party was minimal, and but for the haphazard arrangements the badly-organized assassination attempt would never have succeeded.

Sunday, 28 June, was a bright and sunny morning in Sarajevo as the royal train pulled into the station. On hand to greet the royal couple was General Oskar Potiorek, military governor of Bosnia. Confusion occurred almost immediately. The first car in the procession was intended for security detectives, but somehow all but one of them was left behind at the station and only three local police officers were present. Security arrangements were bungled from the beginning.

The Archduke, his consort, and General

Potiorek travelled in an open Viennese sports car. As they drove along the Appel Quay, the Archduke, whose attitude towards attempts on his life was rather fatalistic, requested that the car be driven slowly so that he could have a good look at his surroundings. Although the crowds were thin, a few cheers rang out as the procession passed. Near the central police station, as General Potiorek was pointing out a new army barracks, a tall young man, Čabrinovič, suddenly hurled a hand grenade directly at the sports car from a nearby group of onlookers. The grenade bounced off the folded roof of the car and fell into the street, exploding under the next car in the procession and wounding several officers and about twenty of the crowd. As the Archduke's chauffeur accelerated towards the town hall, however, Franz

Right: Gavrilo Princip, who wiped out two lives and an era.

At that very moment a short young Bosnian, Gavrilo Princip, took out his revolver. A policeman tried frantically to grab his hand, but was struck by someone nearby. Emerging from the crowd at a distance of only four or five paces, Princip fired twice into the car. The first bullet mortally wounded the Archduke in the jugular vein. The second bullet entered the Duchess's abdomen. Duchess Sophie sank to the floor, her face between her husband's knees. The Archduke murmured, 'Soferl, Soferl, don't die. Live for my children.' Then he passed into unconsciousness. The car raced towards the Konak, Governor Potiorek's official residence, but the bumpy drive only worsened their condition, and the royal couple were pronounced dead shortly after arrival. As the bells of Sarajevo began to toll, none could have realized that their mournful clamour heralded four years of bloodshed and the death of millions.

Franz Ferdinand was far from popular in Vienna; but his death raised issues of far-reaching significance. Investigations eventually showed that the assassinations at Sarajevo had been organized by the Black Hand, a Serbian secret society headed by 'Apis', a shadowy figure who was also chief of Serbian military intelligence. The Serbian Prime Minister, Pasič, and possibly others in the Serbian government heard rumours of the existence of a plot against the Archduke; but Pasič had made only a half hearted attempt to warn Vienna against the Bosnian visit. The collective and direct complicity of the Serbian government was not proved, and after two Balkan wars in recent years, the Serbians were probably not anxious for further fighting. However, the responsibility for the murders was not assigned quickly or accurately enough to satisfy the Austrians. Serbian territory had been the base from which the assassinations were carried out, and there was a case for strong Austrian measures against Serbia.

The motives behind the double murder will probably never be fully known, but extreme Serb nationalists regarded Franz Ferdinand with fear because he advocated concessions to the South Slav minority of Austria-Hungary. The Black Hand felt that these concessions might detract from Serbia's position as a rallying point for South Slav discontent and as the nucleus of a future South Slav state. Thus the Archduke had to be eliminated. Furthermore, 'Apis' at least may have intended the killings to provoke war between Austria and Serbia, calculating that Russia, traditional patron of the small Slav nations, would ally with Serbia to force concessions from Austria. The Serbian press and public hardly bothered to conceal their pleasure at the murder of two members of the hated Austrian royal house. Thus, with tempers strained on every side, Austrian reprisals against Serbia could be expected.

In fact, the assassinations at Sarajevo could not go unchallenged if Austria-Hungary was to continue as a great power. The implications of the crisis were manifold. If Austrian reprisals resulted in Habsburg domination of Serbia, this would bring Austria-Hungary too close to the Dardanelles for Russia's comfort. For generations the

Ferdinand ordered a halt to see who had been injured by the attack. Until this was ascertained, the imperial car was a sitting target for a further assassination attempt. It was now discovered that Duchess Sophie's neck had been grazed, but she was otherwise unhurt.

The Archduke arrived at the town hall in an outraged mood. His wife's celebration had been spoiled. He immediately decided to visit one of the officers wounded by the grenade, who had been taken to a military hospital. The visit to a local museum would then proceed as arranged. Duchess Sophie had not originally intended to visit the museum, but now she insisted on remaining with her husband.

Setting out again, the imperial procession drove along Appel Quay at high speed. At this point another curious error occurred: evidently the chauffeurs had not been informed of the unscheduled visit to the hospital, for the first car turned right at the corner of Appel Quay and Franz Josef Street, and the second car followed. Potiorek shouted angrily to the driver of the third car that he was making a mistake. The chauffeur braked sharply, and the car stopped.

Straits had been the principal Russian interest in the Near East, for they were Russia's lifeline to much of the world beyond her borders. If, on the other hand, Serbian independence could be maintained, a decisive step would have been taken against the growing German and Austrian influence in the Balkans and Turkey.

Austria-Hungary was allied to Germany, Serbia was the protégé of Russia, and Russia was the ally of France. Italy and Rumania, although formally allied with Germany and Austria-Hungary, had shown signs of undependability. As for Britain, she had ententes – but not alliances – with France and Russia. These inter-relationships meant that potentially the Sarajevo crisis might escalate into a European war.

The Rise of Nationalism

In addition to the power manoeuvres of the great alliances, the Sarajevo incident took place in a period of virulent nationalism. Britain and France were powers that on the whole were sated and secure as a result of their colonial expansion. Their empires had brought them markets, raw materials, and prestige. Part of Russia's growing energies had been devoted to eastward expansion. Germany was different. She had become a nation only in 1871, too late to gain a share of the richer colonies. To Germany, as a young nation flexing its muscles and seeking its fortune, the situation was bitterly unjust. Germans thought that Britons and Frenchmen were denying them their rightful share of colonial influence. This was a situation that the Reich did not intend to tolerate indefinitely. Austria-Hungary was also in a sullen and confused mood, as pressures for change mounted among the minorities of her polyglot empire, and as Russian strength became a growing challenge to her Balkan policy. By 1914, many in Vienna had concluded that only a decisive move against Serbia, the stalking-horse of Russia, would sufficiently discourage South Slav disaffection and provide a unifying cause which might prolong the life of the enfeebled Habsburg empire. To such men, Sarajevo was a golden opportunity. The situation was the more fraught with danger because Germany and Russia also possessed influential factions which looked to war as a safety valve for national emotions, ambitions, and frustrations.

Kaiser Wilhelm II and Emperor Franz Josef led the Central Powers. Neither believed that military action against Serbia would lead to world war.

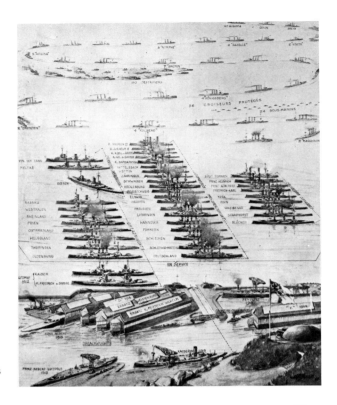

Left: British naval strength in 1914. **Right:** Germany's challenge to British naval hegemony was a major cause of the war.

'A Nightmare of Coalitions'

A closer look must be taken at the position of Germany. The outstanding issue in Europe for a generation had been a deadly-paradox, described by Cyril Falls as 'the arrogance which disguised Germany's anxieties.' Many would have judged the German future rich with promise, but Germany's anxieties'. Many would have judged as A. J. P. Taylor has noted, economic might in peacetime 'must have brought Germany the mastery of Europe within a few years', Germany saw only the fact of her 'encirclement' by the Franco-Russian alliance. Ironically, her reactions to her neighbours fed the very fears that had caused them to combine against her. To understand how this came about, we must examine the history of the preceding four decades.

The Rise of Germany

In 1871 Prussia defeated France and united the other German states into an empire. The German chancellor, Bismarck, felt the containment of a seething France was vital, and with this aim in mind in 1873 he associated Germany with Austria and Russia in the Three Emperors' League. By 1882 Italy had joined the alliance formed between Germany and Austria-Hungary in 1879, followed by Serbia in 1881 and Rumania in 1883. Then in 1887, Russia, by now estranged from Austria, negotiated her own treaty with Germany. France watched impotent as she was isolated from Europe by these manoeuvrings.

However, in 1890 the arrogant and unstable Kaiser Wilhelm II became jealous of Bismarck's prestige and dismissed him. Swiftly all Bismarck's worst fears were realized. Russia, rejected by the Kaiser in favour of Austria, allied herself with France, and at a stroke the Bismarckian policy of containment of France was destroyed.

It has been said of Bismarck that his aim toward Britain was to keep her 'in friendly isolation from Germany and unfriendly isolation from France'; but after his departure from office, Anglo-German relations soon deteriorated. This mounting ten-

sion resulted in Britain and France reconciling their major differences in the 'entente cordiale' of 1904. No formal alliance was established, but especially after the 1907 Anglo-Russian 'arrangement', France, Russia, and Britain became known as the Triple Entente, and formed an alliance in fact if not in name.

In 1905, Japan, already allied to Britain since 1902, defeated Russia in a war begun in 1904 over rival claims to influence in Korea. This momentarily strengthened Germany's position in the balance of power. However, in the same year German strong-arm threats to France over the future of Morocco drove the British and the French into a closer relationship. The next increase in tension occurred in 1908 when Austria annexed Bosnia and Herzegovina, thereby risking an Austro-Russian war by outraging Russian sensitivity on the subject of the Balkans. Germany, however, backed Austria and deterred any aggressive move by Russia. At this point, with France having been alienated in 1905 and Russia in 1908, with Britain still in disagreement with Berlin, and with Italy's attitude still uncertain, Austria remained Germany's only friend in Europe. Relations with Vienna assumed crucial importance if the Germans were not to be totally isolated.

In 1911 Germany increased her pressure on France by dispatching a gunboat to the Moroccan port of Agadir, but she was forced to climb down by British support of France. Between 1908 and 1911 German naval strength had been increasing faster than ever, and despite a degree of outward friendliness, Britain, traditional bastion of naval power, viewed these developments with suspicion.

The Arms Race

The level of armaments was now increasing throughout Europe. Haunted by fears of a sudden outbreak of war, politicians allowed their generals to formulate ingenious but fatally rigid war plans and mobilization procedures. Flexibility and manoeuvre took second place, and by 1914 Europe was a powder keg awaiting a spark.

Opposite above: The British battle cruiser *Inflexible* was ready to fight in 1914. **Below:** Britain's feared dreadnoughts lead the fleet out to sea: 18 July 1914.

Nun bin ich wieder gerne Soldat.

Many reservists were delighted to have the opportunity to wear their uniforms daily. But the war was not to be as glamorous as some supposed.

Laurence Lafore wrote of Austria and the crisis of July 1914: 'In a situation where coolness and skill were needed, alarm and clumsiness took their place and brought about the fatal steps to catastrophe.' In fact, heavy-handedness and bungling were not the prerogatives of Austria alone.

The initial reaction of Conrad von Hötzendorff, Austro-Hungarian Chief of Staff, to the Sarajevo murders was to move swiftly against Serbia. 'The hour has struck for the Monarchy,' he said, though he realized that immediate action was not feasible, since the necessary mobilization of forces would take about sixteen days. Conrad was opposed on practical grounds by Count Tisza, the Hungarian Prime Minister, who asked if German support would be forthcoming. Berchthold, the Austro-Hungarian Foreign Minister, was in urgent need of some bold measure to bolster his own sagging prestige. He decided to obtain advice from Berlin.

The Blank Cheque

The Sarajevo crisis was greeted in Berlin with conflicting counsels. Many Foreign Ministry personnel, seeing a potential chain of disaster, took a more moderate line than the military. However, on 5 July the Kaiser, seconded by Chancellor Bethmann-Hollweg, gave Vienna a 'blank cheque' for action against Serbia. As Szögyény, the Austro-Hungarian ambassador in Berlin, reported: 'Action against Serbia should not be delayed . . . Even if it should come to a war between Austria and Russia, we could be convinced that Germany would stand by our side . . .' Germany would be sorry to see Austria miss 'the present favourable moment' for strong measures.

Those who spoke thus in Berlin apparently felt that Austrian inaction, vaccillation, or delay would so reduce the prestige of the Dual Monarchy as to lead to severe repercussions, even the break up of the empire. The Kaiser himself was outraged at the shedding of royal blood, parti-

cularly that of the Archduke, a personal friend. He may have thought that Tsar Nicholas, similarly indignant, would keep Russia aloof from the crisis. Nevertheless, at the beginning of July the Kaiser had commented, 'The Serbs must be disposed of, and soon.' The German historian Fritz Fischer has suggested that the actions of the German government in early July perhaps show that Germany was using Sarajevo as an excuse to launch a preventive war against Russia; but this interpretation is highly controversial, and one can argue with equal success that Germany, feeling herself and Austria surrounded by hostility, saw Sarajevo as a fortunate chance to reassert her support for her ally. For even though Austria was a partner of dubious strength, Germany wanted to keep her away from the Franco-Russian alliance system.

Many historians have argued that the Germans, either naïvely or disingenuously, thought that the approaching conflict might be confined to Austria and Serbia. Russia, Berlin reasoned, might be in a position to do little more than bluff ineffectively, though her strength was growing daily. It was widely felt that Russian ambitions in the Balkans and elsewhere made war with Germany inevitable sooner or later. The question was: could Germany wait until the Russian colossus turned on her?

By 14 July Tisza had substantially agreed to Conrad's arguments for a forward policy. Discussions in Vienna on 7 July showed that there was considerable fear on the part of Austria that if she did not now settle accounts with Serbia, German support in future was problematical. Some even feared a German-Russian settlement at Austria's expense. From Berlin Szögyény emphasized that Russia was preparing for eventual war and, as the German Foreign Secretary, Jagow, reiterated, that in a few years Russia would 'overwhelm us if she is not forestalled'.

If Austria allowed herself to become enmeshed in diplomatic negotiations over the assassinations, her enemies would have time to out-manoeuvre

The Austrian cavalry was an extravagant echo of a glorious past.

her. Thus it was decided to send Serbia an extremely stiffly-worded memorandum. If, as Austria expected, Serbia were uncooperative, an excuse for war would be provided. Despite Berlin's impatience toward the leisurely pace of Austrian preparations against Serbia, it was decided to lull foreign suspicions by allowing the usual annual holidays to be taken: Moltke, the German Chief of Staff, remained at Karlsbad until 25 July, and the Kaiser enjoyed his customary summer cruise.

The Austrians elected to delay their memorandum to Serbia until the completion of the state visit to Russia of the French President and Prime Minister, lest their presence in Saint Petersburg be used to stiffen the Russian position at the moment of crisis. On 22 July, perhaps acting under the influence of the French, the Russians had warned Austria not to present Serbia with unacceptable demands.

On 23 July the French state visit to Russia was completed. Immediately Vienna sent a strong memorandum to the Serbs. The note contained ten demands; the most important required that Serbia allow Austria to suppress local agitation against Austria-Hungary and take action herself

Austrian army uniforms were romantic and splendid.

against those involved in the Sarajevo crime. Emperor Franz Josef said on reading the terms: 'Russia cannot accept this . . . this means a general war.' He spoke prophetically, but no one listened. Sazonov, the volatile Russian Foreign Minister, echoed these sentiments when he learned of the contents of the Austrian note. The note was to be answered within forty-eight hours, although the Russians tried unsuccessfully to get the limit extended by another two days. But on 25 July, just before the time limit expired, Belgrade accepted most of the Austrian demands and offered to submit to arbitration those which infringed her sovereignty. Thus the Serbs had very cleverly put Vienna in the wrong by appearing in the guise of sweet reasonableness. As Lafore drily put it, 'Butter remained visibly unmelted in their mouths.' Yet they did not expect their reply to satisfy Vienna, for three hours before the reply was given, they had ordered mobilization.

Mobilization

On receiving the Serbian response, Austria-Hungary immediately broke diplomatic relations, and planned to commence war on 10 August, when mobilization would be completed. The Kaiser, however, returned from his cruise, and on 28 July learned the full story of events during his absence. Whether from sober second thoughts, or merely panic, his reaction was that Belgrade's compliance with most of the demands meant 'every reason for war disappears'. He suggested that in order to satisfy her honour, Austria should occupy the Serbian capital and then negotiate. However, his attempt to restrain Vienna was negated by the officials in Berlin. Bethmann-Hollweg did not relay the message until the evening of 28 July, and he omitted the crucial sentence that war was no longer necessary. By this time, Austria had already declared war on Serbia.

After the Serbian reply of 25 July, Ambassador Szögyény had telegraphed to Berchtold that Bethmann-Hollweg and Jagow were still advising the Austrians to act immediately and confront the world with an accomplished fact. Later, as British intervention in the dispute became more likely, Bethmann panicked and sent a series of telegrams to Vienna urging restraint. But Moltke was urging Vienna to push forward! Divided authority in Berlin assured recklessness in Austria, her junior partner.

The Serbian mobilization strengthened the hands of extremists everywhere. Only a few hours later, on 25 July, Austria ordered partial mobilization on the Serbian front, to begin on 28 July. On 25 July both Germany and Russia themselves began to prepare for mobilization. When her mobilization began on schedule on 28 July, Austria declared war on Serbia. War had come at that moment because Vienna felt in danger of being diverted into unwanted negotiations with Serbia.

Meanwhile, a double miscalculation had been made. Just as Austria expected Germany to neutralize a threat from Russia, the Russians hoped that their alliance with France, and British diplomatic pressure, would isolate Vienna. In fact, though Serbia was sometimes a nuisance and an embarrassment, Russia could not see her

President Poincaré visits Tsar Nicholas II and the Russian fleet: 25 July 1914.

protégé eliminated without in effect abdicating as a great power. However, the Russians had advised Belgrade to conciliate the Austrians and rely on the justice of the great powers, but little notice was taken of this counsel. The Serbians were aware of their influence on Russian attitudes; and indeed, Sazonov warned Pourtalès, the German ambassador in Saint Petersburg, that 'if Austria swallows Serbia we will make war on her'.

France was prepared to fulfill her treaty commitments to Russia, but on the whole she played a moderating influence throughout the crisis. In a sense, she could do little else, for although the French state visit to Russia lasted only from 20–23 July, the French leaders, Poincaré and Viviani, were away from Paris from 15–28 July, during which time policy-making machinery was paralyzed.

The British Commitment

Although there was no alliance between the two countries, the British had a strong moral commitment to France, more especially because of secret negotiations in recent years. Yet throughout the crisis, the British government was preoccupied with the domestic issue of Irish Home Rule. Given the mood of the times, neither government, Parliament, nor the people would have sanctioned an announcement that Britain stood firmly behind France and Russia in the event of general war. Grey, the Foreign Secretary, hoped that this very lack of commitment would weaken the forces pulling towards war in both Germany and Russia. What made British entry into the war unavoidable was the unprovoked German violation of the neutrality of Belgium, which Prussia, Britain, France, Austria, and Russia had guaranteed some seventy-five years earlier. The country was able to unite behind this total disregard of treaty obligations. For centuries a vital British interest had been to prevent the Low Countries from being dominated by a great power. German conquest of Belgium and France would have made this likely if not certain.

Between 24 and 26 July, Grey made various proposals for mediation of the Austro-Serbian dispute. Again, the temporizing effect of Berlin and Paris on Saint Petersburg and Vienna was overestimated. To add to the confusion, Britain warned that she might not stand aside from the conflict. Yet as late as 1 August, Grey refused a definite commitment to France on the grounds that the terms of the Franco-Russian alliance were unknown to the British government.

There is evidence that the German General Staff expected British participation in the war; but they did not worry much about it, influenced in part by the British Army's difficulties in the Boer War. More important, Germany expected to be able to knock France out of the war before British aid, if it were given, could be effective.

War with Serbia

The Austrian declaration of war against Serbia was followed on 29 July by the bombardment of Belgrade. Russia was deeply affected. Already, on 28 July, the Tsar had ordered partial Russian mobilization on the Austrian front, in this way trying to make it clear that Russia would not stand

Sir Edward Grey, the British Foreign Minister, who went bird watching shortly before the outbreak of war.

Previous page: When the Austrian navy mobilized, its ships were launched into the Adriatic.

aside if Austria attacked Serbia. The previous day, 27 July, Messimy, the French Minister of War, attempted to persuade the Russians to proclaim general mobilization and take the offensive, but the Tsar had restricted himself to bringing pressure to bear by partial mobilization. Meanwhile, the Russian generals themselves were also persuading the Tsar that any measures short of full mobilization were impracticable. Russian mobilization would take many weeks; and the generals argued that it must be started during the crisis in order to be effective if war later ensued. Tsar Nicholas agreed to commence general mobilization on 31 July; but later on 29 July, as a result of a message from the Kaiser, the Tsar reverted to his policy of partial mobilization. Nicholas was a man of naturally vaccillating temperament, and as the crisis gathered strength, he reversed himself once

more on 30 July, in the belief that German general mobilization would begin at any moment. The French government had called on Russia to present a cautious and non-provocative attitude towards Germany, but the transmission of this message may have been bungled or deliberately misinterpreted by Paléologue, the French ambassador to Russia. At this point the Russians lost their nerve and ordered mobilization before the Germans, who in turn ordered their own mobilization. Austrian general mobilization then followed on 31 July.

In fact, on 31 July Germany only declared a state of war emergency and demanded that Russia 'suspend every war measure against Austria and ourselves within twelve hours'. Falkenhayn, the Prussian Minister of War, felt that because German mobilization would be so much quicker than that of Russia, Germany could afford to wait a few days. But Moltke was adamant. Having received no satisfaction from Russia, Germany declared formal general mobilization and war against Russia on 1 August.

By now French involvement was certain. On 31 July, Germany sent an eighteen-hour ultimatum demanding that France define what her position would be during a German-Russian war. On 1 August, Vivani replied that 'France will act in accordance with her interests'. Meanwhile, the French General Joffre had been pressing for mobilization, and on the afternoon of 1 August the cabinet yielded. As it happened, even if the French had agreed to neutrality, the Germans had decided to demand the occupation of the French fortresses of Verdun and Toul as a pledge of good conduct – a humiliation which they knew no French government could tolerate.

The Schlieffen Plan

Why was it necessary for Germany to pick a quarrel with France? The answer lay in the rigidity of the German offensive plans. Moltke related in his memoirs that when the Kaiser questioned whether Britain would enter the war if Germany attacked only Russia, the general replied that war with Russia alone was impossible. Germany had only one war plan, and it could not be changed. This was the famous Schlieffen Plan, and it called for a swift knock out blow against France via a German sweep through Belgium, followed by a rapid transfer by rail of the victorious troops to the eastern front for the expected longer campaign against the Russians, who would take the six weeks required for victory in the West to complete their mobilization. On 2 August, therefore, Germany demanded passage through Belgium for her armies, a demand which was firmly refused. On 3 August, Germany declared war against France. The German war on two fronts had begun.

By 4 August, the threat to Belgium was uniting the British, and Grey issued an ultimatum demanding that Germany respect Belgian neutrality. When the ultimatum expired without result, war between Britain and Germany began at midnight, German time.

Why did the War Break Out?

How the war broke out is a subject for endless discussions and limitless conclusions.

After the Balkan wars, Austria's military men were afraid of Serbia's increased population and military might. In Germany, the soldiers looked with apprehension on Russia's swift recovery from her 1905 defeat by Japan. The feeling grew that war, if it had to come, would be more favourable to Germany and Austria now than later. Russia, for her part, was more and more concerned at increasing German influence over Turkey; if the 'sick man of Europe' were rejuvenated in the Balkans, Russian ambitions would be thwarted. Thus mutual fears and rivalries helped to create a situation in which swift escalation to war was possible.

Divided interests accelerated the advent of war. In Germany, for example, the desires of military, business and governmental circles conflicted in

Von Falkenhayn, the Prussian Minister of War. He wanted to wait. The Kaiser didn't.

many ways. As A. J. P. Taylor wrote, 'it was easier. . . to drift with events' than to take positive action. To make matters worse, in 1914 each of the great powers lacked a statesman who could see beyond the immediacy of events and pull his country back from the abyss. Emperor Franz Josef was almost senile, and both the Kaiser and the Tsar were unstable and impetuous. The British were preoccupied, and the French were without a leader through much of the crisis. Sir Edward Grey, the British Foreign Secretary, spent most of the month of July bird watching, and, with regrets, had to give up his pastime to return to London when the crisis deepened.

In addition, the sudden nature of the July crisis made improvisation necessary. Grey and Sazonov in particular confused the issue by making repeated suggestions before all the other powers had

had the opportunity to consider their previous proposals. Perhaps most remarkable of all, a mood of fatalism overcame many in the summer of 1914. It was as if men knew that peace in Europe was too happy a state of affairs to last.

Was Germany at Fault?

Although she felt that time was working against her and considered a preventive war more and more seriously, Germany had no long-term war plan timed for 1914. Such specific planning would have required an assertiveness and consistency which was lacking in both Bethmann-Hollweg and Moltke, not to mention the Kaiser. Under-writing Austrian grievances was an easy alternative. Even so, German support for Vienna was a crucial influence on the coming of war, for without the backing of Berlin, Vienna could never have acted as she did. Not all of this support was conscious, however, and Austria knew exactly how to play on divisions within the German ruling elite to get her own way.

Germany's situation was bitterly ironic. The Franco-Russian encirclement, which drove her on to war, was probably far less solid than she imagined. There were plenty of influential people in both countries who opposed the alliance. Russian strength might well have faltered due to revolution, as in fact occurred in 1917. Domestic affairs in France would soon have weakened her military strength.

Rivalries for trade and colonies had been important causes of the tensions which eventually snapped in 1914. However, by the actual year these issues had ceased to be predominant since, for example, Britain and Germany were developing markets in different parts of the world.

Despite the build-up of alliances and armaments, few men expected a long war, and hardly anyone envisaged the more than four years of relentless bloodletting and upheaval which lay ahead. This revealed an amazing collective lack of responsibility, imagination, or foresight. At the same time, many saw war as a means of reweaving the tattered social fabrics of the nations, or of achieving the aims of subjugated nationalities; few thought of the vast social changes that 'total' war itself would bring about.

Pacifist and internationalist forces were overwhelmed by the sudden upsurge of patriotism in every country on the eve of war. Fostered by popular education, nationalism was a force stronger than men realized – until it was too late. Also important, particularly at a subconscious level, were ideas of irrationalism, violence, and nihilism. Men such as Sorel and Nietzsche, as well as Darwin and Freud, saw their ideas applied or distorted to serve the cause of war.

No single explanation can account for the outbreak of war. The complex problems and suspicions combined with the immediacy of the crisis finally overwhelmed both politicians and generals.

Opposite: Kaiser Wilhelm II and von Moltke during the mobilization. They knew that speed was necessary if the Schlieffen Plan was to succeed.

Uhlans, the elite of the German cavalry, were to prove powerless in the face of the machine gun.

CHAPTER TWO
The War Unleashed

The outbreak of war was greeted by cheering crowds in every belligerent capital. The popular mood in every country was one of nationalistic self-righteousness, and everywhere the war was expected to be short, glorious, and victorious. By 4 August 1914, all but one of the great European powers was at war; Italy had declined to enter on the side of her erstwhile allies, Germany and Austria.

The Great War was one of mass armies. In 1914 the German army numbered 856,000 men in peacetime, rising to 3,800,000 when trained reserves were mobilized. If necessary, almost 4,000,000 additional men could be made available. The French army consisted of 736,000 men in time of peace, but upon mobilization this could rise to a maximum of over 3,500,000. In fact, about 1,650,000 French troops were engaged in the opening campaigns. In all, millions of men were placed in uniform in the service of the elaborate war plans, which each side possessed.

The war had opened according to plan for Germany. As her war blueprint, the Schlieffen Plan, had instructed, five armies, the *crème de la crème* of German military might, were hurled through Belgium into northern France. The French eastern fortresses were thereby circumvented, and the Germans now supposed that they could fall on the French armies west of Paris and inflict a quick and crushing defeat. But Moltke could not resist adjusting the Schlieffen Plan. The eventual result was that the plan misfired, and with it collapsed the German dream of lightning victory.

To meet the German threat, the French war plan, Plan 17, called for an offensive regardless of cost (*l'offensive à outrance*). The French were to strike into Alsace-Lorraine and east of Metz. Another French force under General Lanrézac, and the British Expeditionary Force (BEF) under Field Marshal Sir John French, was to move into Belgium if, as happened, Germany violated the neutrality of that country; otherwise they would have proceeded straight towards Metz.

Toujours Chic

In placing inordinate emphasis on offensive action, the French forgot the principle that superiority in numbers at any point must be paid for by adopting defensive positions elsewhere. The French also feared that their infantry, previously whipped up to an enthusiasm for attack, would be unable to stand on the defensive against the German army, which they considered more highly trained than their own. The result was that the French rushed forward, heedless of the consequences. General, then Lieutenant, Spears observed:

The sense of the tragic futility of it will never quite fade from the minds of those who saw these brave men, dashing across the open to the sound of drums and bugles . . . The gallant officers who led them were entirely ignorant of the stopping power of modern firearms, and many of them thought it chic to die in white gloves.

If only the French had reinforced the Belgian defences, they might have been able to hold the Germans along the Namur-Antwerp line of fortresses. Instead, the two armies which they threw across Lorraine were repulsed; and when they tried to break through the German centre in the Ardennes, the French were again defeated. Indeed, from 20–23 August, in the Battle of the Frontiers – in Lorraine, the Ardennes, the Sambre, and at Mons – the Allies were decisively routed. The French alone suffered well over 300,000 casualties, which included many of the bravest soldiers or those with greatest initiative. More than one officer in ten was already a casualty, and at Flaxon on 19 August, the French Twenty-sixth Division lost two-thirds of its officers. Without the promotion of many able men from the ranks, these losses would already have been irreparable.

The BEF at Mons

The British Expeditionary Force was by now fully involved in the campaign. Under Field Marshal Sir John French, the BEF had crossed the Channel between 12 and 20 August. Almost 90,000 soldiers took part. Their mood was mainly one of optimism; they had no idea that slaughter was their destiny.

After concentrating near Maubeuge, on 22 August the infantry dug itself in and prepared for action in the pit headgears and slagheaps of the drab little Belgian mining town of Mons. British reconnaissance planes had reported many German troops moving towards Mons; and the British waited with a 'keenness whetted by the first sight of the enemy', in the words of John Terraine. The twenty-third of August was a Sunday, and as they hurried to Mass, the inhabitants of Mons eyed the British troops with amiable curiosity.

French had placed his men along the line of the Mons-Condé canal. The position to be defended was a salient to the north east of Mons itself. The

The outbreak of war was greeted jubilantly in every belligerent capital. In Vienna the cheering began even before the war, when Austria-Hungary broke off diplomatic relations with Serbia.

General Joffre led French forces in China and Africa and was appointed Chief of the General Staff in 1911.

overall defensive position was far from easy, for the canal, while providing no real obstacle to the German advance, was difficult to defend in view of its shallowness and the many bridges which crossed it.

Early on 23 August, the Germans under Kluck moved in. About thirty thousand British faced nearly ninety thousand Germans. The focus of the German attack was the bridge at Nimy, the northernmost point of the salient. After a short but fierce bombardment, the Germans attacked frontally, suffering heavy casualties from British musket fire, which was so accurate and rapid that the Germans mistook it for machine gun fire. The Germans were 'the most perfect targets' because of their method of advancing in close order. As a British sergeant described it, the Germans advanced 'in solid square blocks, standing out sharply against the skyline, and you couldn't help hitting them'. Another soldier reported that the first company of Germans 'were simply blasted away to Heaven by a volley at seven hundred

Above: In Germany even the weapons were bedecked with flowers. **Right:** Not every German soldier was as enthusiastic about the war as his Kaiser would have wished.

yards, and in their insane formation every bullet was almost sure to find two billets'. In fact, Mons became a series of strong German attacks being met with equally strong British defences. A German account emphasized that the enemy, 'Well entrenched and completely hidden . . . opened a murderous fire . . . finally the whole advance stopped . . . with bloody losses the attack gradually came to an end.' Nevertheless, under the pressure of a prolonged German attack, in early afternoon the British forces were driven back to new positions south of Mons, and by late evening a new British line had been established. Due to their exhaustion, the Germans had been unable to force their passage across the Mons canal, and this inconclusive result was typical of the day's fighting.

At 11:00 p.m. on 23 August, as the British prepared to dig in before the next day's battle, word reached them that, in a supremely uncoordinated move, the French Fifth Army under Lanrézac was breaking off fighting to the right of the British positions and had decided to withdraw. The success of the German advance and the failure of the French offensives had bred caution, and the BEF, finding it futile to stand alone, now retreated to the Maubeuge-Valenciennes line. Many of the troops were confused, for they had seen Mons as a great victory and knew nothing of the dire warnings coming in of a superior German concentration of forces. Kluck's army had been held up for a day at the price of sixteen hundred

Crown Prince Rupprecht of Bavaria was the son of King Ludwig III of Bavaria. He commanded the German Sixth Army in 1914.

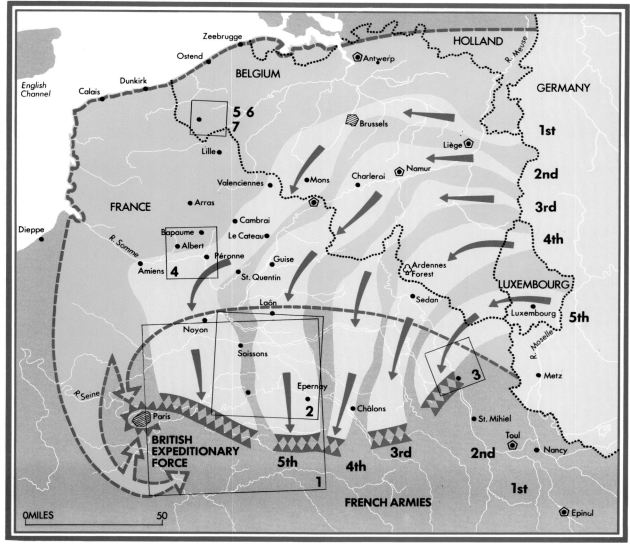

Schlieffen's planned invasion

Actual invasion

1 1st Marne 5-9 September 1914. See chapter 2

2 2nd Marne 18 July - 7 August 1918 See chapter 13

3 Verdun 21 February 1916- August 1917 See chapter 7

4 Somme 1 July - 19 November 1916 See chapter 7

5,6,7 1st, 2nd & 3rd Battles of Ypres
21 October - 22 November 1914 See chapter 4
22 April - 24 May, 1915 See chapter 6
31 July - 20 November, 1917 See chapter 12

⬡ FORTS
Schlieffen's plan included seizure of the French and Belgian ports before the encirclement of Paris took place. In 1914 the wheel was turned more sharply. The plan failed because it was partially abandoned.

33

Right: British recruits march to Waterloo Station, led by a brass band from Doctor Barnardo's Orphans' Home. **Far right above:** The cream of French manhood feared no one. **Far right centre:** The first British volunteers arrived in Le Havre less than a fortnight after the outbreak of war.

Left: Field Marshal Sir John French led the BEF across the Channel. **Right:** The German juggernaut rolls through Belgium. **Centre above:** The Germans met heavy resistance at Mons, but pressed the Allies back into France. **Below:** The British cavalry retreat from Mons. **Far right:** Many French prisoners were taken.

Right: In memory of the 1,000 English and 300 Belgians who fell at Antwerp, October 1914.
Below: The battle of the Yser Canal near Ypres.

Gedenkblatt zur Erinnerung an die Gefangennahme von 1000 Engländern und 300 Belgiern bei Moerbeke westl. Antwerpen 9/10. 10. 1914. durch II. Batl. bayr. Landw. Inf. Regts. Nr. 1.

Der europäische Krieg 1914.

Nr. 16.

Nr. 10160.

Neuruppin, bei Oehmigke & Riemschneider.

Die Schlacht am Yser-Kanal bei Ypern.

Die nach Eroberung der Festung Antwerpen geflüchteten belgischen und englischen Truppen sammelten sich an der Küste des Kanals auf der Linie Ostende - Dünkirchen, wo sie Unterstützung durch französische und frische englische Truppen fanden, ferner durch die aus Afrika und Indien herangezogenen Spahis, Sikhs, Gurkahs, Afridis und Patlans. Unsere Armee rückte sofort hinterher und es entspann sich in der Gegend von Ypern ein mörderischer Kampf. Englische und französische Kreuzer beschossen vom Kanal aus den rechten Flügel unserer Truppen, wurden aber durch verschiedene Volltreffer unserer schweren Geschütze zum Rückzug gezwungen. Die Schleusen bei Nieuport wurden von den Engländern zerstört und dadurch ein Teil des Geländes unter Wasser gesetzt; es konnte dies den Vormarsch unserer Truppen vielleicht etwas verzögern, aber nie aufhalten, die Pioniere hatten sehr bald Brücken geschlagen. Unter schweren Verlusten an Mannschaften und auch an Geschützen wurden die Verbündeten fortwährend zurückgedrängt, feindliche Vorstöße brachen in sich selbst zusammen, was auf ein Erschlaffen der Truppen schließen läßt. Ein vollständiger Sieg unsererseits dürfte nahe bevorstehen.

British casualties. The total German losses are not known, but must have been much higher.

An aura of mystique surrounds Mons, the opening British engagement of the war. According to legend, the BEF was even aided by the intervention of angels! The significance of Mons for the Allies was that, as Cruttwell wrote, the battle was 'neither a victory nor a defeat, but a delaying action which achieved its purpose'.

Despite his many faults, General Joffre, the French Commander in Chief, was an indomitable and unflappable man. His armies had suffered grievous defeat and immense losses, but his soldiers maintained a surprisingly high morale. Now Joffre decided to take a defensive position and reduce the enemy by attrition. He would re-group his forces in retreat, while looking for an opportunity to take the offensive when the Germans least expected it. To act prematurely, however, 'would have run the risk of being turned into a hopeless rout', as Joffre himself wrote later.

The Long Retreat

Thus, from 24 August to 5 September, the Allied armies retreated. Along the way, the British engaged the enemy at Le Cateau, and the French at Guise-Saint Quentin. Yet Joffre's stolid optimism might have been misplaced, if not for the fact that the German supreme commander, Moltke, received exaggerated reports of German successes on every battlefront. Moltke became overconfident; indeed, he deluded himself that final victory was within his grasp. Thus he drastically reduced the strength of the German right wing. Although he could therefore no longer make an encircling movement west of Paris, in the euphoria of his mood, this hardly mattered. On 25 August, he decided to send four western divisions to the eastern front. These successive weakenings of the German western position had a decisive influence on the outcome of the Battle of the Marne some twelve days later.

At the end of August, Moltke felt ready to try to envelop the French by means of Crown Prince Rupprecht's army on the left and those of Bülow and Kluck on the right. Now fate took an ironic hand. The German armies had advanced so swiftly that their supplies had failed to keep pace. The armies were too big to live off the land, and the troops, already exhausted from incessant fighting and marches, faced hunger as well. Sir Basil Liddell Hart observed that now 'so much grit had worked into the German machine that a slight jar would suffice to cause its breakdown'. This jar was to be administered at the Marne.

Suddenly, Moltke became concerned at reports of ominous French troop movements. At the same time, and in the absence of adequate communications, Kluck interpreted the spirit of his orders in the way he thought best, and he advanced across the Marne. Prompted by General Galliéni, the military governor of Paris, Joffre moved to take advantage of this overreaching movement. The French Sixth Army under Maunoury was sent against Kluck's right, while the BEF and the Fifth Army, now commanded by Franchet d'Espèrey, attacked in the north.

By 5 September, when it was already too late, Kluck realized that German successes had been .

General von Kluck, whose lack of courage to carry out the Schlieffen Plan led to disaster for Germany at the Marne.

exaggerated, and that the Allies were recuperating more quickly than he had dreamed possible. Meanwhile Maunoury continued to advance, and when he encountered German forces under Gronau on a line extending from Vincy to the Marne, the Battle of the Ourcq ensued. This fierce display of fighting marked the first engagement in the Battle of the Marne. The results were inconclusive, since the German advance by day was countered by their withdrawal from exposed positions by night. However, Cruttwell assesses the significance of the Ourcq as being that 'the sting . . . had been partially drawn by the vigorous and unexpected initiative' of the Allies.

The Marne

Much of history is decided by luck and timing, and the Marne was no exception. On 7 September, Bülow decided to utilize two of Kluck's corps to complete a wheeling movement. But Kluck, by now seriously concerned about the fighting north of the Marne, instead decided that the corps would retire behind the Petit Morin river. The result was a widening gap between Bülow's right and Kluck's left, and into it moved the BEF, now six divisions in strength, and the French forces of Conneau and Franchet d'Espèrey. The advance of the BEF was snail-like in its slowness and caution. This was due to the shock of previous casualties, the suspicion that the Germans were preparing a giant ambush, and the lack of imagination or resolution on the part of the high command. Nonetheless, this steady advance was crucial to the coming Allied victory.

Maunoury was pressing his attack with vigour, and a division was brought from the east to help

Above: French reinforcements were called up to defend Paris at the Marne. **Right:** The BEF rests before digging in at the Marne.

Left: A transport brigade is hit by shrapnel near the Marne.

Below left: The 1st Cameronians cross a pontoon bridge at la Ferte: 10 September 1914. Below: The Germans were stopped at the Marne. This time it was their turn to be taken prisoner.

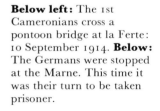

Darf Belgien Englands Aufmarschgebiet werden?

Above: German propaganda claimed that Belgium would be occupied by Britain and used as a launching pad against Germany's Rhine cities and the Ruhr Valley, the industrial heartland of Germany. This excuse was used to convince Germans that their invasion of Belgium was pre-emptive and therefore justifiable. Although such a ploy was never considered since the Germans occupied most of Belgium so quickly, it was seriously discussed by Britain during the early stages of World War II.

Right: A German artist's impression of the savage hand-to-hand fighting which took place in the early stages of the war.

him. On 7 September, the resourceful Galliéni swiftly conveyed two of these needed regiments to the battlefield in an armada of more than one thousand commandeered Parisian taxicabs. This stroke, although it captured the public imagination, had no important influence on the fighting, but was significant for its demonstration of the potentialities of motorized transport in war.

Between 6 and 8 September the Allies were unable to gain a decisive victory. On 7 September the BEF forced its way across the Grand Morin river, and the next day the British crossed the Petit Morin and advanced to within four or five miles of the Marne. Franchet d'Espèrey and his cavalry also crossed the Petit Morin, but without encountering the Germans. Meanwhile Foch's Ninth Army was driven back and lost control of the passages of the Marshes of St Gond.

However, cumulative forces were telling on the German position. By 8 September, Bülow was despondent and tired, and his troops were more exhausted and ravenous than ever. Bülow reported that the German Second Army was 'no longer capable of forcing a decisive victory'. Moreover, the anticipated breakthrough in Lorraine had failed. Now Moltke sent Hentsch, head of intelligence for France, to tour the German armies, to assess the situation and to order retreat if necessary. Hentsch found Bülow badly shaken; and on 9 September, influenced by the French capture of Marchais-en-Brie and reports of British columns advancing to the Marne, Bülow decided to pull back his forces. The same day, the battle with Maunoury was broken off, and on Hentsch's order the First Army also retreated. By 11 September a German general withdrawal to the Noyon-Verdun line along the river Aisne was in progress, and here the Kaiser's forces regrouped among their prepared defences. The German retreat had also been hastened by rumours that forty thousand British and eighty thousand Russian troops were landing on the Belgian coast; ironically, only three thousand British marines had arrived.

On 11 September, Joffre wrote that 'the advance must be pursued energetically, leaving the enemy no respite'. Yet, having summoned their last strength to meet the clash of armies, the Allied infantry, debilitated by their arduous retreat, were incapable of further extensive effort. In addition, on 9 September the weather, previously hot, had turned to cold and rainy mists. Munition supplies were low or non-existent. Many

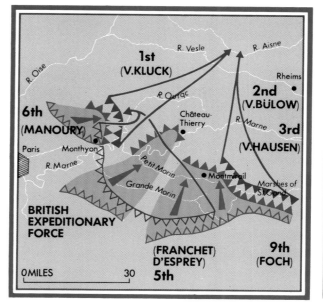

ALLIED ⋈ GERMAN

Front-line positions 5 Sept, 1914

Front-line positions 9 Sept, 1914. The Allies having regained the lost ground. Subsequently the Germans retreated to the Aisne, which they reached 14 Sept, 1914

bridges over the Marne had been destroyed, and the roads were clogged with traffic. But the main victory, a strategical and psychological hammering of the Germans, had been achieved.

Moltke is alleged to have told the Kaiser on 13 September that as a result of the Marne episode, 'Germany has lost the war'. Whether or not this statement was actually made, it was true to the extent that Germany had seen the irrevocable failure of her most basic strategic concept, that of quickly winning the war in the west in order to turn east with all her might. The Marne was only a partial tactical success for the Allies. Few German prisoners were taken. As Sewell Tyng, an historian of the Marne, has noted, the battle 'left the victors masters of the field, but did not impose on the vanquished the sense of hopeless inferiority that is the mark of decisive defeat'. Even so, the Marne ranks as the premier strategical victory of the war, for with their success the Allies had made a long and costly war on two fronts unavoidable for Germany.

Thus ended the opening phase of the war on the western front. Churchill was to capture its significance exactly when he wrote:

The measured, silent drawing together of gigantic forces, the uncertainty of their movements and positions, the number of unknown and unknowable facts made the first collision a drama never surpassed. Nor was there any other period in the War when the general battle was waged on so great a scale, when the slaughter was so swift or the stakes so high.

Prisoners from the Battle of the Marne.

CHAPTER THREE
Eastern Clashes- Tannenberg and Serbia

In accord with the demands of the Schlieffen Plan, the Western front had seen the main initial concentration of German forces. While Moltke's armies expected to overwhelm France in six weeks, Austria-Hungary and East Prussia would have to bear the brunt of the Russian attack. Conrad, Austria's chief of the general staff, commented that he hoped Moltke would not leave him too long 'in a nasty mess'.

In the east each power seemed bent on taking the offensive. For Conrad in particular, the offensive was a veritable obsession. Austria expected to remove the Serbian thorn from her side in about two weeks; Vienna was not unduly worried over dealing with a 'kingdom of pig-breeders'. Certainly the Serbian campaign was expected to be finished before the Russians hacked their way through Galicia. However, when put into action, the Austrian plans bogged down. In addition, because Russian mobilization was swifter than had been expected, Conrad had to transfer troops from the Serbian front to face the more formidable foe.

Because the Serbian capital, Belgrade, lay along the frontier with Austria-Hungary, the Serbs half expected the first Austrian attack in this direction. Elaborate defensive preparations were made, and even before the outbreak of war, the government and the royal court were evacuated inland. As it happened, however, the Austrian war plan called for attack from the west and northwest. The intention was to create a movement of envelopment which would strike a deathblow at the heart of the enemy.

A Serbian Disaster
As war began, the Austrians were optimistic. Their troops were fresh for battle, but those of Serbia were already dog-eared from two recent Balkan campaigns. Austrian equipment was also superior. On the other hand, Serbian morale was also high as the tiny nation steeled itself to defend its hearths.

On 11 August the Austrian Second Army crossed the Sava river and easily took the town of Šabac. But next morning, as the Fifth Army crossed the Drina, it encountered heavy fire from two Serbian divisions. Next day, Serbian harassment from high defensive positions brought the Austrian offensive to a temporary halt, but it subsequently moved forward, sustaining enormous losses.

The Austrians were led by Potiorek, the mismanager of the archducal visit to Sarajevo. On 19 August, after Serbians under Putnik launched a counteroffensive, Potiorek unsteadily withdrew his forces back across the Drina, and by the twenty-fourth the Austrians had completely evacuated Serbia.

On 7 September, Potiorek was able to cross back into Serbian territory. This time he inflicted severe casualties on the enemy. In one horrendous disaster, a Serbian division, which had entered Hungary, was trapped as it tried to recross into Serbia. Five thousand men were mown down in a few hours. Even so, Putnik managed a counterthrust at Sarajevo, causing Potiorek to pursue him for seven weeks in an effort to ensure the safety of the Bosnian capital.

By 25 October Bosnia had been cleared of Serbian forces, and Austrian predominance in men and supplies had had its effect. Yet as Potiorek drove back the enemy, his pursuit was so relentless that it reduced his own forces to physical and spiritual wrecks. Somehow he managed to take the offensive again in the first week of November, and his task was helped by the heavy rain and ice which played havoc with the Serbian supply lines. On 2 December, by a happy coincidence the sixty-sixth anniversary of the accession of Franz Josef, Belgrade was captured. Austria now became overconfident. Though Serbia was practically destitute of reserves of ammunition, the courage of her men endured. Next day, 3 December, the Serbs threw themselves with suicidal abandon at the Austrians – and the Austrian lines caved in. By 13 December, Potiorek was once more driven back across the Sava; Belgrade was relieved on 15 December.

Austria had sustained over one hundred thousand casualties; in addition, her troops had abandoned countless weapons which were invaluable to the Serbs. Yet Serbia was unable to press forward her advantage. The oncoming winter, the ravages of typhus, and the loss of more than half of her crack troops (including one hundred and seventy thousand dead and injured) produced a stalemate which was to last for many months.

The Eastern Front
From the beginning of the war, the Russians had received a stream of French demands and pleas for an attack on East Prussia as soon as possible. The French emphasized that every thrust in the east was a relief of pressure from the west. Finally, yielding to their ally, the Russians attacked before their armies were fully concentrated.

Left: The tenacity of the Serbs was tremendous.

Right: Serbian infantry put up a stout defence against overwhelming odds.
Far right: A Montenegrin infantryman. Montenegro supported Serbia when war broke out.

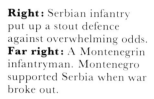

Although thousands of Serbs were taken prisoner, their comrades in action fought on.

East Prussia was the site of numerous estates of the Prussian aristocracy. Germans regarded the territory with fierce pride as a bastion of the Teutonic way of life against the hordes of barbaric Slavs beyond. These atavistic feelings made the Germans determined to hold the province at all costs. Fortunately for them, although they were greatly outnumbered by Russian forces, the Germans were much superior in the education and training of their men, in the excellence of their command, and in their logistical support. Germany also had the advantage of better transportation facilities. In Fuller's picturesque description, the Russian soldier was 'a big-hearted child who thought out nothing and was surprised by everything'. Less appealingly, Russian troops were a reflection of their own corrupt and inefficient society.

East Prussia Invaded

On 17 August the Russian general Rennenkampf led the First Army in force westwards into East Prussia in the direction of Königsberg. Three days later he defeated the Germans at Gumbinnen, about ten miles inside the frontier. Mackensen's Seventeenth Corps took to their heels 'in fearful panic', as one observer tells us, and the Russians captured over seven thousand German prisoners. Yet this was only a tactical incident in the overall picture, and the fumbling Rennenkampf was

about to order a retreat himself, when he heard that the Germans were withdrawing instead.

Because of failure of nerve and general bungling, the German Eighth Army commander, Prittwitz, popularly known as 'Fatty' because of his legendary girth, was now replaced by his brother-in-law, Hindenburg. Ludendorff was brought in as chief of staff. By now the Germans had decided to concentrate against the Second Russian Army under Samsonov, which had crossed the German frontier on 20 August. In this the Germans were taking the calculated risk that they could deal with Samsonov before the cautious and slow-moving Rennenkampf could intervene. Cruttwell suggests that Rennenkampf's incompetence may have reflected a covert sympathy for Germany, the land of his ancestors. His inaction can also be explained, however, by his dislike of Samsonov and his unwillingness to cooperate with his rival. In any case, the German plan was aided by the fifty-mile chain of the Masurian Lakes, which formed a natural barrier between the two Russian armies.

Hindenburg Takes Command

When Hindenburg arrived to take command, the First Corps, led by a German general with the unlikely name of François was already detraining to the west of Tannenberg. For a considerable time François was heavily outnumbered by the Russians, but in the end the latter played into German hands. Samsonov, thinking that the German Eighth Army was routed, and hurried along by Jilinsky, commander of the Northwestern Army Group, pushed forward faster than ever, but then stopped to rest on 25 August. Actually, by 22 August the fighting capacity of Samsonov's men had already been drastically reduced by their marching in scorching heat through desert terrain without proper food. According to one German eyewitness, 'Whole

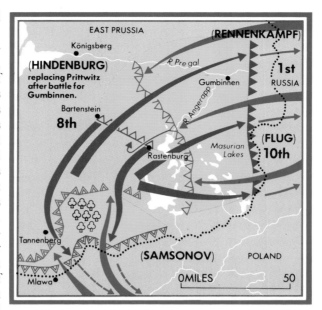

Russian advance until 20 Aug 1914 – Germans withdraw

Advance until 27 Aug

8th moved to counter-attack. 29 Aug Russian retreat

8th counter-attack Russian 1st & 10th. 12 Sept-Russian retreat

army corps advanced . . . without bread or oats, and had to have recourse to their reserve rations . . . the march discipline was bad . . . Nerves were so shaky that the troops fired at every airman . . .'

On 25 August, Ludendorff, who was still worried about Rennenkampf in the background, ordered François to attack Samsonov and envelop his left wing. Lacking full artillery support and ammunition supply, François demurred. Ludendorff angrily insisted, but just in time, intercepted Russian communications revealed that his fears about Rennenkampf were unfounded.

The Russian Lines Crack

The twenty-sixth of August was a day of fierce fighting. Samsonov had resumed his advance, but Mackensen and Below drove him back. By the evening, the Russian position was becoming untenable. Contact between the two Russian divisions was broken, and during the night the situation deteriorated into complete chaos. Orders

were issued and countermanded as crisis followed crisis. One Russian corps, the Twenty-third, was described as 'terribly exhausted . . . they had been three days without bread or sugar'. Though he was trying to save himself from envelopment rather than to envelop the enemy, Samsonov decided to continue the battle as a holding action until Rennenkampf could arrive to turn the tables on the Germans. However, although on 26 August the German troops were themselves too tired to press their advantage and pursue Samsonov with vigour, part of one Russian division had been pinned down around Lake Bössau. In a state of utter exhaustion and panic, many Russians drowned. This incident was a portent of the slaughter to come.

On 27 August, François was ready for action. Relentlessly battered by his heavy artillery, the Russians, pitifully hungry and now lacking any will to fight, were hurled back from their positions, suffering horrendous casualties in the process. Seeing the full gravity of their situation, on the evening of 27 August Jilinsky ordered Rennenkampf to move forward. The order came too late and carried an insufficient note of urgency.

On 28 August Ludendorff ordered François to relieve the pressure on Scholtz's Twentieth Corps, but François again disobeyed orders, being determined to cut off Samsonov's line of retreat. The Germans were fortunate that François acted as he did, for otherwise a large part of the Russian forces would have escaped the trap into which they were forced on the following two days. As it was, Samsonov was hemmed in on three sides, and as Cyril Falls remarked, for the Germans 'it was like heading stock into a corral . . .' Meanwhile Ludendorff was again haunted by the spectre of Rennenkampf. He wrote, that Rennenkampf's 'formidable host hung like a threatening thunder cloud to the northeast. He need only have closed with us and we should have been beaten'. In reality, Ludendorff greatly overestimated Rennenkampf's strength; no coup de grace was ever to come from that quarter.

The Tannenberg Triumph

Samsonov's position was nonetheless desperate. Rennenkampf was moving forward so ponderously as to be useless. Only two of Samsonov's corps, the Thirteenth and Fifteenth, were any longer able to fight with any effect. His communications were badly disrupted. In desperation he moved to take personal control at the front. It was too late. Defeat stared at him unblinkingly, and Samsonov was gripped by a fathomless melancholy. A general retreat on 29–30 August developed into a cataclysmic disaster. Many troops were surrounded in forests and marshes, where they wandered helplessly about, some despondently trying to regroup. Countless soldiers starved to death or were killed by German troops who were combing the forests. In places, Russians in sufficient numbers and with the strength born of desperation managed to break through the German cordons; but the overall picture remained unchanged. One Russian column met a typically gruesome end: 'From two directions searchlight beams shone forth . . . Immediately after there followed machine gun

Paul von Hindenburg takes command after the retreat in East Prussia. General von Below stands third from the right, next to Hindenburg.

Samsonov led the disastrous Russian attack.

46

Left: Germany's heroes. From left to right: Field Marshal von Mackensen, General von Ludendorff, Hindenburg, and General von Seeckt, subsequently Head of the Reichswehr and Architect of the Wehrmacht. Oskar von Hindenburg, the Field Marshal's son, stands behind Ludendorff.

fire and a few rounds of rapid shrapnel fire . . . Five times the Germans repeated the same manoeuvre and each time the column melted and melted.' The Germans had taken ninety-two thousand prisoners; François' corps alone captured sixty thousand. At least thirty thousand Russians were dead. German losses numbered between ten and fifteen thousand. Their booty included a vast supply of guns which the Russians could ill afford to lose.

An important witness was missing from the climax of the debâcle. Late on 29 August, after spending the evening walking and wandering in a forest, Samsonov slipped away from the staff officers who were accompanying him. Minutes later, a single shot rang out through the wood. Unable to face the Tsar or his men again, General Samsonov had killed himself.

Although Hindenburg had described the German netting of the Russians as 'harvesting', the victors themselves were reduced to the last stages of exhaustion by the six days of fighting. At the suggestion of either Hoffmann or Ludendorff, a name was found for the battles: Tannenberg, in verbal revenge for a defeat which in 1410 the Poles and Lithuanians had inflicted on the Teutonic Knights.

The two German corps which Moltke had inadvisedly transferred from the west had now arrived on the eastern front, and here they proved invaluable, despite the fact that their continued presence in the west would probably have reversed the outcome of the Marne. Reinforced by the new arrivals, Hindenburg was able to defeat Rennenkampf, though he failed in his primary objective of cornering the First Russian Army on the coast and destroying it as he had done with that of Samsonov. True, Rennenkampf lost between thirty and forty-five thousand men as prisoners, but he was able to evade the Germans by retreating with the bulk of his troops. Nevertheless, in the Battle of the Masurian Lakes, 8–9 September, Rennenkampf was driven out of East Prussia. His own nerve cracked, and he fled in ignominy by car to Kovno (Kaunas), eighty miles away.

Tannenberg was a great and imaginative victory for Germany, but the damage it did to Russia has been exaggerated. Although she sustained extremely heavy losses, Russia was not irreparably crippled. As it occurred, the battle was not the result of deliberate planning. The German army had sought to hurl back the Russians, not to surround them, and the idea of their envelopment emerged later, made possible by the passivity of Rennenkampf's army.

Perhaps, however, the most lasting aspect of Tannenberg was its valuable lift to German morale. East Prussia had been saved. As a result, Hindenburg became and remained a folk hero. This was ironic, for Tannenberg was planned by the brilliant young staff officer, Hoffmann, and was won in large measure because of the initiative and sure judgment of François. As for the French, they expressed their condolences to Russia because of the sacrifices made in the name of alliance; but Paris could not help but rejoice that the Russian offensive had led to a fatal weakening of the German western front. On the Marne, Moltke's pigeons came home to roost.

Above: The retreat to
Tannenberg was a
bloodbath for the Russians.
Left: Tens of thousands of
Russians were slaughtered
at Tannenberg.

Opposite above: Russian
soldiers kneeled to pray
before the Tsar on their
way to the front. **Opposite
below:** Field Marshal
Paul von Hindenburg, the
victor of Tannenberg.

Above: Hungarian cavalry press forward on Russia's southern flank. **Right:** A wire implacement is stormed near Lemberg.

Previous page: Almost a hundred thousand Russian soldiers were captured by the Germans.

Austria and Lemberg

Farther to the south, in Galicia, Austrian troops had entered Russian territory on 10 August. Ten days later Conrad ordered a northward offensive to meet the Russian armies, which had attacked Galicia once they were certain that the major initial German concentration was to be on the western front. Immediately Conrad was thrown off balance, for he had expected a slower and more ineffective Russian mobilization than in fact occurred.

On the morning of 28 August the Austrian Twenty-seventh Division was ambushed, and over eight thousand men were lost. Conrad was now a seriously worried man. Two days previously the Russians had advanced on the Austrians in such force that a general panic had set in with many troops fleeing to Lemberg, where they demoralized the civilian population. At the same time, the Slavs in the Austro-Hungarian army showed their disregard for the Habsburg cause, many of them willingly surrendering to the Russians or supplying them with strategic information. No wonder Conrad wrote to Emperor Franz Josef that he was 'now going through the most terrible moments' of his life.

No doubt Franz Josef was too. The aging Emperor, after over sixty years in power, could envision all his efforts coming to a tragic end.

Lemberg and the Austrian Front

Fortunately for the Austrians, the Russian South-western Army Group under Ivanov vastly over-estimated the Austrian strength facing them in the region of Lemberg, and therefore did not press the advantage of their recent victory at Zlotchow. Liddell Hart comments that had Ivanov 'pushed on at once it is likely that he would have crashed through the shaken Austrians as through a paper screen'. Although Grand Duke Nicholas, judging the situation more accurately, ordered the Russian advance to continue, the Russians had lost two precious days in dithering, in which time the jittery Austrians had had a chance to pull themselves together. Yet misinformation from aerial reconnaissance did much to undo the Austrian plans, and meanwhile on 30 August the Russians under Brusilov were victorious in breaking the line of the Austrian Second Army. Everywhere the cry was heard, 'The Cossacks are coming!' A few days later the Galician capital of Lemberg (Lwow), the fourth largest city in the Habsburg Monarchy and an important centre for communications, fell after being encircled by Russian forces from the north and east.

After several intermediary bouts of vicious fighting, on 10 September the two armies clashed along a wide front. The Russians placed great significance on the outcome of this affray. Influenced by the result of Tannenberg, Nicholas decided to concentrate on the defeat of Austria-Hungary, and only secondarily on that of Germany. On 31 August he ordered Ivanov to destroy the Austrians without regard to cost in life and limb. This was easier said than done, for though the Austrians were suffering frightful casualties from the armies of the Tsar, the Russians' slow advance allowed their armies to remain intact; and, when cornered, the Austrians

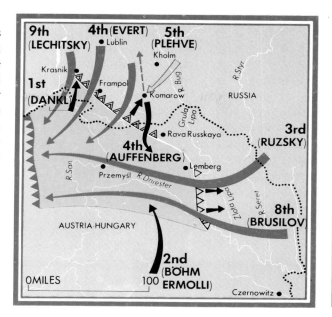

Position & advance 25 Aug
Overpowered by Russian 3rd & 8th armies

Position & advance 26 Aug
Russians repulsed 29 Aug

Position mid-Sept 1914

Battle of Lemberg ended in complete rout of Austrians

were still able and willing to engage in bloody attacks in which both sides were slaughtered with macabre impartiality. Eventually, however, the Habsburg soldiers' spirits broke under the impact of a Russian holding action from the east and an attack from the north. On 11 September Conrad had no choice but to abandon the fight and withdraw his armies beyond the River San.

The victories around Lemberg were great triumphs for Russia, and they did much to erase the shame of Tannenberg from the public mind. Austria had been left with two hundred and fifty thousand casualties, and Russia had captured over one hundred thousand prisoners. Barbara Tuchman judges that the Russians had 'accomplished a mutilation of the Austro-Hungarian Army, especially in trained officers, from which it was never to recover'. Indeed, the Austrian retreat continued in increasing chaos for more than three weeks. To the ravages of sickness and disease were added long arduous marches. Austrian morale suffered a crushing blow; their attempts to invade both Serbia and Russia ended ignominiously. In Berlin muttered complaints were heard that the Fatherland was 'fettered to a corpse'.

Thus, wracked by internal dissensions and denuded of many of its best and most reliable officers, the Austrian rout in Galicia was com-

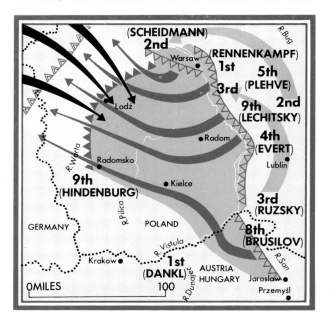

1st Battle of Warsaw

Front line 9 Oct, 1914. 2nd & 3rd armies moved north forcing Central powers to overextend communication lines

Advance by 11 Nov

2nd Battle of Warsaw

Counter-attack 11 Nov - 17 Dec

plete. This left the Germans worried lest the coal-fields and industries of Silesia, vital to the war effort, fall to the Russians. Their fears were well placed, for in fact the French were urging exactly such an action upon their eastern ally.

The Push Toward Warsaw

As Russian armies ominously regrouped, the Germans decided to take protective measures. Hindenburg reasoned that with a surprise thrust he could cross the Vistula and capture Warsaw. A fortress city, Warsaw was an important defensive position; in addition, denying it to the Russians would remove an excellent base from which to launch an offensive into Silesia.

Meanwhile the Russians had reversed their plans and had now decided to give top priority to the destruction of German forces before taking any further measures against the Austrians. Grand Duke Nicholas planned an enveloping movement close to Warsaw. Hindenburg, he prophesied, would be driven off and into Austrian forces further south. Hindenburg knew of part of this plan via the usual Russian carelessness in sending vital radio and telegraphic messages un-coded. As a result the German advance was ploddingly careful, being slowed down further by the same knee-deep Polish quagmires of mud which had ensnared Napoleon.

On 10 October the German Seventeenth Corps encountered and defeated a strong Russian force at Grójec. It was here that the Germans discovered detailed Russian battle orders on the body of a dead Russian officer; but the Germans were unable to act fully on this information, since the Russian plan was already in full swing. Desperate fighting took place with Russian troops who were forcing their way across the Vistula. Late on 11 October Ludendorff prepared to retreat. Con-rad's forces were of little help to him, for by now the Austrian communications had been severely disrupted by snow and ice. In any case, the Austrians resented German high-handedness and were prepared to assert their independence of action even if it meant failure for the common cause. Conrad was eager to place blame for defeat in any quarter but his own, and he complained that 'flighty and rambling operations' on the part of the German Ninth Army were responsible for Russian successes.

Eventually Austrian *amour propre* was partly satisfied, and as the Germans moved north, Austrian troops replaced them and prepared to face the Russians around Ivangorod. They were to attempt to push the enemy out where their German ally had failed to do so. For four days, in vicious and strenuous hand-to-hand combat, the Austrians tried their utmost to break into the Russian positions. Their failure did not detract from the outstanding bravery which they showed under appalling conditions.

Now German-Austrian bickering flared up to new heights. The Germans, more and more fear-ful of a Russian offensive in Upper Silesia, abandoned the Austrians to their fate and struggled back to their own territory. The Rus-sians had once more overextended themselves. Their supplies ran out, their men were exhausted; their horses dropped in their tracks.

A New Offensive in Poland

On 1 November Hindenburg was appointed Commander in Chief of all German forces in the east. Immediately he began preparations for a new offensive in Poland. He still had hopes that a knock-out blow could be delivered against Rus-sia, though this in itself would not end the war. Rather, the German hope was now to defeat Russia and then crush France before the new British recruits were sufficiently trained for battle. However, Falkenhayn, now chief of staff, could not spare Hindenburg troops from the West until December, by which time the second Ger-man attack on Warsaw had forfeited the advan-tage of surprise. Meanwhile, Hindenburg had to muddle along as best he could.

By 11 November the Germans were ready to advance. On the south bank of the Vistula, Mackensen wreaked havoc on a lone Russian corps. Communications between the Russian First and Second Armies were felled. The Second Army tried to protect the area of Lodz and deal Mackensen a glancing blow, but Mackensen caught up and shoved the Russians back on Lodz in disarray. Lodz, a city of half a million in-habitants, was an important billeting area and an industrial centre, and the Russians set great store in holding it. Yet by now the Russian Second Army was hemmed in on three sides.

From 18–25 November, a confused, whirling murderously vicious battle took place. Thousands of the injured froze to death. Somehow the Russians held on to Lodz and prepared to entrap fifty thousand Germans who were cut off from their fellow troops some twenty miles away. Characteristically Rennenkampf bungled the operation. He failed to close off the German way of escape to the north, and Scheffer was able to break out. As the savage winter extended its frozen grip, the rival armies prepared for yet more battles to come.

54

Above: Hungarian hussars are forced to retreat. **Far left:** Polish cavalry, under Russian command, rush to defend Warsaw. **Left:** A Russian field gun digs in to face Hindenburg's onslaught.

CHAPTER FOUR
The Widening War

Left: The Germans dig in, confident that they would complete their conquest of Belgium.

In September 1914, at the First Battle of the Marne, a decisive and irreparable blow was dealt to German strategy in the west. In consequence, on 14 September Moltke was relieved and was replaced by Falkenhayn, though the change was not openly admitted until 1 November.

After the Marne, the Germans had retreated to defensive positions on the Aisne. When the Allies eventually caught up with them, they attacked these positions forcefully. Heavy but indecisive fighting lasted from 13 to 18 September. The western front stabilized, and each side tried, and failed, to envelop the other. The armies collided in a series of devastatingly fierce battles, during the course of which the BEF moved towards the Flanders town of Ypres. As the left flank of this Ypres-bound movement reached the coast, Falkenhayn decided to penetrate the position before further British troops arrived.

The Germans had considered their western flank vulnerable to attack, for to their rear was Antwerp and the 'tattered, weary and shaken' Belgian field army of at least sixty-five thousand troops. Falkenhayn resolved that the city must be captured; and although it was strongly fortified, the heavy German siege artillery made short work of the defences. In brief, as one history relates, 'the operation was a walkover', and Antwerp

fell on 9 October. Nevertheless, if the Belgians had not held out until further resistance was impossible, the German troops surrounding Antwerp would have been thrown into the general affray at least five days earlier. In that case the Allies might have been broken altogether before it was possible to hold the Germans at Ypres.

On the British side, Sir John French was full of confidence. He firmly believed that the BEF was stronger and the German army weaker than at Mons the previous month. On 10 October, the order went out that the BEF would advance to meet the enemy. Unhappily for the British, however, their estimate of German strength was highly optimistic. Similarly sanguine was Foch, the commander of the French northern group of armies. Obstinate, wilful, but exuding 'gusts of optimistic encouragement', as Liddell Hart put it, Foch was certain that the Germans would be unable to extend and secure defensive positions to the coast. German cavalry could delay, but not prevent, a general Allied thrust, and the French plan was to envelop the German flank. Foch made the further mistake of underestimating the exhaustion of the Belgian divisions. His urgings to attack had a hollow ring among men whose leadership had been decimated.

Already, however, the BEF was advancing from

Above: The 2nd Scots Guards, equally confident, test their trenches. **Left:** The Cloth Hall in Ypres in 1914 before its destruction.

Ypres to the La Bassée canal. Undaunted by the failure to capture Lille, on 18 October Sir John French was still cheerfully expecting an advance on Brussels. Reality wore a different face. Though British forces were shortly to be strengthened by the Indian Corps and other reinforcements, the Germans were able to field men in even greater numbers. Already on 10 October, the first of these new German units had left for Belgium. They included large contingents of students 'flaming with patriotism and enthusiasm', as Falls describes them. These raw young recruits, sometimes called the 'schoolboy corps', were scythed down by the grim harvester of battle, and the Germans referred to their slaying as *Der Kindermord von Ypern*, or 'the massacre of the innocents at Ypres'. Nevertheless, these doomed young men fought with such fanatical fury and dedication that their inexperience at times was overcome, and they annihilated battalion after battalion of Allied troops.

By the week beginning 17 October, both French and Germans had begun to weigh each other's strength more realistically. Foch now concluded that the gap in the German line had closed and solidified, whereas previously he had sought and expected to find such a gap between Lille and Antwerp. Falkenhayn and Duke Albrecht of Wurttemberg, the Fourth Army commander, also now understood in approximate terms the size of the force opposing them. Now, counselling against manoeuvring, Foch informed Rear-Admiral Ronarc'h, commander of a brigade of French sailors, that 'Your mission is to stop the enemy in his tracks.' To Joffre, Foch appealed for reinforcements; French, he cautioned about the need for a defensive line behind the main BEF. To everyone, Foch was an inspiration.

British aerial reconnaissance was meanwhile reporting the westward advance of German troop columns. The situation was somewhat confusing, and much of French's false optimism is explained and justified by the fact that while he received a stream of reports indicating that strong German opposition was to be expected, this was counterbalanced by the numerous Allied successes in forcing back the Germans with a minimum of effort. What French did not understand, however, was that the German light cavalry or *Uhlans* was acting both as a screen and a scouting party for the columns, which were marching behind.

Early on 19 October, the German Forty-fifth and Forty-sixth Divisions encountered the enemy. Excited by this first martial experience, the new recruits prepared for action. To their intense disappointment, no thrilling engagement followed. Instead, there was skirmishing and intermittent exchanges of shell and rifle fire. The morning ended with an air of anticlimax.

In the afternoon, the two German divisions moved forward towards the villages of Kortemark and Hooghlede. The Forty-sixth Division intended to capture the ridge of Hooghe, but when the Germans arrived they found that the French dragoons had dispersed.

By the evening of 19 October the Germans had taken all the Allied positions covering the Yser and had mercilessly bombarded the remaining French and Belgian defences in Dixmude and Nieuport. Next day, the 20th, the main German offensive was to begin, with the Fourth and Sixth Armies advancing together. Albrecht was confident that the day would end in an Allied rout.

North of the La Bassée canal, Rupprecht and his men heavily outnumbered the BEF. Their intention was to break out between Béthune and Armentières, but first the British positions overlooking Lille had to be wiped out.

On 20 October, two German battalions moved towards the village of Le Pilly, where an Irish battalion faced them. As the Germans loomed up out of the morning mist, the well-trained Irish pumped their deadly fire into the oncoming Westphalian ranks. For five hours the Germans struggled continuously to enter the village. Eventually the Irish position became untenable, for they were isolated in the crossfire of Germans to the south and east. Nevertheless, in the afternoon when the German assault was resumed, the plucky Irish battalion fixed their bayonets and soldiered on at gruesome sacrifice. As the day ended, the hapless battalion was erased from the map. Two hundred and fifty-seven men were dead, and all but 50 of the remaining 290 were wounded. Only 30 men slipped out from under the German net and returned to their lines.

The Flanders Swamp

As luck would have it, torrential rains were turning the plain of Flanders into a swamp. This naturally made fighting very difficult, and air reconnaissance was prevented, so that as yet Sir John French was ignorant of the decimation of the Irish. Other reports showed that the Allied lines were generally being held, and Lieutenant General Sir Douglas Haig was able to send news that his troops were moving into the battle zone of

The 129th Baluchis on the outskirts of Wytschaete.

Ypres. Such German prisoners as had been taken were young and badly trained. These factors initially bolstered French's optimism, though his spirits soon deteriorated. As this happened, it appeared to the angry Joffre, that French's new mood of despair was due to fears that a repetition of the retreat to the Marne was getting under way.

On 21 October, Haig was disgusted to learn that British and French troops had retired from the key position of Passchendaele – later to achieve bloody immortality – with only slight resistance. To make matters worse, that afternoon the nearby French cavalry was ordered to retreat. While at first resisting such folly, its commander had to obey when the order was repeated. Gloom prevailed. Passchendaele had fallen to the Germans from sheer bungling of orders, and now the Forest of Houthulst had been yielded without a fight.

The position was better on the strategically vital Messines ridge. British forces under Allenby were attacked by Rupprecht's cavalry on the morning of the 21st, but a potentially disastrous confusion of orders was resolved in the nick of time.

Once more the Germans resumed the offensive on the ridge, but they were unable to get very far. However, they caused many casualties, and the British had partially to withdraw, because of the shortage of men and ammunition which was beginning to be felt.

At Dixmude, the French were 'having a hellish time', as British reconnaissance colourfully reported. The German Fourth Army followed the Sixth in attacking everywhere, with some tactical success but with no general breakthrough.

On the Yser, Beseler decided to attempt by stealth what he had failed to achieve by assault, and took his Germans across the river under cover of darkness. The ploy was successful, for when morning came the Allies were unable to dislodge the Germans.

By 22 October Foch, despite his dynamism and inspirational coordination, concluded that the initiative was passing to the enemy. Striving to reinforce Anglo-Belgian cooperation, he simultaneously approved a French offensive under d'Urbal. Circumstances appeared to be thwarting Foch's initial instructions, but then an Allied counterattack was victorious over the Forty-fifth Division. By 24 October, French troops had secured a line from Dixmude to Zonnebeke; yet the British defence continued over much the same ground as previously, and Foch's plans for a general counteroffensive remained unrealized. Yet neither was the campaign proceeding according to plan for Germany, which now decided to attack at three points: around Dixmude; to the east of Ypres; and between La Bassée and Menin.

At Dixmude, it seemed that the forces of nature were smiling on the Reich. Chill winds and water

Armoured cars were called up to support the British defenders of Ypres.

Top left: The Belgians fought hard in the face of the German advance. **Top centre:** The Germans brought up artillery which dated back to 1896. **Top right:** French troops (and their war dogs) held fast. **Left:** In the face of horrific devastation and carnage, the French attack . . . and attack again. **Above:** General Haig was disgusted to learn of the Allied retreat.

were as effective as German shells in weakening the French defenders. On the night of 24–25 October, artillery bombardment steadily pounded at the town, followed by wave after wave of German assaults. As dawn broke, the Germans drew back; Dixmude lay in ruins. Both sides were utterly exhausted by their exertions.

On the 25th, the Germans made repeated attempts to break through on the Yser. The Allies remained fiercely determined that they should not pass. Each side battered and hacked away, and the casualty lists grew longer.

Along the low ridge of Ypres meanwhile, the German 'schoolboy innocents' were attacking and encountering the resistance of the French. One French regiment managed to cripple the German advance, but additional German troops moved forward and retook Zonnebeke.

By 24 October, Albrecht's aim of breaking open the British line had met with success. Strangely, the Germans, as if unaware of this, failed to press home their advantage. Meanwhile the British were reinforced by French cavalry under Dubois, and the line was stabilized. Furthermore, the British somehow held the Messines ridge. Fighting raged throughout the day. The unhappy Germans began to think that a decisive break in the Allied line was impossible, while the Allies for their part were continuously suffering under an endless outpouring of German firepower, backed by seemingly limitless reinforcements of troops. The stark horror of the endless rounds of battle is captured in a description given by Brigadier Farrar-Hockley, historian of the First Battle of Ypres: 'As each body of Germans is destroyed, we surge forward and take on the next, shooting and charging alternately, bayoneting the survivors until by sheer exhaustion and losses we come to a standstill.'

On 25 October, fresh British troops began to arrive at the front; and French infantry reinforcements were not far behind. Overjoyed, French reported home, 'My anxiety is over.' Only hours later, Sir Horace Smith-Dorrien blunted French's mood of euphoria by reporting that he feared the imminent breach of his section of the Allied line. Not many men or supplies were at hand to fill the threatening gap, yet miraculously the line was still holding the next day. Subsequently two thousand additional British troops shored up the previously weakening link.

Throughout 25–26 October, the salient of Kruiseecke was hammered and pulverized by German bombardments. Scores of men were buried and smothered as earth fell in on them. Despite this ordeal, the nerve-shattered survivors somehow reassembled. French's optimism waxed again, for Foch was still his incorrigibly optimistic self, and the French reinforcements had arrived. Now the Allied attack could be resumed. But on 29 October, the Germans themselves again took the offensive, their main attack beginning the next day. Yet on the evening of the 28th, the Belgians had played their last trump by opening their sluicegates and flooding a two-mile area from Dixmude to the sea to a depth of three or four feet. In the most literal sense, the German advance was bogged down. One account relates that 'it seemed to the Germans as if the whole country had sunk

with them and behind them'. Yet for the Belgians, outwitting their enemy had been achieved at a ghastly price. Thus far in the campaign they had already lost twenty thousand casualties, about 35 per cent of their armed forces.

The thirtieth of October saw a day of incredible devastation. As night fell, however, deep dissatisfaction was registered on each side. Rupprecht, expressing himself 'profoundly disappointed' with the course of events, renewed his resolve to take the Messines ridge. The German commanders demanded an even stronger offensive. At the same time, Foch was shoring up the sagging British morale, advising his allies to 'hammer away, keep on hammering and you will get there'.

The Middle of an Earthquake

On 31 October, after prolonged bloodshed and firing so intense that, as one sergeant put it, 'The ground was literally shaking as if we were in the middle of an earthquake', the Germans assailed and later captured Messines ridge. At Gheluvelt, nearly five miles southeast of Ypres, the British position began to crumble, and for a time all seemed lost; but by a desperate summoning of Allied reserves, the Germans were again driven back. Earlier the rapid British firing had again given the impression that machine-guns were being used.

The next day, 1 November, the Allies had anticipated further horrendous German attacks. The juggernaut, however, did not materialize, and the Germans bided their time until the Allies had exhausted themselves in localized attacks. Their inactivity was, in fact, mainly due to despondency at the endless chain of sufferings and losses without decisive result. Foch's attacks on 1 and 2 November were bold and imaginative, but for eleven more days Falkenhayn refused to take no for an answer. Finally, the additional miseries of snow and flooding, added to his preoccupation with events in the east, forced him to call a halt to the slaughter.

On 10 November, the Germans finally captured Dixmude, but the gain was meaningless, because by now the flooding of the Yser bank had been completed. Next day the fighting flared up to a climax of destruction. After further skirmishing, the Battle of Ypres formally ended on 22 November.

Ypres was the last occasion in 1914 when the Germans tried to break through the Allied positions to reach and capture the Channel ports. The attempt had been made, and had failed.

Ironically, Ypres itself, the occasion of the carnage, was a poor defensive position, in fact a bottleneck. The German emplacements on the hills above were far better, as also was a north-south position just to the rear of Ypres. But the town had become a symbol of the Allied cause, just as Verdun hypnotized the French later in the war. Ypres had to be held, at no matter what price. Over fifty thousand British had been killed or wounded, and the French losses were at least as great. Between 13 and 25 October alone, Germany sustained one hundred and thirty-four thousand casualties. One historian estimated that Ypres took a toll of a quarter of a million dead and maimed.

L'INGORDO
TROP DUR

Top left: Marshal Foch. **Left:** An *Uhlan* with a captured colonial soldier. Racist propaganda played an important role in convincing Germans that the French were incapable of defending themselves. German *Kultur* would triumph over French barbarism. **Top right:** Allied propaganda against Germany was grotesque. Already charged with eating babies and impaling them on spikes, 'the Huns' were supposed to have laughingly cut off the hands of their mothers. No lie was too great, no distortion too bizarre. **Above:** An Italian caricature of the Kaiser, greedily devouring the world.

欧洲大戦乱画報（其二十四） 日本軍之青島総攻撃我軍巨砲之威力＝戦慄ス

Above: A Japanese propaganda poster depicting their attack on Tsingtao. **Right:** A more realistic impression of Japanese armed forces before the seizure of Tsingtao.

By now the entire western front had become the scene of a futile, stale and repetitive struggle. Between November 1914 and the spring of 1917, at least half a million of the flower of European manhood fell – while the result was that the lines of battle varied less than ten miles in either direction. This fact, which in retrospect seems to us unimaginable in its callous irrationality, stands out as the ugliest and most senseless occurrence of a peculiarly unlovely war. Falls explains that stalemate occurred because 'The assault could never be driven through into open country fast and clearly enough to prevent new lines of resistance being established and the defence congealing about the bulge.' However, the squandering of life remains inexplicable.

Ypres itself was nevertheless an example of mass heroism. Its indomitable veterans were, as Sir John Edmonds wrote, 'tired, haggard, and unshaven men, unwashed, plastered with mud, many in little more than rags'. In the midst of a vast exercise in destruction, the human spirit of the survivors prevailed against incredible odds.

The Entry of Japan

Meanwhile, on the political front, the war had been spreading to include a number of other belligerents, the foremost of which was Japan. Both Britain and Germany made early efforts to keep the war from spreading to the Far East; and on 1 August Grey had specifically told the Japanese that if Britain joined in the approaching conflict, she did not expect to need the help of her Asian ally. Indeed, initially Japan agreed that she would observe neutrality in any war confined to Europe; she would enter the war only if a third party – in this case, Germany – attacked British interests in the Far East. This position accorded with the renewed Anglo-Japanese alliance of 1911. In addition, Japan implied that she would only go to war if Britain asked her to do so.

On the other hand, the British Admiralty had decided that Japan would be needed to 'hunt out and destroy German armed cruisers who are attacking our commerce' in the Pacific. On 6 August, Grey informed the Japanese of this. This position was of course completely contrary to the one which Grey had taken only five days earlier. After reflecting on the course of events, on 7 August the Japanese cabinet decided to join the fighting on the side of the Entente.

Japanese motives were self-interested. As the Foreign Minister, Kato, emphasized to his colleagues, Japan could exploit the situation to gain both the fortress and port of Tsingtao and certain Pacific islands at Germany's expense. Thus, on 9 August, Kato told the British that Japan would have to participate in the war on more than a token basis in order to destroy German power in the Far East. Grey, by now worried at unleashing Japanese power in China or the Pacific islands, made it clear that London wanted Japanese help to be restricted to naval operations; and accordingly the British withdrew their request for Japanese aid. But the Japanese were adamant, and in the end Grey had to admit that it was for Japan alone to decide the nature of her actions.

On 15 August Japan issued an ultimatum to Germany, calling on Berlin to agree by 23 August to withdraw her naval might forthwith from Japanese and Chinese waters, or to disarm those ships that could not be withdrawn immediately. Germany was also to hand over to Japan within a month the German leased territory of Kiaochow, in the Shantung province of China. As the Japanese nebulously put it, Kiaochow would be held by them 'with a view to' its 'eventual' restoration to China. Meanwhile, despite pressure from Britain, Japan refused to give specific assurances as to the limits of her ambitions.

No German reply to the ultimatum having been received, on 23 August Japan declared war against Germany. Almost immediately she moved against the German Pacific islands and Tsingtao, which fell on 7 November. The islands in particular were an important strategic gain. America and the Pacific Dominions, as well as Britain herself, looked with suspicion on this further accretion

General Liman von Sanders, German adviser to the Turkish army. His efforts to bring the Ottoman Empire into the war on the side of the Central Powers succeeded.

Above and opposite above: Uniforms of the Chinese army. Although the Japanese invaded China to seize Germany's colonial possessions, China did not enter the war until 1917.

His Excellency Djemal Pasha with his Chief of Staff, Fuad Bey. Djemal Pasha had no enthusiasm for fighting Britain and France.

to Japanese strength. Japan had plunged into the Great War – as an unwanted ally.

Several factors made it likely that if Turkey became a belligerent, she would do so on the side of the Central Powers. German influence over the Turkish army was strong; indeed, it had recently been reorganized under the direction of General Liman von Sanders. Moreover, Enver Pasha, War Minister, the pugnacious leader of the Young Turk revisionists and himself already of pre-eminent stature in Turkish life, was a convinced Germanophile. Strengthening ties of trade and commerce linked the two nations. The Kaiser himself was eager for Turkish support in connection with the Berlin-Baghdad railway scheme, and he loudly proclaimed his sympathy for Mohammedan aims. Above all, Russia, a member of the Entente, was the hereditary enemy of that pan-Turkish irredentism which was coming to the fore at Constantinople. Pan-Turanian expansion could only be achieved at Russian expense.

On the other hand, the Minister of Marine, Djemal Pasha, at first leaned in sympathy towards the Entente. French influence was felt through her investments in the country, and the British held a powerful position in naval circles. Furthermore, the condition of the country as a whole had been debilitated by a series of recent wars. Probably most Turks wanted either neutrality, or war against only the hated Romanovs, though popular opinion was outraged at the British appropriation of two Turkish battleships which had been constructed in an English shipyard.

As early as 2 August, Enver committed himself to a secret agreement under which Turkey would intervene on the German side if Russia took the part of Serbia. It was agreed that if Greece allied herself with the Entente, Turkey would receive the Greek Aegean islands and Crete in the event of German victory. Yet Turkey did not commit herself to immediate participation in the conflict; and, simultaneously with the secret negotiations

Allied Movements 1914

▷ 21 October
▷ 11 November
◣ 22 November

Little large scale movement during two months fighting. Although forced to give up ground to the Germans, the Allies were not forced out of the salient

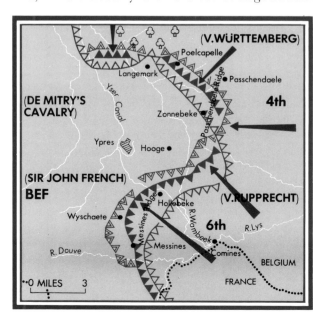

with Germany, Enver approached the Russians with an offer of alliance in return for the cession to Turkey of western Thrace and the Aegean islands. Russia, needing whatever Balkan support she could get, was unreceptive, though she proposed certain concessions which were intended to keep Turkey neutral. Instead, they merely whetted the Turkish appetite for gains. To make matters worse, Allied diplomacy towards the Turks worked at cross-purposes because of their differing interests in the Near East. For all these reasons, despite initial hesitancy because of British participation in the Entente, by early in September it became obvious that Turkey was gravitating towards the Central Powers. In August, the German cruisers *Goeben* and *Breslau* had evaded their British pursuers, entered the Dardanelles, and had been 'purchased' by Turkey complete with befezzed German crews. This transparent ruse had shown which way the wind was blowing; and the Marne and the Russian

victories in the East only delayed the inevitable. By October, Djemal had reconciled himself to an anti-Russian policy, and in return for a large German loan, Enver and Talaat Bey, the Interior Minister, had promised to stand at the side of Berlin. The pro-neutral or pro-Entente Turkish ministers were disunited and ineffectual.

On 28 October, without a declaration of war, the Turkish fleet under the German Admiral Souchon bombarded Russian ports on the Black Sea, and by 5 November all three major Allies were at war with the Ottoman Empire.

Turkish entry into the war meant that considerable Allied forces had to be diverted to defend Egypt and the Caucasus. In fact, Turkey's strategic location threatened the Russian lifeline to the Mediterranean and that of Great Britain to India and the Far East. Furthermore, it was feared that the Turkish alliance with the Central Powers would lead to the disaffection of the Mohammedan millions within the Indian Empire.

The German cruisers *Goeben* and *Breslau* enter the Dardanelles, evading their British pursuers. Their German crews were given fezzes when the ships were incorporated into the Turkish navy.

In addition, the smaller Balkan states might now be tempted to align themselves with Germany.

Nevertheless, Turkey was to pay dearly for her impetuous entry into the war. Already poor, backward, and inefficient, her price for losing was reduction to an Anatolian rump-state. Before they leaped, the Turks did not look hard enough.

Thus Japan and Turkey had joined the conflict, though on opposing sides, and the Great War had spread beyond the confines of Europe. In the meantime, however, several countries had declared their intention of abstaining from the war. Of the European nations, Norway, Sweden, Denmark, the Netherlands, Switzerland, and Spain were all successful in maintaining their neutrality throughout the war.

The Role of the Neutrals

The role of a neutral was by no means easy, the British blockade affected all their interests in varying degrees and often prevented the neutrals from taking full advantage of the increased demands for goods from warring nations. On the other hand, in the United States, which remained a neutral until 1917, the upsurge in trade with the Allies as a result of the wartime situation contributed significantly to creating a climate in which influential sections of the country felt a vested interest in an Allied victory. Though often precarious and equivocal, the position of the neutrals was not untenable. As most of them realized fully, they were fortunate indeed to escape the disastrous loss of life sustained by the belligerents.

Because they had entered the war for ostensibly defensive reasons, in one sense the absence of specifically stated British or French war aims is hardly surprising. Their first priority was to win; and because of the nature of the early course of the war, for much of the time this meant, in effect, the clearing of the enemy from occupied Allied territory. The German rape of Belgium had been the rallying point behind which the British had marched into the affray; therefore the restoration of Belgium was an inseparable part of the Allied cause. Similarly, the German armies had to be pushed out of northern France; and once the war began, if not before, the overwhelming majority of Frenchmen dreamed of the reunion of Alsace-Lorraine with France, though the territory had been German since 1871 and was an ethnic and linguistic crossroads.

Early in the war, few men agreed with Kitchener that a long struggle lay ahead before victory could be achieved. If the war were to end by Christmas, then victory itself would define specific war aims. Not until the end of 1914 did this optimism irretrievably fade before the spectre of havoc which the fighting had invoked. By then, with the chance of rapid victory irrevocably lost, all the belligerents intensified their search for allies, and in doing so were forced to clarify what they were fighting for – and against. Moreover, as the war and the concomitant suffering grew ever longer and more frightful, appropriate spoils of victory had to be found. Somehow the holocaust had to be justified, to be made worthwhile; somehow the maimed and weary soldiers had to be inspired to struggle on. As Allied resources

evaporated under the voracious demands of total war, American financial and material aid became increasingly indispensable, and the evolving aims of war were influenced in part by the desire for American approval.

Thus the British fought to restore the Low Countries to their age-old status of buffers; the French to free their territory and regain their lost provinces; and the Russians to maintain their momentum, to survive as a great power, and later merely to remain together as a political entity.

In October 1914, the Russian Ambassador in Paris, Isvolsky, asked for a statement of French war aims. He was told that German power must be destroyed. The following month, Paléologue, Isvolsky's opposite number, was received by Tsar Nicholas. Besides discussing the 'necessary' destruction of Austria-Hungary, the idea of a separate Hanoverian kingdom in northwest Germany was mooted. Paléologue also mentioned that 'perhaps' France would favour an extension of her territory to include the German Rhineland, although in fact the Quai d'Orsay remained non-committal on this point. Thus as the autumn wore on, the debate on Allied war aims did become more specific; but there was still no comprehensive or agreed list of aims, nor any concrete plan for their achievement.

In England the liberal press, once it was reconciled to the idea of participation in the war, emphasized the more righteous reasons for the conflict. Gardiner of the *Daily News* spoke of fighting to free the German masses from the Prussian yoke. As early as 14 August, H. G. Wells dubbed the affray 'The War to End War'. By November, both Asquith, the Prime Minister, and Grey had emphasized that the Allies must fight to prevent either 'continuance or recurrence of an armed brute power in Central Europe'.

As the fighting continued, with ever-lengthening casualty lists as silent witnesses to the slaughter, the propaganda services of each side harped upon the brutality of the enemy. For the Allies, the natural corollary of their image of the Germans as brutes was that 'the Huns' were unfit to be colonial masters. Gradually the idea gained strength that these German dependencies, considered unready or unable to rule themselves, should be taken in so-called trust, by the (as they saw themselves) morally superior Allies. The colonial issue illustrates well the almost imperceptible and natural emergence of certain aims. The 'realists' were also pleased with the reflections of the 'idealists' on the colonial problem, since for reasons of strategy they badly wanted areas such as German Southwest Africa. For these and other reasons, by early 1915 the British had conquered most of the German territories in Africa.

While Allied annexationism proceeded apace, it was different from the ambitions of Germany in terms of power politics. Klaus Epstein wrote that '*only* German annexations threatened the complete overthrow of the European balance of power; and *all* German annexationist plans were certain to violate the now fashionable principle of nationality'.

The emergence of war aims underlined the divisions among the Allies themselves. For example, Britain and France bickered over the

71

future of the German Cameroons. While France was more concerned for the future of Poland than for Serbia, Britain was relatively unconcerned about both. There were fewer French than British who worried about national self-determination. The French hoped to soothe their Russian ally by securing the principle of freedom of the Straits; the British were more dubious. However, in September 1914, by the Treaty of London it was agreed that when peace terms might be discussed, 'no one of the Allies will demand terms without the previous agreement of each of the other Allies'. Yet for all this, it must be underlined that, as A. J. P. Taylor pointed out, 'There was no serious exchange of ideas between the Entente Powers on war aims during the first winter of the war.' Allied ideas on the shape of the future world were embryonic and tentative.

On the German side, the aims of war were defined earlier and in more detail. Whether or not one accepts the Fischer-Geiss thesis that Germany was literally 'grasping at world power',

German aims were undoubtedly far-reaching. In many circles, for instance, the idea of *Mitteleuropa*, or German domination (either by outright annexation or economic control) of the Balkans and the Near East, and also of much of Eastern Europe, was expected to provide a vast area for development and exploitation, comparable to the British and French colonial empires. The paucity of German colonial holdings was also bitterly resented, and dreams arose of a powerful bloc of German territory in the centre of Africa: the *Mittelafrika* concept.

In early August, the Kaiser hinted that after the expected German victory, the Polish Kingdom would be re-established, divorced from Russia and closely linked to Germany. At the same time, Bethmann-Hollweg encouraged Finnish separatism and considered the idea of a Ukrainian buffer-state. By 21 August, the Chancellor was speaking of Belgium, Holland, and Poland as German protected states or *Schützstaaten*, and almost three weeks later, when a decisive German triumph in

Flying Officer Bruno Büchner stands before his aeroplane, one of the few the Germans left to defend their East African colony.

the west seemed imminent, Bethmann formulated his September Program, a kind of provisional shopping list of German needs and desires.

According to the Chancellor, Germany's first priority was 'to achieve security for the German Reich in west and east for all imaginable time'. To do this, it was necessary to weaken France to the point where 'her revival as a great power' would be 'impossible for all time'. Similarly, 'Russia must be thrust back as far as possible from Germany's eastern frontier and her domination over the non-Russian vassal peoples broken.' With France and Russia sapped of strength, Germany would be the dominant European power.

The September Program also listed specific war aims. France was to cede the Briey orefield and possible other pieces of territory to Germany, while French Flanders was to be joined to Belgium. Belgium itself was to make certain territorial concessions and 'must be reduced to a vassal state, . . . economically a German pro-

vince'. Holland 'must be left independent in externals, but be made internally dependent on' Germany. Luxembourg would be incorporated into the Reich. An economic association to include France, Belgium, Holland, Denmark, Poland, Austria-Hungary, and possibly Norway, Sweden, and Italy would be created under German leadership to 'stabilize Germany's economic dominance over *Mitteleuropa*'. The issues of *Mittelafrika* and Russia 'will be considered later'.

The program outlined above is an indication of the massive shift in the continental European balance of power that Germany considered necessary to her own future as a power of world stature. But the September Program was never rigidly followed; and after the definitive failure of German western strategy at Ypres, Bethmann-Hollweg seriously considered a compromise peace with Russia in order to turn westward with free hands. Although this idea was shelved because of opposition, Germany's war aims, while flexible, remained grandiose.

CHAPTER FIVE
Navies and Armies Clash

During the Great War the Japanese, seeing their opportunity, took the lion's share of the German Far East and Pacific colonies. These colonies were also important because Tsingtao, the capital of Kiaochow, was the headquarters of the German East Asiatic Naval Squadron, commanded by the formidable Vice Admiral Graf Maximilian von Spee.

During October 1914 it became evident that a major part of this squadron was heading for South America, where Germany had powerful interests. To the Germans, this course seemed prudent in view of the Japanese declaration of war against Germany. Such action brought two further advantages: it was thought unlikely that the Japanese would pursue the Germans so far afield, in view of possible complications with the United States, and the journey could be accomplished in relative ease and secrecy by journeying via the myriad islands en route.

The British were anxious lest subsequently the German fleet might round Cape Horn and cause havoc to the vital South American-European trade in meat and maize. The Admiralty resolved that this danger must be averted at all costs, for if her foreign trade and food imports were seriously disrupted, Great Britain would be brought to her knees in a matter of weeks. Thus the German vessels must be found and destroyed.

Coronel, to the south of Santiago, Chile, was the scene of the first round in a double clash of navies. On 31 October the British light cruiser *Glasgow* anchored in Coronel Bay. She had taken a battering in tremendous gales during her journey from the Falkland Islands, and was now in need of a brief respite in port for repairs. Next day, however, the *Glasgow* sailed away, aware from telegraphic signals that a German ship was nearby. Soon she joined the rest of the British fleet some forty miles west of Coronel.

As it happened, Spee had moved south to forestall the *Glasgow* at the same time that the British commander Rear Admiral Sir Christopher Cradock, had voyaged north to fight what he supposed to be the isolated German light cruiser *Leipzig*. Although both navies sought the encounter, the actual battle was full of mutual surprises.

The British ships, *Good Hope*, *Monmouth*, *Glasgow*, and *Otranto* spread out in linear formation. On the afternoon of 1 November, the German armoured cruisers *Scharnhorst* and *Gneisenau* approached on the horizon; the *Leipzig* was not, after all, alone. To this German concentration was added the *Dresden*. The British were at a heavy

disadvantage: against two elderly armoured cruisers, an armed merchant ship, and a light cruiser, the Germans pitted two modern armoured cruisers and two light cruisers, with the danger of a third, the *Nürnberg*, in the background. Moreover, the German ships were manned by expert professional sailors, whereas the British seamen were mostly recent recruits. Cradock could have avoided action by retiring southwards; Cruttwell guesses that his motive for not doing so was his hope that before his inevitable destruction he might damage the German fleet sufficiently to enable the British ship *Canopus*, 300 miles to the south, to finish the job.

Cradock was a true son of Nelson. Fearlessly he prepared for battle against overwhelming odds. As evening fell, the German guns blazed fire, and thunderously the British boomed their reply. Yet, outlined in the sunset, the British ships were doomed. In under an hour the *Good Hope* found a watery grave. Torn by an explosion, her hulk blazing like a charnel house, the British flagship disappeared from sight. Lumbering on into the darkness, the burning *Monmouth* was annihilated by the *Nürnberg*. Both British ships went down in grim defiance, with the loss of every single man aboard, 1440 in all. Somehow the *Glasgow* contrived to escape, while the *Otranto* had only played a minor role. The German ships were barely scratched, and their only casualties were two wounded. Here was a German victory at the very moment when Allied morale needed a fillip to counter Turkish entry into the war.

Britain did not sit down under the humiliation.

Opposite: The *Scharnhorst* in the foreground, with the *Leipzig*, *Nürnberg* and *Dresden*, sailing off the Chilean coast: November 1914.

Admiral Sir Christopher Cradock, who sailed into disaster in 1914.

(Map legend:)

Coronel

OMILES 600

1.11.14. Battle of Coronel (German Victory)

SOUTH AMERICA

Atlantic Ocean

Pacific Ocean

8.12.14. Battle of Falklands (British Victory)

Falkland Islands

Magellan Straits

Cape Horn

Right: The German cruiser *Dresden*, which the British finally cornered and sank in March 1915. **Below:** The German disaster in the Falklands. The *Inflexible* and its crew assist the survivors of the *Gneisenau*.

Admiral Lord Fisher, newly reappointed as First Sea Lord, was fiercely determined to hunt down Spee wherever he went. Yet Spee had tasted victory and liked its flavour. As the French say, *l'appétit vient en mangeant*. After much delay, Spee decided to pull off another coup by attacking the Falkland Islands, a position of tremendous strategic importance due to its use as a coaling station and radio communications centre. He was partially encouraged by several reports that the islands now lay undefended.

Meanwhile, on 7 December, Vice Admiral Sir Frederick Doveton Sturdee, Commander in Chief of British naval forces in the Pacific and South Atlantic, had arrived with his squadron for coaling in the Falklands. Next day the *Gneisenau* and *Nürnberg* were sighted. The Germans had seen a tremendous pall of smoke rising from the harbour, but thinking that the stocks of coal were being destroyed on their approach, they proceeded. Too late, the German vessels spotted the British battle-cruisers lying at anchor in Port Stanley. Swiftly they and the rest of the German fleet sped south-east. Ironically, several of the British ships were still coaling, and had Spee boldly attacked, he might have done considerable damage.

Sturdee, calm and unhurried in the best tradition of Drake, but nonetheless relentless, followed in pursuit. Caution lest his ships be damaged seriously led Sturdee to fight at long range, and this considerably lengthened the duration of the battle. Nevertheless, he had it mostly his own way. In the afternoon, the *Scharnhorst*, already burning uncontrollably, was pulverized by the *Inflexible* and the *Invincible*. Rolling on her side, the *Scharnhorst* sank. Firing haphazardly to the end, the *Gneisenau* went down with flags flying and sailors cheering the Kaiser. The Germans had proved themselves as brave in defeat as they were haughty in victory. Then the *Nürnberg* fell victim to the *Kent*, and the *Leipzig* similarly to the *Cornwall* and the *Glasgow*. Only the *Dresden* escaped, to lead a charmed life as the last German cruiser at sea, until she too was cornered the following March.

Some two hundred German sailors survived the rout, but eighteen hundred died, including Spee and his two sons. British casualties were only thirty. The Falklands was Coronel in reverse, but now the threat from German surface raiders was over. Britannia once more ruled the waves.

Stalemate in the East

In the eleven days preceding Christmas, Joffre's hopes of a breakthrough in the west were once more disappointed. The Tenth Army attacked at Arras, while the Fourth Army concentrated in Champagne. Falls has stated the bald truth in describing this French offensive as 'a mere killing match', useless from every point of view; yet it was one which dragged on until 17 March. The French fought with gallantry and fortitude, but nonetheless made no strategic impact on the Germans. The resulting casualties numbered at least one hundred and eighty thousand, about evenly divided between Germans and French.

On the eastern front, the winter campaign was an anticlimax to the great clashes of the autumn. German reinforcements during December led to

Damage done to HMS *Kent* after the Battle of the Falklands.

Admiral Lord Fisher, the First Sea Lord, who was determined to hunt down Graf Spee. His friends called him Jackie. The Germans probably had another name for him.

the fall of Lodz on 6 December, for as usual the Russians were short of supplies and especially munitions. Yet Hindenburg failed in his bid to smash through the Russian fortifications to the west of Warsaw, and indeed, the line remained unyielding until the summer of 1915.

In Galicia, the Austrians were still struggling rather unsuccessfully to push the Russians back. Despite a few hopeful advances, Conrad was unable to disrupt the Russians along the line of the Dunajec, and the full force of winter now added to the difficulties of further operations. Meanwhile, Falkenhayn strongly emphasized the decisive importance of the western front as opposed to that in the east. He believed that the war could never be won until Britain and France were defeated. Apprehensive of a repetition of Napoleon's disastrous experiences in 1812, he urged a separate peace with Russia in order that the whole of German might could be swung westwards. But Hindenburg and Ludendorff pressed the argument that knocking Russia out of the war first could be achieved; and when this was done, Germany would have acquired vast supplies with which to turn fully to the west. Moreover, Germany had to bolster her Austrian ally in the east. These latter arguments were convincing to Chancellor Bethmann-Hollweg and Jagow, and in January 1915 Falkenhayn was finally forced to give way. The war in the east would continue with high priority.

On 9 February the German Eighth and Tenth Armies moved forward from their positions at Lötzen and the Masurian Lakes. Their object was to make a pincers movement and thus to encircle the Russian Tenth Army. Due in part to the now-familiar interception of Russian uncoded radio messages, the Germans were able to force a break in two places. In the Winter Battle of Masuria, they cornered at least seventy thousand Russians

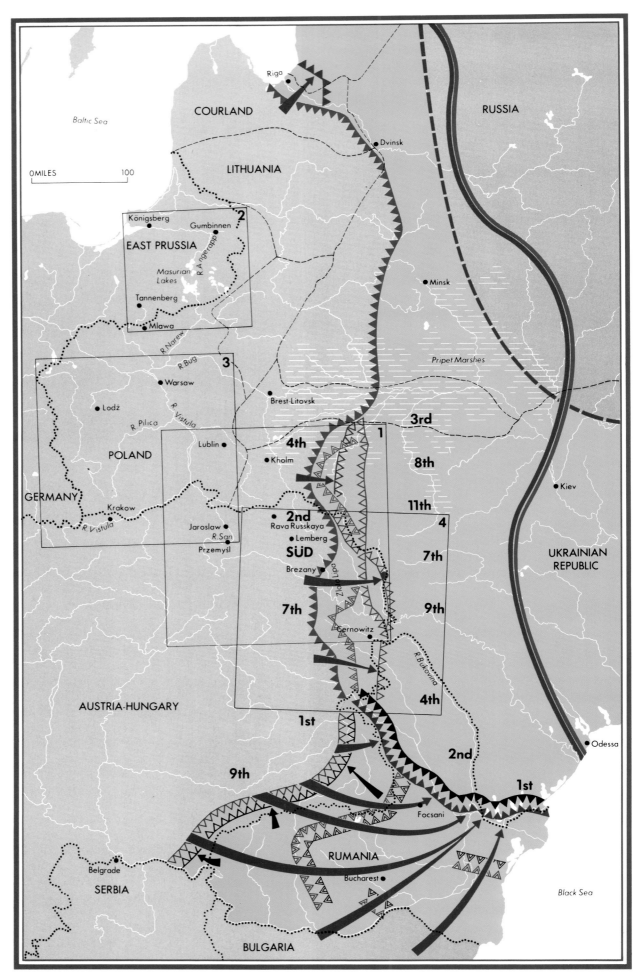

Brusilov's offensive 1916

Front line 4 June

Advance by 4-10 June

Advance by 20 September

Rumanians join war on strength of Russian victory. Depth of their invasion by 8 Sept, 1916

9th army counter-attack Position by 26 Nov, 1916

By 17 Jan, 1917 Rumanian armies shattered and most of their country lost

Push back into Russia by 3 Aug, 1917; Riga taken 21 September

During breakdown of Brest-Litovsk treaty negotiations Germans advance deep into Russia & Ukraine

Line set by Brest-Litovsk treaty 3 March, 1918

States recognised as independent by treaty

1 Battle of Lemberg 25 Aug-Mid-Sept, 1914 See Chapter 3
2 Tannenberg 20 Aug-12 Sept, 1914 See Chapter 3
3 1st & 2nd Battle of Warsaw 9 Oct-17 Dec, 1914 See Chapter 3
4 Kerensky offensive July 1-3 Aug, 1917 See Chapter 11

Above: Austrian artillery in Galicia. **Right:** Polish troops in action: December 1914. **Far right:** A German barricade dividing a village north-west of Arras, April 1915.

German trench mortars in action.

in the forests surrounding Augustovno (Augustow). However, as Edmonds points out, another Tannenberg was avoided, since the German encirclement was accomplished with only one division, and the insufficient number of German troops meant that the majority of Russians were able to escape. Furthermore, the Russians did not slide into panic as they had at Tannenberg. Yet to the Germans, the important fact was that their hallowed East Prussia was once more cleared of the enemy.

The Struggle for the Carpathians

Yet if East Prussia were free, the Carpathians were not. Vienna was by now convinced that if Italy joined the Entente, the war was lost, and Austria sought a tremendous victory in Galicia in order to prevent Italian and Rumanian entry into the war. As it turned out, no such victory came, and the expected interventions followed. For their part, the Russians believed that if Austria-Hungary could be defeated, the shock would cause German morale to collapse. Thus both sides independently decided to force an action in the Carpathian Mountains, gateway to the Hungarian heartland.

The ice-covered Carpathians provided an unenviable site for a winter offensive. Roads which now were frozen proved equally impassable later, when the thaw had made them muddy and slimy. Before this occurred, however, untold thousands, including whole companies at a time, died of exposure on the march. Finally the campaign became a series of misery-laden attacks up

sheer slopes that would have defied an army of mountain goats. In fact, the whole Carpathian episode degenerated into what the official Austro-Hungarian history admits was 'a grisly folly'.

On 23 January the Austro-Hungarian Army took the offensive by means of a general attack on the passes of Dukla, Lupków and Uzsok. The German South Army simultaneously attempted to take the passes of Verecke and Wyszków. On the defensive stood the Russian Eighth Army. The offensive lasted only a few days, then petered out, a dismal failure caused in large measure by the disruption of supply lines in the miserable weather.

Late in January, the Russians in turn went over to the attack, ran into difficulties, but made some progress. Despite this, Conrad planned a further offensive for late February, for he feared the blow to morale and the effect on the southern European and Balkan neutrals if he did nothing to relieve the Russian siege of the fortress of Przemysl. Yet again the hapless troops were defeated by the weather, by then known as 'General Winter'. Przemyśl fell on 22 March, and with it the Russians gained one hundred thousand prisoners. Slav obstructionism in the Austrian ranks reached a new peak, and Habsburg morale hit rock bottom. Furthermore, the Russian troops surrounding Przemyśl were now freed for a counterattack which gained considerable ground. They were halted and the line stabilized only by the arrival of German reinforcements in April. This in itself was symbolic. For the exhausted and demoralized Austrians, the winter fighting was their last major effort independent of Germany.

Previous page: 1500
Russian prisoners receive
bread rations in Augustowo.

The ill-fated *Lusitania*.

The Sinking of the Lusitania

On 7 May 1915, a sudden disaster broke upon a horrified and astonished world. A German submarine had sunk the steamship *Lusitania*, pride of the Cunard Line, with the loss of 1198 lives.

On the morning of 1 May the *Lusitania*, a British vessel, had left New York for the trans-Atlantic crossing to Liverpool. Many Americans were on board – despite a solemn black-bordered advertisement which had appeared in the New York papers.

The advertisement had caught the eye of many newspapermen and thrill-seekers, and as the mighty liner steamed out of harbour, an air of premonition hung over Pier 54. Some of the more morbid photographers present were selling pictures of the ship and proclaiming, 'Last voyage of the *Lusitania*!' Ominous telegrams warning passengers to cancel their berths added to the electric atmosphere. One which was addressed to the multimillionaire Alfred Vanderbilt cautioned, 'Have it on definite authority the *Lusitania* is to be torpedoed.' Yet few on board the powerful vessel, the largest and fastest steamer on the Atlantic run, paid heed. Vanderbilt himself scoffed at any thought of danger. After all, as many reasoned, why would anyone attack a harmless luxury liner, especially one including many Americans whose goodwill was sorely needed by the Central Powers? Who would foolishly attack a ship whose passenger-list included a gaggle of VIPs?

As the *Lusitania*'s passengers settled down to their opulent voyage, they little realized that in the hold were 4200 cases of small-calibre rifle ammunition and over 100 cases of empty shrapnel shells and unloaded fuses. Such a small amount of material hardly constituted an imminent danger to the German war effort; yet nevertheless the Germans defined these goods as contraband of war. Moreover, the passengers included a group of Canadian volunteers en route to the front.

As the *Lusitania* made its way across the Atlantic, approximately fifteen German submarines were restlessly patrolling the ocean depths. In their fear that the Allied blockade would strangle their economy, on 4 February the German government had proclaimed that the waters surrounding the British Isles constituted a war zone wherein, after

17 February, 'every enemy merchant ship . . . will be destroyed without its being always possible to avert the dangers threatening the crews and passengers on that account'. In view of alleged Allied misuse of neutral flags, 'Even neutral ships are exposed to danger in the war zone.' The *Lusitania* was sailing straight towards her doom.

On the night of 4 May, the 32,000-ton Cunarder moved swiftly through the invisible midpoint of its voyage. At the same time the German *Unterseeboote* (U-boat) U-20 appeared off southern Ireland, and during the next two days sank three ships, though without loss of life.

On the evening of 6 May the *Lusitania*'s captain, Turner, 'a seadog's seadog', as one authority called him, received a terse radio message from the British Admiralty: 'Submarines active off south coast of Ireland.' Elaborate safety precautions were undertaken; lifeboats were readied, bulkhead doors and portholes were secured, and after a further warning message, it was decided to take a mid-channel course. Meanwhile the ship's lookout had been doubled.

In the early afternoon of the following day, the Irish coast appeared on the horizon. The fog which had persisted earlier had now lifted. The *Lusitania*'s journey was nearly over. Now was sighted a familiar landmark, the Old Head of Kinsale. At that very moment – 1:40 p.m. – Kapitänleutnant Schweiger of the U-20 sighted the *Lusitania* in his binoculars. Swiftly the U-boat submerged, shortly to move in for the kill. The *Lusitania* became a sitting (or rather, moving) duck, for as he proceeded on a steady course at eighteen knots, Turner had unwittingly manoeuvred the ship into the position of an ideal target.

At two o'clock, most of the *Lusitania*'s voyagers had finished a leisurely luncheon. While some lingered in the Louis Seize dining saloon, others had adjourned for their coffee to the exquisite late-Georgian lounge. Many had emerged to take a stroll on deck, for the air was pleasant and the sun had come out. In the distance an orchestra played the 'Blue Danube'.

At 2:09 p.m., the U-20 unloosed a single of its deadly torpedoes. Heading straight for the British ship, the 290 lb missile cleaved through the water, leaving a trail of white foam in its wake.

Suddenly a lookout saw the danger to starboard. His shouted warning was superfluous. At precisely 2:10, the torpedo thudded into the starboard side behind the bridge, to the accompaniment of a terrifically powerful explosion. Suddenly the 790-foot vessel sharply lurched to starboard. Among the passengers, complacency gave way to fright. Several lifeboats, ready for launching, were thwarted because the *Lusitania* was moving too rapidly for evacuation measures to be taken safely. Already one boat had gone over the side, and its hapless occupants fell into the sea.

As the *Lusitania* listed ever more sharply to starboard, lifeboats to port crashed onto the deck in steady succession. Panicky passengers scurried about, many of them wearing their lifebelts incorrectly. As water surged onto the sinking starboard deck, several voyagers leapt overboard. By now a few of the boats had been safely launched – but not nearly enough. Amid the anguished cries of women and children, a grotesque note of black comedy was provided by a trio of Irish maidens distractedly warbling 'There Is a Green Hill Far Away'. Screams and oaths were intermingled as unanchored objects skidded and hurtled across the decks. In his ship's log, Schweiger laconically noted, 'Great confusion on board . . . They must have lost their heads.'

Now the *Lusitania*'s end was near. Suddenly her rudder and propeller heaved into the air, the bows thrust deeply into the water. Eighteen minutes after the torpedo had sunk home, as one survivor saw it, the *Lusitania* sank forever beneath the waves 'with a thunderous roar as of the collapse of a great building during a fire'. A scene of pandemonium spread across the surrounding mile of water. The sea was full of boats, some secure and some capsized. Flotsam and jetsam and hardy swimmers abounded, but the scene was rendered hideous by a steadily mounting number of lifeless floating bodies.

Eventually the roll of death amounted to 1198 of the 1959 passengers and crew. Of those dead, 128 were neutral Americans and 94 were children. The Allied press shrieked with outrage, while the *Frankfurter Zeitung* inadvisedly crowed about the German Navy's 'extraordinary success'.

Those in charge of the wheels of Allied pro-paganda quickly capitalized on the monumental German blunder, and no effort was spared to bring America into the war on a crest of passion. *The Times* stormed that the sinking 'has placed the whole German race outside the pale'. President Wilson's intimate adviser, Colonel House, urged immediate war in the absence of a full German apology. Many Americans railed against Germans and 'hyphenates' in general, but Washington kept its head. After a warning to Germany to cease unrestricted submarine attacks on merchant vessels, American neutrality was maintained for two more years. Still, the *Lusitania* incident occasioned an emotional outpouring of sympathy for the Allied cause. As such, in the words of Gaddis Smith, 'it was a sensitive barometer forecasting future American behaviour.'

The official inquiry into the disaster found that two torpedoes had fatally damaged the *Lusitania*, but German and other evidence suggests that only one torpedo found its target. The inquiry skimmed over the question of Admiralty carelessness, for one may well ask why the ship was not sent via a more northerly route when submarines were first observed off southern Ireland; why was the *Lusitania* unescorted even by patrol boats? Why did she carry war material at a time when the Germans were desperate enough to stop at nothing? Whatever the answers to these questions, the story of the *Lusitania* provides perhaps the outstanding example in the war of a misconceived policy with repercussions that besmirched Germany's good name.

Some of the few survivors of the *Lusitania*.

Disaster in Gallipoli

Liddell Hart and others have emphasized that the keynote of the Allied campaign against Turkey was one of shortsighted lethargy. In retrospect, Liddell Hart considers that an Allied attack on the Dardanelles should have been pressed home at the beginning of November 1914 – for at that time and for at least three months afterwards, the Turkish defences remained an obsolete patchwork.

In view of the long and tangled arguments that developed over the merits of a naval versus a combined land-sea operation against the Straits, it is both tragic and ironic that the chance was missed to field an army against the Dardanelles without the use of Allied troops already committed to the field. In August 1914 the Greek Prime Minister, Venizelos, had offered the Allies such forces, but they were refused because of Grey's unwillingness to offend Turkish susceptibilities.

As early as August, Churchill, as First Lord of the Admiralty, had seen the importance of forcing the Straits. On 25 November, at the first meeting of the War Council, he proposed a naval attack on the Dardanelles. The idea was shelved, but a month later the Secretary of the War Council and general *eminence grise*, Sir Maurice Hankey, urged a knockout blow against Turkey as a means of forcing her withdrawal from the war, of aiding Russia, and of influencing events in the Balkans. Indeed, by the end of 1914 many influential men, including Lord Fisher, the First Sea Lord, and Lloyd George, then the Chancellor of the Exchequer, looked for a means of breaking the deadlock, which the war had reached in the west, by use of force, particularly naval power, in another theatre of operations.

The argument for a new eastern front was immeasurably strengthened by the arrival on 2 January of a Russian appeal for a British diversionary action against Turkey to relieve the Ottoman pressure on the Tsarist positions in the Caucasus. As it turned out, however, within days the moment of greatest Russian need had passed because of the victory of Sari Kamish, and the Russians withdrew their request. Yet the Dardanelles idea had been given the fillip it needed, and the project moved forward with a momentum of its own.

Now Churchill telegraphed to Vice Admiral Carden, commander of a British squadron in the Aegean, with reference to the merits of a naval assault. Carden replied, 'I do not consider Dardanelles can be rushed. But they might be forced by extended operations with large numbers of ships.' Seizing on this last sentence, Churchill got the War Council to agree on 15 January to 'prepare for a naval expedition in February to bombard and take the Gallipoli peninsula, with Constantinople as its object'. Churchill took this provisional decision (*prepare* being the operative word in the sentence just quoted) as definite and final, and pushed aside the doubts of others such as Fisher. Robert Rhodes James has shown that Churchill took the sole initiative, pressing Lord Kitchener, the Secretary of State for War, for the British Twenty-ninth Division for use after the naval attack. However, not until 10 March did Kitchener agree to this.

Left: Australian troops on board HMS *London* heading toward their landing at Gallipoli. **Below:** French battleship in action in the Dardanelles, 1915.

Above: The Turks moved their howitzers up and down the coast to compensate for their lack of artillery. **Above right:** The *Suffren*, one of France's contributions to the Allied fleet at Gallipoli. **Below:** HMS *Queen Elizabeth*.

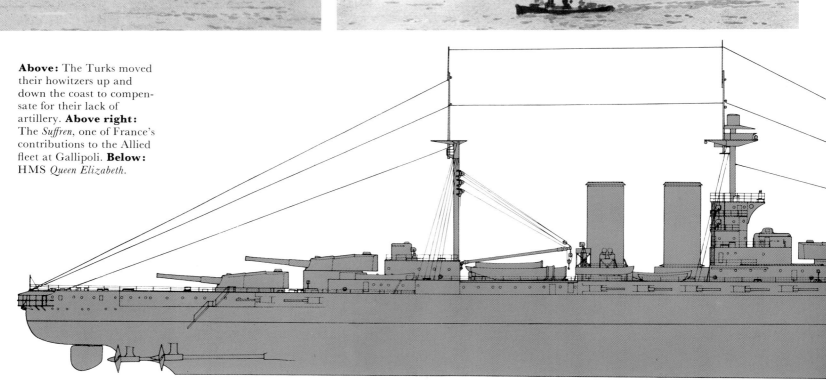

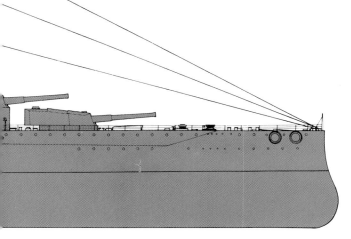

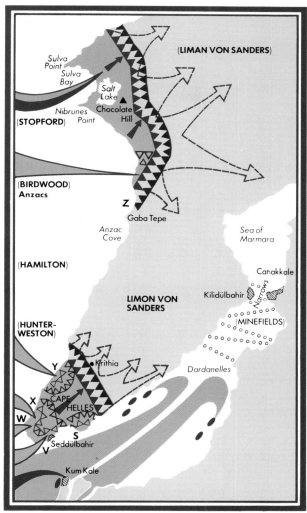

Allied naval attempt to force the Dardanelles: 18 March, 1915

Feint attack to screen the landings at Cape Helles 25 April, 1915

British landings 25 April, 1915

Footholds gained 25 April, 1915

British landing at Suvla Bay 7 August, 1915

Furthest advance by 14 August after much costly fighting

Original objectives

On 19 February the naval attack commenced. Bad weather then caused a delay until 25 February, but on the 26th the task of destroying the intermediate Gallipoli defences began. The results were extremely disappointing. After light opposition to a few tentative marine landings, early in March Turkish resistance became much stronger. Yet on 18 March, urged on by promptings from London, the Anglo-French assault on the Narrows began in earnest. A minesweeping operation took place simultaneously, but on 8 March the Turks had been able to lay a new set of mines, one of which now destroyed without warning the French battleship *Bouvet* and almost all her crew of over six hundred men. In the end, mines destroyed or put out of action six of the nine Allied battleships taking part.

Meanwhile, General Sir Ian Hamilton had been appointed commander of a Mediterranean Expeditionary Force of some seventy thousand British, Australian and New Zealand (ANZAC) and French troops. On 22 March he and Rear Admiral Sir John de Robeck, who had replaced Carden as naval commander in the area, agreed on the need for a combined land-sea operation. Yet with the advantage of hindsight one might argue that a further naval attack on the 18th would have succeeded; certainly the Turks, short of heavy shells and ammunition, had thought so. Indeed, if Constantinople, the Turkish capital, had fallen then, Turkey would probably have sued for peace, for in this area lay her only source of munitions.

On 25 March, worried by the recent naval assault, Enver formed an army to defend the

Top left: The Allied naval attempt to force the Dardanelles was doomed to failure almost from the outset. **Left:** The Allies bombarded the Dardanelles unceasingly in the hope of softening up the Turks.

Rear Admiral Sir John de Robeck.

Dardanelles under General Liman von Sanders. Through mismanagement and dilatory measures, the Allies allowed Sanders a month to complete his defences and bring up his troops. The entire Allied operation was bedevilled by conflict of wills at home, lack of coordination and divided command at the front, and a complete inability to know when to cut losses.

By 20 April the Allies were ready at last. The unfavourable weather, like an omen of disaster to come, caused a temporary delay. At dawn on 25 April, the Twenty-ninth Division landed at five small beaches – designated S, V, W, X and Y Beaches – at Cape Helles, on the southern end of the Gallipoli Peninsula; the ANZACs moved above Gaba Tepe, ten miles farther north on the western side of the peninsula. A British feint was made at Bulair, while the French made a mock diversion at Besika Bay and a temporary landing at Kum Kale on the Asiatic side of the Straits.

The ANZAC landing at Gaba Tepe got off to a bad start. The strong current carried the landing boats a mile north of the projected disembarkation area and to a much less favourable spot. Nevertheless the ANZACs came ashore to only light fire; but the smallness of the – evermore to be known as ANZAC Cove – led to impossible crowding and intermingling of units. The Turkish counterattack, inspired by Colonel Mustapha Kemal, later Atatürk, developed the fury of a whirling dervish, and the ANZACs were thrown back with heavy casualties.

Farther south, three of the British landings were comparatively easy. At W Beach, however, all was dark and silent as the men headed for shore, but as they clambered onto the land, Turkish rifles spewed fire, while many British were enmeshed in underwater wire as they went over the sides of their boats. Eventually the landing was made, but the strain and the decimating losses were sufficient to exhaust the troops for the rest of the day.

If the 'W' landing was difficult, the one at V Beach (Sedd-el-Bahr) was worse. As three thousand troops approached the shallow cove, its cliffs towering above, the Turks prepared their welcome. In the words of Liddell Hart, 'hell yawned'. Lying in wait, the Turks held back their fire until the boats had almost reached land. Then, their bullets ripping across the water with devastating accuracy, the Turks swiftly made the sea run red with British blood.

At S Beach, after making a successful landing, the battalion followed its orders, which were to wait for the troops from other beaches to join it before proceeding further. If these troops from S and X Beaches had instead moved to V and W sites, they could have overwhelmed the Turks. Similarly, at Y Beach two thousand men idled the day away; they sat on the cliff and, as Falls said, 'enjoyed the scenery' for want of orders or coordination. Next day, even as the Turks retreated, in a mood of alarmism the troops re-embarked. The official history acknowledges the great opportunity which was lost: 'It is as certain as anything can be in war that a bold advance from Y Beach, on the morning of the 25 April, must have . . . ensured a decisive victory.' Cruttwell sees in the wasted chances 'the most dramatic day of the whole World War'.

In the end it was passivity that triumphed. At Helles, for example, it was initially decided to rest the tired troops and await the arrival of French forces before attempting any advance. By 28 April a new attack was hazarded, but the Turks had greatly augmented their numbers, and the Anglo-French line broke close to the shore, to be

Above: The Turks, under Mustapha Kemal, conducted a brilliant defence against the Allies in Gallipoli. **Left:** British troops awaiting evacuation near Cape Helles.

Below: The ANZACs fought bravely but suffered heavy casualties at Gallipoli.

saved only by a shell from the *Queen Elizabeth* which landed smack in the middle of the advancing Turkish force and flattened it.

In the first phase of the Gallipoli campaign, Allied casualties were more than twenty thousand (of these, over six thousand were killed) out of a force of seventy thousand. The Turks were slaughtered in their turn, as when, on 1 and 3 May, they surged forward, bayonets fixed, and were sliced down by the thousand. Bravery and heroism on both sides were legendary. On 6 May the Allies returned to the attack, but, short of shells and observation aeroplanes, their position was undermined by the exhaustion of their troops. On 18 May, ten thousand more men fell in a Turkish attack of suicidal fury.

In London, public furor at the bungled campaign helped to bring down the Liberal government. After this, the new Coalition government of 25 May gave greater support to the Gallipoli project in terms of both men and supplies. Balfour had replaced Churchill at the Admiralty because of the latter's role in the campaign. Nevertheless, Hamilton continued to fight on in bursts of effort; in any case, it would have been hard to withdraw the troops because of the lack of natural cover and the shortness of the summer nights. Yet the steadily increasing Turkish build-up made an Allied defence equally difficult. Some bold new stroke was obviously needed.

During the summer a new scheme took shape. ANZAC forces, reinforced by British and Indian troops, would break forth towards the Sari Bair Mountains after diversionary thrusts had been made. New troops would be landed at Suvla Bay, three miles north of Anzac Cove, and an attack would be mounted on the Turks by an army with a 2:1 superiority in numbers.

S. L. A. Marshall notes that 'no other amphibious operation was ever floated from such an inordinately complex and unnecessarily ramified plan'. The reason for such complexity in the Suvla Bay operation remains a mystery. Still, the site itself was well chosen for a landing, for the Turkish defences were only lightly manned; Suvla provided an excellent anchorage for the fleet; the nearest ridges could not completely command the shore and thus abort the operation almost before it commenced; and the landing room available on the large sandy beaches meant that the enemy need not be presented with any concentrated target.

Despite the muddles that accompanied it, the Suvla operation almost succeeded. Early on 7 August, ANZAC forces came within an ace of capturing the commanding heights, but the Turks were saved by the disastrous inexperience of the British troops, the incompetence of their commanders, and their prostration from the merciless heat. During 7–8 August there was a breakdown in Allied supplies. On 6 August the men had come ashore with only one canteen of water each; now they lay helpless and parched while fresh water in plenty lay offshore in tankers. Cruttwell adds that 'the plague of flies was such that food was blackened by them as it was raised to the mouth'. Not surprisingly, dysentery was rampant.

On the night of 8–9 August, Kemal's reinforcements began to arrive, and when the Allied attack

On entend
le canon
Constantinople...

GERDA·WEGENER·

Opposite top: The successful defence of Gallipoli became a symbol of Turkish national pride.
Opposite bottom: Turkish artillery battered the Allies and drove them back to the beaches.
Overleaf: Devastation at Cape Helles after the battle.

This French cartoon cynically portrays the Sultan cringing with his harem when the guns of Gallipoli were heard.

got under way, it was thwarted by these fresh troops. Early on 10 August, Kemal's forces hurled the Allies from their positions. Further Allied thrusts were futile because of what the German official history called 'a ring of ever-increasing strength round the British position'.

As opposition grew at home, the Gallipoli campaign faltered and subsided into the now-familiar trench fighting. By the end of the year, Allied evacuation was rendered inevitable, for the Central Powers had recaptured the Berlin-Baghdad railway project, thus enabling them to deliver supplies quickly to their Ottoman ally. Amazingly, not a single casualty resulted from the with-

drawal – a weird end to a campaign in which the Entente lost over a quarter of a million men as casualties or prisoners, and in which the Turks bore losses nearly as great, including sixty-six thousand killed.

On 28 December, the British government recognized the futility of Gallipoli by formally resolving that the war would be decisively settled in the west. Fuller's summation stands as a poignant but just epitaph: at Gallipoli 'there was no judgment; no clear strategical analysis of the initial problem; no proper calculation of its tactical requirements; and no true attempt to balance the means in hand with the end in view.'

CHAPTER SIX

Italy: Egoism at War

On 3 August 1914 as the cataclysm of war struck Europe, and Italy declared her neutrality despite long-standing defensive obligations to the Central Powers through the alliance forged in the days of Bismarck, the intentions of Italy had long been in doubt; and as early as 1902 she had anticipated 1914 by an agreement of neutrality with France in the case of individual attack. The Italians justified their policy on the grounds that Austrian action against Serbia violated the alliance with Italy, since Vienna had acted without consulting Rome. Further, the entry of Great Britain on the Entente side had resulted in conditions which Italy had not envisaged and under which, so Rome argued, she was relieved of her commitments. Germany and Austria-Hungary accepted, at least outwardly, the accomplished fact of Italian neutrality, but they made anxious overtures to ensure that Italy did not go over to the Entente. In fact, in the race to acquire allies, or at least to deny them to the foe, Italy was wooed by both sides.

Thus she was able to follow a policy which Salandra, the Italian Prime Minister, contrasted with one of sentiment and aptly called *sacro egoismo*. Literally this meant 'sacred egoism'. More broadly it referred to a line of action of exclusive or innate self-interest, and to a policy which aimed at maximum acquisition of territory and prestige at minimum cost.

In Italy's pursuit of *sacro egoismo*, the Allies were from the beginning at an advantage. Italy's longings were directed primarily towards the seven hundred and fifty thousand Italian-speaking inhabitants of *Italia irredenta* ('unredeemed Italy'), an area consisting of part of the Austrian South Tyrol (including the Trentino) and Istria, along with the Habsburg Adriatic port and the hinterland of Trieste. Thus Italy's territorial ambitions were mostly directed against the Dual Monarchy; but despite pressures from Berlin and threats and blackmail from Rome, Vienna refused to cede these territories. Dubious exceptions to this refusal were a probably insincere offer of part of the Trentino in March 1915, followed by a larger concession in May – when it was already too late to keep Italy out of war. On the other hand, the Allies had less to lose (even though they had to be careful not to offend Slav susceptibilities by a magnanimous offer to Italy), so they could promise the Italians considerable gains in return for their aid in achieving victory. Moreover, as 1915 dawned, the Allies became more desperate to break the bloody deadlock in the west via a thrust

into Central Europe from the south, and their offers to Italy increased. However, there were accompanying hints that full belligerency rather than mere neutrality would be exacted in return.

At the same time, other factors drove Italy towards war. Popular Italian sentiment, though hoping for Italian non-belligerency, was firmly in favour of an Entente victory against Austria, Italy's feared and hated rival in the Adriatic and the Balkans. Further, the war faction was dominated by the articulate middle class and included important industrialists and publicists (such as Luigi Albertini of the Milanese liberal newspaper

Opposite: The war between Italy and Austria-Hungary took place largely along their common frontier, the Dolomites. This illustration exaggerates the techniques used but not the terrain over which artillery had to be hauled.

This cartoon shows Italy bravely stringing up the Austrian Eagle. The task was neither so bravely nor so easily accomplished.

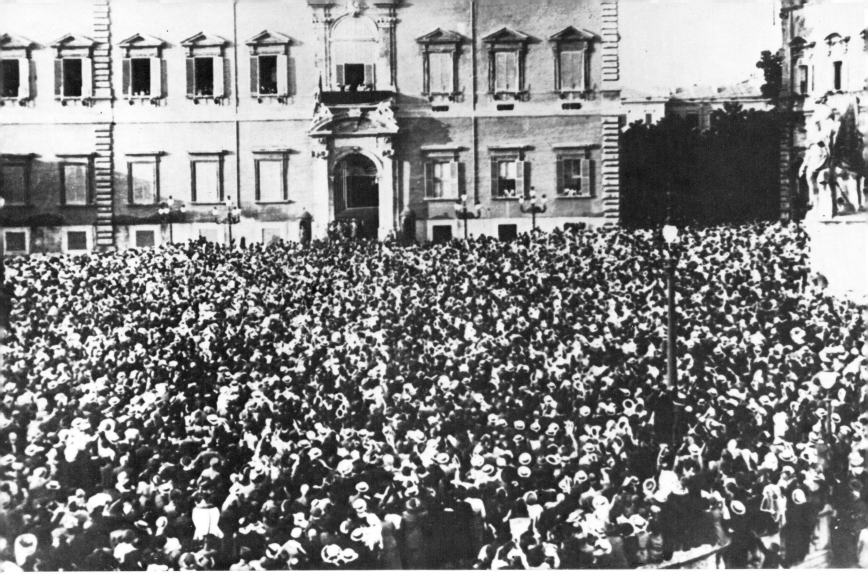

Above: Italians cheer their Queen and Princess outside the Royal Palace when Italy declared war on the Central Powers in 1915.
Opposite top: An Italian peasant goes off to war.
Opposite bottom: The Italian Air Force played a limited role in the first campaigns. The pilot, Gabriele d'Annunzio, centre, was Italy's great nationalist poet. He played a crucial role in the seizure of Fiume after the war.

General Count Luigi Cadorna, the Italian Commander, who was inhibited by both circumstances and temperament.

Corriere della Sera). Finally, many leaders of government and captains of industry felt that the war provided a Heaven-sent, now-or-never opportunity for the realization of Italian ambitions. Retrospectively it is thought that as early as October 1914 Salandra had decided to join the Allies if good enough terms could be obtained, a decision provoked by nationalistic ferment.

Italy Declares War

Propelled by these sentiments, Italy declared war against Austria on 23 May, though not against Germany until 27 August 1916. In her pocket lay the Treaty (or, more correctly, the Pact) of London, signed on 26 April 1915 by Italy, Britain, Russia, and France. Though the terms were theoretically secret, their gist was widely rumoured. The Allies had promised Italy that in the event of victory she would receive all of the South Tyrol (Alto Adige) south of the Brenner Pass; Istria (including Trieste) and the northern Dalmatian littoral; the Albanian port of Valona and an Italian protectorate over that country; legalization of her position in the Dodecanese Islands, off the Turkish coast; and a loan of £50,000,000. Moreover, if victory led to a partition of Turkey, Italy would receive a sphere in Asia Minor, as well as suitable booty if Britain and France appropriated the German colonies. In return, Italy was to join the war against all the enemy within one month. In fact, however, this proviso was almost immediately violated by Italy's dilatory declaration of war against Ger-

many, a delay caused mainly by her financial problems.

Thus Italy had joined the war: but the worth of her participation was at best dubious. The Libyan War against Turkey only three years earlier had cost Italy dearly, and in 1915 her military resources were still depleted. Further, Italy lacked sufficient heavy industry and resources of investment for large-scale production of military material. Despite these obstacles, however, she managed to triple the size of her armed forces to nine hundred thousand men by the spring of 1915.

In May 1915, with the Austrian and German offensive in Galicia gaining momentum, some Habsburg divisions could be spared for the Italian front. Seven of these were facing Italy by 23 May. Four days later, General Boroević von Bojna, a Croatian whose valour had been shown at Przemyśl, took command of the Austrian Fifth Army against the Italians. A believer in the importance of solid defences, Boroević immediately ordered that the Austrian troops should construct positions, place obstacles in front of them and remain there.

Italy was poorly placed to open a campaign against her northern neighbour. The contortions of their common frontier left Austria in a position to partition Venetian provinces along the geographically convenient wedge of the Trentino. An Italian offensive into the mountainous Alpine frontier region would be, most literally, an uphill battle against the Austrians poised above her, and, even if successful, would result in no great strategic gain. In the east, the terrain was relatively (and only relatively) less difficult, but it was irregular, bleak and barren country in which any army would find it hard to make headway. As Edmonds emphasizes, Italy's single great advantage was that her lines of interior communication were shorter than those of the enemy. Yet, although troops might be swiftly dispatched between the Trentino and the eastern frontier of the Isonzo River, there was always the danger of an Austrian attack on the rear positions.

It seemed to both sides that the Isonzo front was the easiest area in which to bid for a decision. Even there, however, the Italians were acutely aware that the Austrians, controlling the river crossings and dominating the heights, were well prepared to riddle and decimate any Italian move forward. Piero Pieri notes the paradox of the Italian position: 'The river could not be crossed until the mountains had been seized, and the mountains could not be seized until the river had been crossed.'

Nevertheless, during 1915 the first four Battles of the Isonzo took place. Seven more were to occur before the war was over. For Italy, the campaign became an exercise in futility. At the loss of a quarter of a million men, she failed to prevent the Central Powers' success against Serbia and succeeded in diverting only a dozen Austrian divisions from the east.

In each case the Isonzo fighting was marked by an Italian offensive, for Austria, coping with the campaigns against Serbia and Russia, chose to stand on the defensive. The Italian aim throughout was the immediate gain of the Carso (Karst or Kras) Plateau and the town of Gorizia (Görz), though the ultimate objective remained Trieste and, beyond it, the Danubian plain via the Laibach (Ljubljana) Gap. By this means, the Italians hoped to fulfil their promise to Russia of 16 May to try to join up with the Serbs.

Cadorna's Offensive
Although General Count Luigi Cadorna, the Italian commander, showed perhaps excessive caution and therefore lost several opportunities for action, his methods were circumscribed by the strategic and political facts of life already mentioned. Falls points out a tremendously inhibiting factor: the number of men killed in the Isonzo campaign as a proportion of total casualties was very high indeed, due to the deadly effect of shell explosions disintegrating and scattering the rocks of chalky composition which littered the terrain. An additional trial was the chill mountain wind or *Bora*, to which was later added the lashing autumn rains and bitter winter.

Yet on 24 May, Cadorna launched into a general offensive along the whole front. By 16 June, when the initial phase of operations had ended, the Italians had made some gains in their positions for further tactical operations. However, it was already clear that the campaign would be one of ghastly attrition. Sure enough, the First Battle of the Isonzo 23 June–7 July and the Second 18 July–3 August were both costly and fruitless. Over one hundred thousand casualties were calculated, the majority of them Italian. In the Third

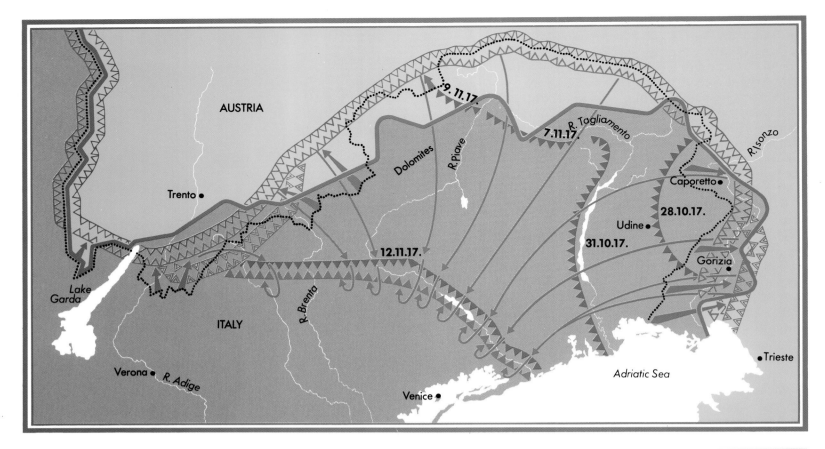

ITALIAN   AUSTRIAN

Gains and positions at
the end of 1915

Gains in the East and
losses in the West 1916

Italian retreat to the
Piave 1917

The stand on the
Piave 1918

ITALIAN   AUSTRIAN

Armistice line
November 3 1918

Above: The wide, flat
expanse of the Champagne
district was fought over
many times during the first
year of the war.

Battle, 18 October–3 November, and the Fourth,
10 November–2 December, Cadorna introduced
heavier artillery, but its support proved ineffectual against determined and strategically
fortified Austrian defenders. Thus the Italians
displayed 'magnificent valour', as their admiring
enemy termed it, to little avail. Casualties –
again predominantly Italian ones in these two
battles numbered about one hundred and ninety
thousand. The final bitter irony was that for the
Habsburg Empire, the Italian campaign proved a
rallying-point for its diverse nationalities such as
no attack against a Slav state could ever have
been. All in all, the dispassionate observer might
have remarked that in 1915 Italian egoism walked
hand in hand with folly.

Stagnation in the West

Meanwhile, undeterred by the repeated failure
of attempts to break through on the western
front, Joffre decided in March 1915 to launch yet
another offensive, this time in Artois with the
heights of Vimy Ridge as its objective. However,
to launch the attack, it would be necessary first
to have the British relieve the two French corps
north of Ypres; and this was not immediately
possible because of the exigencies of the Gallipoli
campaign and a delay in sending British reinforcements. Independently, French himself believed that the relief of Ypres would leave the
BEF with little energy to help in Artois; and he
decided to support his ally by a separate attack at
Neuve Chapelle. A further motivation was the

Taking soup to the men in
the trenches in Artois.

In Memory of

JOHN LEVERS

Private
1552
1st/5th Bn., Sherwood Foresters (Notts & Derby Regt.)
who died on
Thursday, 14th October 1915. Age 22.

Additional Information:	Son of Mr. and Mrs. Levers, of 97, Stockbroch St., Derby; husband of Mrs. E. Rowley (formerly Levers), of II, Moira St., Melbourne, Derby.

Commemorative Information

Memorial:	LOOS MEMORIAL, Pas de Calais, France
Grave Reference/ Panel Number:	Panel 87 to 89.
Location:	Loos-en-Gohelle is a village about 5 kilometres north-west of Lens. The Loos Memorial forms the side and back of Dud Corner Cemetery where over 1,700 officers and men are buried, the great majority of whom fell in the Battle of Loos. Dud Corner Cemetery, which stands almost on the site of a German strong point, the Lens Road Redoubt, captured by the 15th (Scottish) Division on the first day of the battle, is located about 1 kilometre west of the village, on the N43, the main Lens to Béthune road. The Loos Memorial commemorates over 20,000 officers and men who fell in the area from the River Lys to the old southern boundary of the First Army, east and west of Grenay, and who have no known grave. It covers the period from the first day of the Battle of Loos to the date of the Armistice. On either side of the cemetery is a wall 15 feet high, to which are fixed tablets on which are carved the names of those commemorated. At the back are four small circular courts, open to the sky, in which the lines of tablets are continued, and between these courts are three semicircular walls or apses, two of which carry tablets, while on the centre apse is erected the Cross of Sacrifice.

Display Record of Commemoration

British commander's wish to improve the somewhat low estimate that the French had formed of British attacking capabilities.

On 10 March, after thirty-five minutes of fierce bombardment to 'soften up' their opponents, the British advanced. The Germans were routed, but soon their brave and adroit retaliation began to yield results. Now the British faltered, giving the Germans time and opportunity to prepare a counterattack which, while it did not gain much ground, at least forced a halt to the British offensive. By 13 March, when the battle ended, losses were approximately equal, with between twelve and thirteen thousand casualties on both sides. British morale remained high. Nevertheless Cruttwell emphasizes the 'short sighted extravagance' of this British 'gamble' in view of the BEF's shortage of ammunition.

On 9 May, after the dreadful interlude of the Second Battle of Ypres, the French offensive in Artois began. Joffre was fortified by the knowledge that the Central Powers' primary attention was in the east, in the major offensive of Gorlice-Tarnów. Brave and well-versed in warfare, the troops now crashed through the German defences, and the thirty-third Corps under General Pétain almost reached the crest of Vimy Ridge. But German reinforcements and a mistaken withholding of French reserves caused the whole shape of the battle to change. The scene altered to one of lengthy and wretched bloodletting which consumed at the very least one hundred thousand French and seventy-five thousand German casualties before the fighting ended on 18 June.

By now the French General Staff had decided that only when the enemy was 'so worn down that he has no reserves available' could victory be grasped. The remedy for the disease of slaughter was . . . more slaughter.

Above left: British artillery, Vimy Ridge.
Above: A French Colonel, the battle flag of his regiment in his hand, leads an attack in Champagne in 1915. Left: The 1st Cameronians prepare for a gas attack.

Overleaf: Italian incursions into Austrian territory were stopped at almost every turn.

At the same time, at Aubers Ridge and Festubert the British were achieving only disappointing results. Throughout this period, especially because of the demands of Gallipoli, ammunition continued to be in short supply. Yet optimism remained unquelled, since the BEF knew that at least they had diverted German forces which would otherwise have been used against the French.

Now a long lull in major operations ensued. The western front lay in stagnation. During this time, the Germans transferred four divisions from the east after successfully concluding their summer offensive. In addition, using civilian forced labour, they rapidly strengthened their defences for the expected onslaught.

Joffre had by now decided that the spring Artois operation had failed because, large as it was, it lacked the necessary magnitude. Moreover, he concluded that the attack had been mounted too narrowly and on only a single front. Now he intended that the Allies should attack broadly on separate fronts, destroying the German power to concentrate reserves and threatening both sides of the German salient. Buoyantly optimistic as ever, Joffre exulted that this would 'compel the Germans to retreat beyond the Meuse and possibly end the war'.

After three days of preparatory bombardment, the French again attacked on 25 September in Champagne. Joffre urged his men to let the enemy have 'neither quarter nor rest until the achievement of victory'. Stirringly he told them, 'Your *élan* will be irresistible'.

As the French moved forward, Joffre described the scene as a 'whirlwind of fire and steel let loose'. Yet after a fierce initial assault, there was no great breakthrough to the Meuse and Belgium, and the Germans counteracted by a second and reinforcing line of defence two to four miles behind the first one. This entrenchment mostly remained intact. Seeing that the result was a deadlock, Joffre halted the offensive on 30 September, but he had by then taken eighteen thousand prisoners and, as Falls says, given the Germans 'a scare to remember'. Early in October the fighting was renewed, but the results were still inconclusive.

Simultaneously the French had plunged into Artois, where the results were even worse than those in Champagne. On 28 September, one division once again attained the crest of Vimy Ridge. However, bad weather ruined any further assault, and the campaign was also affected by the demands of the Salonika operation, which had been theoretically determined on 11 September. Fighting was halted 30 September and renewed 11 October, again inconclusively.

As their contribution to the Artois offensive, the British had fought bravely but unsuccessfully at Loos. As so frequently occurred in the Great War, the battle dragged on beyond its logical time limit, neither side knowing when to cut its losses. After this disappointing operation, Sir John French was relieved of his command of the BEF and replaced by General Sir Douglas Haig.

On the western front in 1915, a frightful bill for dead and wounded was presented, and paid in full. Conservative estimates place French losses at one

hundred and ninety thousand, British at sixty thousand, and German at about one hundred and eighty thousand – all for little or no strategic improvement.

In the view of the German official history, the Allied autumn offensive might have succeeded if it had been made a month or two earlier. Yet at the same time the Allies were unprepared for attack. Might-have-beens are always tantalizing, if unproductive. Whether because of destiny or miscalculation, the close of 1915 found the western front impregnable.

Gas Warfare

In the spring of 1915 the Germans introduced poison gas, in an attempt to regain the initiative in the stagnating west. In January Germany had already used gas against the Russians, but the extreme cold had practically nullified its effect. Now, however, the experts advised that at Ypres winds would be favourable for its experimental use. This fitted in well with the German desire to drive the Allies out of Ypres and its surroundings; for as long as they held positions in the area, the French and the BEF were strategically placed for an eventual offensive against Brussels. Conversely, if the Germans held Ypres, they could threaten the Allied flank and complete their conquest of Belgium.

For three weeks before the first gas attack, captured prisoners had reported that Germany had brought to the front 'enormous tubes of asphyxiating gas'. Yet at the highest level the news had been received with scepticism. As the days went by and nothing happened, no defensive preparations were made. It is possible to rationalize this dangerous neglect. The official history itself notes, 'It was presumed that the effect (of the gas) would be trivial and local.' After all, the Allies reasoned, there were Geneva Conventions prohibiting, in spirit at least, the use of such weapons.

(In discussing the ethics of gas warfare, Cruttwell reminds us that the French had burned men alive with liquid fire in the autumn of 1914. Thus behaviour which ordinary people would condemn

Above: A complex chain of tunnels linked thousands of trenches on both sides of the Western Front. **Far left:** A Russian Commander and his Cossack scout officers observe enemy positions near the wall of Cracow. **Left:** French troops drag German bodies from their trenches.

Far left: German troops pause before their advance on Cracow. **Centre left:** Second Ypres, after the battle. **Left:** A French trench at Ypres.

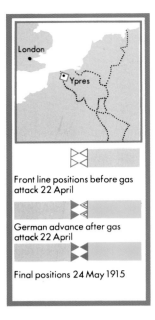

Front line positions before gas attack 22 April

German advance after gas attack 22 April

Final positions 24 May 1915

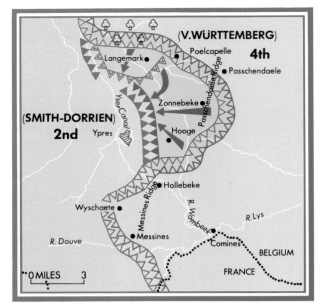

Opposite top: British wounded. A painting by Eric Kennington. **Opposite left:** Gas warfare at Ypres was no laughing matter. **Opposite right:** There was no rest in the trenches – even at night. **Below:** One of Raemaeker's most bitter cartoons, portraying the Kaiser as the friend of war and starvation.

as immoral was not confined to one side.)

On 22 April, the Germans began a formidably heavy bombardment of enemy positions near Ypres. Suddenly, French colonial troops of the Forty-fifth Algerian Division were seen reeling about, some vomiting, all with their throats and eyes burning. Some men managed to gasp the word, 'gaz'. Swinson quotes one eye witness thus: The troops came forward, 'a panic-stricken rabble . . . with grey faces and protruding eye-balls, clutching their throats and choking as they ran, many of them dropping in their tracks and lying on the sodden earth with limbs convulsed and features distorted in death'. As enveloping clouds of chlorine gas swirled about them, first greenish yellow and then blue white in colour, the troops pelted to safety across the Yser canal, or into the town of Ypres itself. Seeing the pandemonium, General Robertson remarked face-

tiously that, 'there must have been something invigorating about that gas'.

The deadliness of the gas lay in its method of scalding and destroying lung tissue. Full recovery, if at all possible, took a very long time. Moreover, the Allied protective measures were at best piecemeal. Wet handkerchieves were used, commonly covered with bicarbonate of soda if it were available. Makeshift respirators were put together from lint and tape. In June a protective helmet was introduced, but the box respirator was not employed until August 1916.

As the Germans joined the pursuit, many of them stumbled into their own clouds of gas, while others cautiously hung behind. Meanwhile the British Second Army commander, Smith-Dorrien, undeterred, ordered the Ypres salient to be held and consolidated by available Canadian troops. On 24 April, after disastrous Allied attempts to attack on the previous day, the Canadians suffered severe casualties from a second German gas attack which reached the salient in the form of a cloud fifteen feet high. Somehow they held back the Germans, who also sustained appalling losses. Nevertheless, by the following day the Germans controlled the heights around Ypres, plus much of the salient. They were to prove very difficult to dislodge without a well-prepared offensive.

As we have seen, the French were meanwhile engrossed in preparation for their Artois campaign of early May, although their efforts to attack at Ypres were both fruitless and muddled. After a bitter quarrel between Sir John French and Smith-Dorrien, the latter was replaced. Smith-Dorrien had recommended withdrawal to the environs of Ypres. Ironically, his successor, General Sir Hubert Plumer, was instructed to pursue the very same course. After further debate produced by opposition from Foch, the retreat was successfully accomplished on 1–3 May.

On 8 May, in a terrific attack east of Ypres known as the Battle of Frezenberg Ridge, the Germans again advanced. In six days of bitter fighting, the British, once more deficient in stores and ammunition, retreated. However, the limited German success was gained so catastrophically that further advances were abandoned.

On 24–25 May, in the Battle of Bellewaarde Ridge, German infantry again attacked, using gas on a larger scale than ever, but without much gain. Both sides were now chronically lacking in ammunition, and the Second Battle of Ypres petered out.

Swinson records that 'Second Ypres' was a new kind of battle, in that materials were matched against men. Falls judges that, though the battle was for them 'the biggest success of the year in the west', the Germans could have won a much greater victory had they possessed the means to exploit to the full the strategy of surprise in their use of gas. In any case, though for the Germans the battle had diverted troops which would otherwise have opposed them in Artois, for its size 'Second Ypres' was one of the deadliest clashes of the war. The grisly toll of losses from the month's fighting numbered 60,000 from the British Empire, 10,000 French and up to 47,000 German troops. In the east, the winter Battle of Masuria had inflicted a total of 200,000 casualties (in-

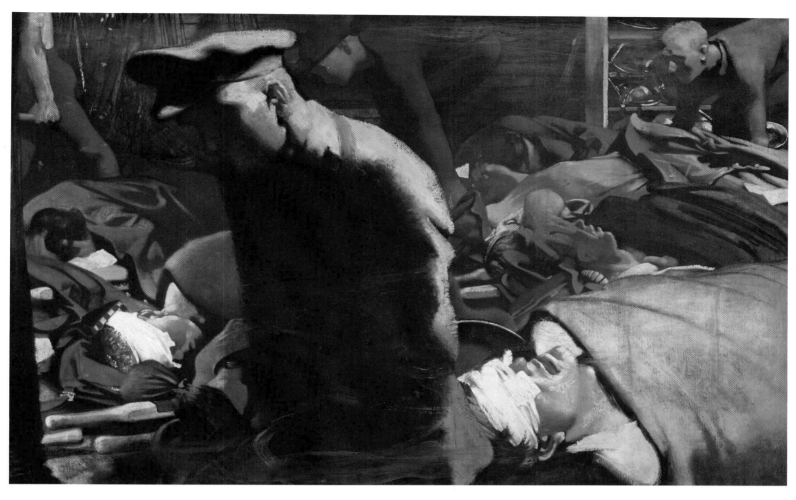

cluding prisoners) on the Russians: and yet the Central Powers had still failed to eliminate Russia from the war. However, many considered that internal forces in Russia were preparing for just such a conclusion. By spring the Russian forces were battered and attenuated. Ammunition and even adequate clothing were lacking, while the soldiers were depressed by letters from home which could scarcely conceal news of the appalling shortages of food and an insidious general corruption. In these circumstances, an immediate Russian offensive was out of the question. And seeing the state that the Russians were in, Germany and Austria decided to seize what appeared a golden opportunity to inflict a serious, if not fatal, blow. Moreover, Conrad for one was still of the opinion that a successful massive thrust against Russia would do more than anything else to influence Italy and Rumania in favour of the Central Powers. The Allied measures against the Dardanelles also demanded a reply in the east.

East of Cracow (Kraków) and not far from Lemberg (Lwów) in the Gorlice-Tarnow area, the Germans steadily built up their offensive preparations. Unlike Hindenburg, Ludendorff or Conrad, Falkenhayn did not believe that the ruination of Russia in one campaign was possible; but he did think (wrongly, as it turned out) that in 1915 the Austro-German onslaught possessed the power to cripple Russia 'for an indefinite period'. On 9 April Falkenhayn took the decision to attack, and supplies and men were transferred en masse from the west.

Now 600,000 Germans and 700,000 Austro-Hungarians faced Russians numbering nearly a million and three-quarters. With considerable superiority in artillery and firepower, on 2 May the German Eleventh Army and the Austrian Third and Fourth Armies moved forward to the attack on a twenty-eight mile front. The Russians, though they expected an offensive, were never sure where it would come. Now they retreated in disorder and panic, and the Central Powers achieved a complete rout on 4 May. The next day General Dragmirov, the chief of staff of the Russian South Western Front, correctly assessed the disastrous position of his forces when he decided to retreat behind the river San. Though Grand Duke Nicholas opposed the idea, further Austro-German successes caused an order for withdrawal.

By 8 May progress was such that General von Seeckt, Chief of Staff of the German Eleventh Army, could exclaim that 'The tactical and strategical breakthrough has fully succeeded'. Two days later, as General Radko-Dmitriev reported that his Russian Third Army had 'bled to death', a general Russian retreat from the Carpathians ensued. Grand Duke Nicholas now pressed strongly for an Allied diversion in the west, hoping to accelerate Italian involvement in the war. At least one authority, Kurt Peball, has described the Central Powers' success thus far as 'the most significant of the war'.

Between 15 and 22 May, the Russians counter-attacked but achieved only local successes. According to some estimates, the Russians had now suffered well over 400,000 casualties and prisoners, and early in June their armies were described as being reduced to 'a harmless mob'. Yet, in contradiction to the hopes of Berlin and Vienna, and despite challenging eastern successes, Italy had now joined the war on the side of the Entente.

Still the Austro-German offensive continued, capturing Lemberg, the Galician capital, on 22 June. Relentlessly, though now more slowly, the Central Powers moved on, taking Warsaw 4–5 August, after extremely fierce Russian resistance. They seized the charred remains of Brest-Litovsk on 26 August. By autumn the Central Powers' offensive had come to a halt and Falkenhayn had decided to stabilize the front – for

Germany and Austria-Hungary had outstretched their communications; Russia had counter-attacked; Italy was making herself felt; a new Allied campaign was in preparation in the west; and Serbia had to be vanquished to relieve the supply routes to Turkey. Hindenburg, however, was determined to attack further, and Vilna fell on 18 September. Still, by December the Russians had been thrown back a considerable distance, as far as Riga in the north and the extremities of the Carpathians in the east.

The end of 1915 saw the close of a year in which the Russians had lost a million casualties and a further million prisoners. In a desperate attempt to save the situation, the Tsar himself had taken supreme command of the armies in September, swearing to, 'fulfil our sacred duty to defend our country to the last'. Somehow, miraculously, the Russian giant had lurched and tottered its way through another year without collapsing. Despite their brilliant victories, the Central Powers had failed to drive the Tsar to sue for peace. Now the care worn and decimated Russian troops rested behind a green and watery barrier of lakes and forests, resolved to renew the fighting with the coming of spring.

From Verdun to the Somme

With the opening of 1916, the Great War had crystallized. With a kind of dull fatalism and dawning realization, the nations pondered on the destruction in lives and materials that was to leave the world, and especially Europe, changed forever. All the belligerents were drawing on their last reserves of men and goods. Their financial resources were for the most part meagre or non-existent. In the latter case, the nations went up to the hilt into debt, struggling to achieve that overwhelming victory which had as yet eluded them.

Yet still the fundamental question remained unsolved: how was a breakthrough in the west to be achieved? Almost everyone was more than ever convinced that the war would be won or lost only on the western front. The alternatives were uninviting. For the Central Powers the eastern campaigns of 1915 had been brilliantly successful, though, like a mirage, decisive victory had shimmered away from them into the vastness of the Russian hinterland. The Russians had, nevertheless, reeled back, and the Germans could afford to concentrate westward sufficient forces possibly to extort a decision in France. For the Allies, 1915 had brought the Dardanelles fiasco, and no great victory anywhere else in compensation. Furthermore, prevailing opinion was that no very suitable back door to the west was to be found in theatres such as Italy, Macedonia or the Baltic. Most important of all, neither side dared risk denuding the western front of troops to win a victory, however great, elsewhere, lest the opponent take advantage of the situation to press home a decisive thrust in France or Flanders. Fearing that the other side would take the initiative, each set of belligerents concluded that an attack was imperative. In the end, the Germans got in their blow first. Falkenhayn for one had been spurred on by the thought that only an attack would delay the Anglo-French build-up of superiority in material.

Pondering on where to attack in the west, Falkenhayn was impressed with what he saw as 'the ever-dwindling power of resistance and the limited ability of the French people to hold out'. Falkenhayn surmised that if France fell, surely Russia would finally cave in and sue for peace. Then England would be left alone – and in all probability unable to continue the fight. (In these larger calculations, Italy and the smaller powers were largely discounted.)

The Carnage of Verdun

Thus the key question was: how to deal the French a death blow? Falkenhayn decided to attack Verdun, the key fortress in eastern France. If Verdun quickly fell, the loss would shatter French prestige irreparably. As the German Crown Prince remarked, 'Verdun is the heart of France'. Yet an actual German breakthrough was not necessary (though there is some evidence that in fact Falkenhayn hoped for this). What was necessary and likely was to trap the French into making Verdun a mystic symbol. If only France would defend Verdun to the last man, the balance of manpower in the west would swing in Germany's favour. Thus Falkenhayn's motives for standing at Verdun were complex. Liddell Hart has argued that perhaps Falkenhayn was an opportunist keeping all his options open. If the French suffered a sudden moral collapse, well and good. If not, he would see what happened next, being not very clear in his own mind what to do. There may also have been the consideration that the British would panic at the threat to Verdun and launch a disastrously premature offensive on the Somme or elsewhere. Naturally the acquisition of Verdun, would strengthen the German front, for the Verdun complex linked the northern and eastern parts of the French line facing the Germans, and the outer defences came within a dozen miles of Metz and Sedan, the keys to any German effort in Champagne. It seems that above all, Falkenhayn was attracted by the idea of threatening Verdun with only a modest number of troops and then drawing the French into a snare where heavy artillery would pound them to dust. What he apparently forgot was that the symbolism of Verdun might work both ways, and that it might not be possible for Germany to decide when to withdraw from the campaign without losing her own prestige. This miscalculation was to prove disastrous for Germany – and for Falkenhayn himself.

In early December 1915, the Allies had decided that each should launch a simultaneous attack as soon as this could be coordinated. Joffre, now supreme commander of all French military forces, proposed an offensive on the Somme. The British supremo, Haig, had reservations, but finally agreed for the sake of Allied solidarity. Meanwhile, the Russians would do their best to retrieve their own position, and the Italians would renew the Isonzo struggle. Anticipating these plans, however, the Germans struck first.

In describing the Verdun campaign, Paul Valéry called it 'a kind of duel before the universe, a singular and almost symbolic tourney'. Perhaps the epic proportions of the horror of the battle made men think and hope that an issue of similarly epic moral purpose was being decided. But whatever the moral implications, Verdun in 1916 was the scene of unsurpassed carnage. The holocaust was never exceeded and seldom equalled. When speaking of the abattoir of the First World War, this description may sound extreme, but it is nonetheless justified.

In contrast with the flat terrain of Flanders or the Somme, Verdun was surrounded by hills and ridges which provided superb positions of defence. On the heights were built three concentric circles of underground forts, their guns emplaced so as to dislodge all but the most vast and relentless waves of infantry. The forts lay five to ten miles from Verdun itself, and in between was placed a veritable network of trenches, barbed wire, and other ingenious impediments. Unfortunately, however, the defences of Verdun had been badly neglected. Many guns had been removed for use elsewhere, and the relative inactivity in this area had lulled the men into a deceptive calm. Lieutenant Colonel Emile Driant made only trouble for himself when he warned the imperturbable Joffre of this.

Perhaps with undeserved luck, the French were

German front 21 Feb, 1916
Initial German attack

Furthest German advance by
July 1916

French counter attack –
positions by Dec, 1916

Final positions Aug, 1917

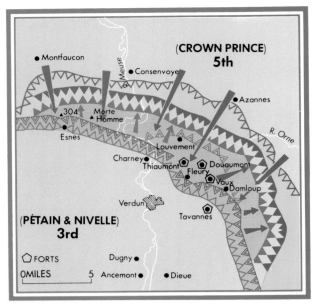

(CROWN PRINCE) 5th

Montfaucon
Meuse
Consenvoye
Azannes
R. Orne
304 Morte Homme
Esnes
Louvement
Charney
Thiaumont Douaumont
Fleury
Vaux Damloup
Verdun
Tavannes

(PÉTAIN & NIVELLE) 3rd

⬠ FORTS
0 MILES   5
Dugny
Ancemont
Dieue

presented at the outset with a hindrance to the German plans. Bad weather caused a nine-day delay in operations. Had this been otherwise, the Germans would have opened the offensive with vastly superior odds, and the French would have had little opportunity to carry out essential repairs to roads and bridges.

On 21 February the German bombardment began. Never in history had such a formidable load of shells and firepower been unleashed. The rumbling from the pounding artillery could be heard one hundred miles away. The violence of the attack was itself enough to annihilate or disintegrate the badly prepared French trenches. One hapless regiment saw eighteen hundred of its two thousand men blown up or mown down. Countless others were buried alive.

Yet already the Germans had made a bad mistake. The Crown Prince, within whose command Verdun was to be fought, wanted to encircle the fortresses by simultaneous attacks on both banks of the river Meuse. Given the French lack of preparedness, this would probably have succeeded. But Falkenhayn decided against releasing the large number of men who would be needed, and only the right bank was attacked.

On the first day of fighting, the Germans moved forward in a probing action. Next day the incredible bombardment continued. Somehow the French held on despite their bloody losses. By the third day, whole units at a time were annihilated and confusion spread. The unfortunate French also added to their own losses by mistakenly shelling some of their own trenches. By 24 February, no amount of heroism could hold the French line. The continuing bombardment smashed it to atoms. Yet despite their gains, the Germans had already met with more opposition than they had expected, and their losses, already great, bred caution. Moreover, between the two sides a barrier intervened the chains of fortresses, including Douaumont, the strongest.

But on 25 February events took a completely unexpected turn. Fort Douaumont, negligently left ungarrisoned, was taken almost absent-

Above left: Aerial view of Fort de Vaux. **Far left:** The Germans attack at Fort de Vaux. **Left:** Lieutenant Rackow, the fanatical German officer who was the first to penetrate Fort de Vaux.

Opposite top left: Gassed in the trenches. **Opposite top right:** Crown Prince Wilhelm. **Right:** The Germans press forward at Verdun.

mindedly by a German patrol. Public opinion in France reeled with shock, while the more sober calculated that the disaster would cost the lives of 100,000 Frenchmen. Throughout Germany, church bells pealed in jubilation at the coup.

Now, at the very moment of France's unfathomable gloom, General Henri-Philippe Pétain arrived at Verdun to take command. Efficient and unhurried, he set himself to organize the men and raise their morale. His encouraging phrase, *ils ne passeront pas* (they shall not pass) became immortal. Under Pétain's inspiration the French perked up. Along the road from Bar-le-Duc, the vital lifeline of Verdun, lorries began to bring a steady stream of supplies. Men referred to this as *la voie sacrée* (the sacred road). During the first week of March alone, 190,000 men trod its path, to add their weight to the struggle.

By 28 February French artillery fire had helped to cause the German attack to falter. During a relative pause in the battle, Falkenhayn considered breaking off the offensive, but rejected the idea because German losses had not yet reached intolerable proportions. Moreover, a new offensive elsewhere would take too long to stage. He therefore agreed to extend the fighting across the Meuse after all.

By about 8 March, the Germans had carved out a holding position across the Meuse, and a titanic battle ensued for possession of the dominating positions. One of the fiercest concerned a ridge with the macabrely appropriate name of Mort Homme. Throughout the spring the battle for its crest waved murderously back and forth.

By April the French counterattacks were both fierce and frequent, but they could only circumscribe the German advance. To add to the impersonal hideousness of the fighting, men by the thousand died from long-range artillery fire, with many infantrymen never catching sight of the enemy. The French and Germans together had already lost over 160,000 men.

Right: The horror of
Verdun was matched only
by the bloodbath of the
Somme. Below right: The
landscape around Verdun
became a surrealistic scene
of twisted limbs and
ravaged earth.

air and morsel of food. The survivors betrayed in their glazed or dilated eyes the nameless horror of their experiences. Some moved about with their frames bent over with physical and nervous exhaustion. Scores of men went mad from strain; others existed in wooden or hypnotic insensitivity. Even the most stolid and brave of men were unlikely to have escaped unscathed.

The French at least had had the advantage of frequent rotation of their troops at the front line. The Germans had never adopted this policy. On the other hand, the fact that higher numbers of Frenchmen than Germans passed through the 'mincing machine' of Verdun had a disastrous effect on the French reserves of manpower. His concern at these developments was among the reasons why Joffre replaced Pétain by promoting him; another was that Pétain was suspected of being too much moved by the catastrophe. He was succeeded by Generals Robert Nivelle and Charles 'the Butcher' Mangin.

On 26 May Joffre had appealed to Haig to bring forward the date of the Somme offensive. If it were left until 15 August, said Joffre, 'The French Army would cease to exist . . .'. Thus the opening of the Somme campaign was set for 1 July.

At Verdun the grisly tale continued. After a week of assaults, on 7 June the Germans captured Fort Vaux, the French northeastern bastion. The fort was surrendered only when its 600 defenders had gone two complete days without water. As they wallowed in putrefaction, their thirst had reduced them to drinking urine.

Yet at this point the Brusilov offensive in the east forced Falkenhayn to transfer needed troops to prop up the Austrians. On 21 June the Germans attacked using phosgene gas. The French held on, but they were at breaking point. Only the knowledge of the imminent Somme offensive held them together, although Verdun had already reduced the French contribution to the Somme from forty to sixteen divisions, of which only five were ready by 1 July.

By 11 July, when the final German offensive at Verdun failed, the scene of the most crucial fighting had been transferred to the Somme. Henceforth the Germans stood on the defensive, though the casualties at Verdun continued to mount.

The total bill for Verdun was between 315,000 and 377,000 French killed or wounded. These were matched by 337,000 Germans. Of the dead, at least 150,000 were never buried, but simply rotted where they lay. No wonder one distracted eyewitness croaked that 'the earth around us was literally stuffed with corpses'.

Jacques Meyer wrote that Verdun 'was a French victory only in the sense of an invincible resistance'. Neither could the Germans claim success. If they had reduced the ranks of Frenchmen, they had lost as much themselves.

In the autumn the French had been able to rally for a limited counter-attack, and Douaumont and Vaux were recaptured, with Nivelle scoring further French successes in December. Yet the futility of the sacrifice of so many lives was underlined by the fact that at the end of the year the adversaries were very nearly at the positions they had held in early 1916.

Finally the Germans overcame the defenders of Mort Homme, only to be faced with French gun emplacements on the ridge known as Côte 304. More German divisions had to be thrown in, however much this went against the grain for Falkenhayn. By May the Germans had more or less cleared the left bank of the Meuse, but at such cost that even Falkenhayn wondered if the fight should be abandoned. Yet German honour made this impossible, as he and others grimly saw upon reflection.

The landscape around Verdun had become a scene of surrealistic and nauseating horror. Deep craters gouged out by shells gaped everywhere. At frequent intervals limbs protruded from the ravaged soil, torn from torsos by the merciless artillery fire. Everywhere, wrote Jacques Meyer, were 'distended bodies that your foot sank into'. The stench of death hung over the jumble of decaying corpses like some hellish perfume. As chaos reigned, many wounded died of gangrene or exhaustion. As the weather turned warmer, the reek of the charnel house invaded every breath of

Battle of the Somme

The Battle of the Somme raged from 1 July to 18 November, taking up all of the British energy in the west for 1916. Here, against some of the strongest German western defences, the Allied attack was undertaken, with the British for the first time bearing the brunt in a major western front offensive. At the Somme was suffered a holocaust of misery and dying equal to that of Verdun, and the casualties were even higher: 650,000 Germans, 420,000 Britons and 195,000 Frenchmen. Together the battles marked the decimation of European manhood.

Topography played an outstanding role in the Somme campaign. The battle area was mostly devoid of important geographical features, with one exception: the Ginchy-Thiepval ridge. Here the German second positions looked down on the Allied lines. Although there was some advantage to be gained from artillery fire uphill, the exposed Allied positions meant that there could be no element of surprise against the foe. However,

Above: Wounded had to be carried off the battlefield under fire.
Right: The British trenches were to become a hell of stench and pain.
Far right: The Germans dug in and held despite heavy bombardment.
Below: The Somme gave the British a chance to go over the top to their deaths.

though they could see from preparations in the spring the battle that was to come, the Germans at that moment lacked the troops to stage a preventive attack. Instead, Falkenhayn decided to deal with the problem of Brusilov in the east, then carry out a decisive counterattack' in the west. In any case, until July Falkenhayn appeared to believe that the Allied preparations were so obvious as to constitute a red herring while the real attack would be staged further north.

Contrary to former theories, Haig fully intended and hoped for a breakthrough at the Somme. Unlike Joffre or, to some extent, Rawlinson, the British Fourth Army commander, Haig was not satisfied with attrition. Yet Rawlinson's doubts made disaster of the British plans. Liddell Hart points out that Rawlinson's advocacy of prolonged bombardment lessened the chance for that element of surprise which would have compensated for limited British artillery and the depth of the German position; while Rawlinson's wish to advance in limited stages hampered the exploita-

Below left: The attacks continued throughout the night. Below: Canadian troops were sent against the Germans – to no avail.

tion of successes by giving the Germans the time to recover and bring up reinforcements. Moreover, it appears that Rawlinson disastrously over-estimated the destructive power of his own long-range artillery.

The Germans had been dug in on the Somme for nearly two years. During this time they had excavated trenches to a depth of forty feet, and these were impervious to damage from all but the heaviest shells. Churchill called these lines 'undoubtedly the strongest and most perfectly defended position' on any battlefield.

'Murderous Fire'

After seven days of heavy bombardment, which the Germans called 'murderous fire', the British had failed to make an impact on the German dug-outs, though by weight of metal alone they had wiped out many of the enemy's front-line trenches. Worst of all, the ground ahead lay covered with barbed wire, which the bombardment had completely failed to break up. It is thus the more odd that the eve of battle found the British optimistic.

Early on the morning of 1 July, nearly 100,000 soldiers advanced shoulder to shoulder from their trenches. Moving forward at a slow walk because of their battle-kit of 66 to 90 lb. in weight, the infantry were perfect targets. German machine guns mowed them down until the ground was littered with corpses. That day, the strength of many battalions was reduced to one hundred men. In terms of losses for the British, 1 July 1916 was the blackest day of the war. Over 57,000 men fell, including nearly 20,000 dead. These casualties numbered 60 per cent of the officers and 40 per cent of the soldiers engaged; and the losses would have been higher had not many soldiers broken ranks and using their common sense, worked or crawled their way forward in small groups.

South of the Somme, and in the context of a smaller attack altogether, the French were brilliantly successful. The terrain was more favourable, their tactics were less wooden-headed, and the German defences in this area were weaker. In addition, the French had concentrated a larger amount of heavy artillery, and to a degree the French attack in this quarter had been unexpected. Troops under Fayolle had almost made a breakthrough. Yet none of this could obliterate the fact that the major attack in the British sector had been a disaster of the first magnitude. Cruttwell criticizes this attack as coming too late in the day, and cites the disadvantages of poor quality ammunition, lack of gas shells, and the spreading of the offensive in virtually equal strength along a too-wide front.

Now, by any reasonable standard, Haig might have been expected to give up the attempt at the Somme. The official history gives the opinion that if as an alternative he had pressed the assault at Messines, which was to achieve success the following year, it would have had 'a far better chance of decisive result, especially if combined with a coastal attack . . .'. Only a few weeks earlier Haig had hinted at such an operation if the Somme offensive 'met with considerable opposition'. By any definition, the opposition on 1 July was 'considerable'! Perhaps obstinacy in the face of disappointment influenced Haig, but it is also certain

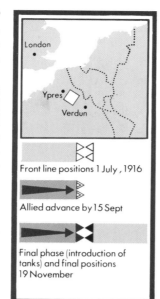

Front line positions 1 July, 1916

Allied advance by 15 Sept

Final phase (introduction of tanks) and final positions 19 November

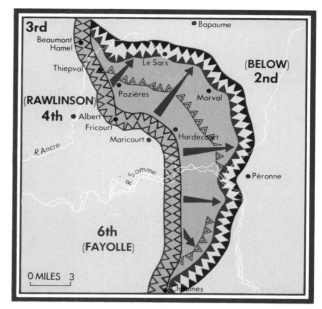

Opposite far left: Soldier on leave to his girl-friend: 'I like your dress but isn't it a bit short?' Her reply: 'Well, in wartime we all have to cut down.' *Poilus* often doubted, with good reason, that their sufferings were shared on the Home Front. **Left:** General Rawlinson, the British Fourth Army Commander. **Opposite below:** On the art of camouflage: 'War, as far as the artillery is concerned, is developing into a fancy dress ball.' Immunity from destruction was the prize for the best costume. **Right:** A well-fortified trench, reminiscent of a coalmine. **Below:** A pause in the carnage of the Somme.

that he had not been told of the full extent of British casualties. Loyalty or sycophancy from Haig's subordinates explains a great deal of his decision to carry on fighting. When on 3 July he did finally learn of the frightful losses, Haig decided to concentrate on the right, and the battle proceeded on a smaller scale.

The second great assault of the campaign began on 14 July. Rawlinson attacked by night, with Bazentin Ridge as his objective. The French and Haig alike were sceptical, the former describing the idea as 'an attack organized for amateurs by amateurs'. But afterwards the French had to eat their words, for the British managed to breach the German second positions. A liaison officer spoke for all when he reported: '*Ils ont osé. Ils ont reussi*'! ('The British have dared; and they have succeeded'.)

This success raised the British hopes, but they were only to be dashed. The higher command reacted with maddening lethargy, and the fruits of victory fell through their fingers. Too much time was given for the Germans to rally, and Haig at least temporarily became resigned to attrition as an end in itself. But at least by this time, the Somme had relieved the pressure on Verdun.

August saw the peak of attrition, *la guerre d'usure*, with slaughter on both sides resulting in fractional gains or none at all. Sometimes the objectives of the fighting were piled high with bodies by the time they were attained. Yet Haig still entertained hopes that by mid-September the Germans would be sufficiently worn down for an Allied breakthrough to be attempted. Meanwhile several fortified positions were secured, and though their efforts to eliminate the salient around Thiepval were unsuccessful, the British were able to reduce its size somewhat during the fighting of early August.

On 23 August German losses of men and destruction of morale reached such proportions that General von Below of the First Army was forced to modify Falkenhayn's earlier ruthless order that 'It must be a principle in trench warfare not to abandon a foot of ground, and if a foot of ground be lost to put in the last man to recover it by an immediate counter-attack'. Indeed, Falkenhayn himself was forced to resign on 28 August. The ostensible reason was Rumania's entry into the war on the Entente side, but actually his departure was due to German losses at Verdun and the Somme without visible compensatory successes. Hindenburg, assisted by Ludendorff, replaced him. They found much evidence of low morale at the front, intensified by depression at Allied command of the air. In the last stages of the campaign there were some desertions and voluntary surrenders, as the Germans saw their own losses surpassing even those of the enemy.

On 4 September the French Tenth Army joined their Sixth Army compatriots in the affray, but their initial successes soon turned into a confused collapse. Meanwhile Hindenburg ordered a holding operation on all fronts, with the object of utilizing 'all other available sources' against Rumania. On the fifteenth, Haig mounted an assault along a ten-mile front from Combles to beyond Thiepval. The battle is known as Flers-Courcelette, and it lasted a week. Tanks were used

The war of attrition cost hundreds of thousands of lives on both sides.

Right: The Somme – the aftermath. **Below:** *Barrage on the Somme* – a painting by Hamlyn Reid. **Bottom:** German machine gunners who survived the intensive barrage cut down their attackers mercilessly.

in war for the first time, but to less than full effect. Subsequently a storm of criticism was directed at Haig, since by using tanks prematurely and in insufficient numbers he revealed their existence without a major gain in return. Yet it was hard to decide when to put the tanks into use, and knowledge of the new weapon might well have leaked out before the moment for their optimum employment had arisen. Moreover, Rumanian belligerency was believed to have strained the German nerves to breaking-point; and it was thought that the introduction of a new weapon might now cause them to snap altogether.

On 25 September the Allies moved forward again. Two days later, and with the help of a single tank, Thiepval fell. The defence was heroic and inflicted highly disproportionate casualties through hand-to-hand fighting. Allied intelligence reported that the Germans had now lost at least three hundred and seventy thousand men (actually an underestimate), and thus Haig was tempted into preparations for another attack towards mid-October. But on 2 October the weather threatened to defeat both sides. Incessant autumn rains brought mud, slime, and yet more mud. This made it impossible to move forward at any certain pace, and objectives had to be gained via small and very costly localized attacks. In Cruttwell's graphic description, 'The battle degenerated into a series of desperate nibbles at a medley of shell-holes hastily strung together and called a trench'. Yet Joffre doggedly insisted that the campaign continue, while Haig urged on the British.

After fighting at Transloy Ridges and Ancre Heights, in mid-November the British achieved success in the area of the Ancre river, a tributary of the Somme. The field fortress of Beaumont-Hamel was captured 'a particularly heavy blow', as Ludendorff noted. The Somme campaign ended on 18–19 November amid abysmal blizzards and torrential rain.

Like Falkenhayn, Joffre had seen his plan of attrition boomerang against his own armies. Verdun had not fallen, but neither had strategic gains been made. Indeed, the British had felt that the Somme was a battle fought in an area devoid of strategic objectives, and one which was launched before sufficient resources had been marshalled. The Allies paid dearly for deficiencies in heavy howitzers and ammunition at the Somme, even though these disadvantages were offset to a considerable extent by the heroic determination of the British Army. This stamina is the more remarkable when one remembers that the British Army had been hastily improvised to fight a highly professional German force.

Perhaps the long-term effects of Verdun and the Somme were the most significant. Certainly the French decimation led to the 1917 mutinies. Beyond this, Pétain and other Frenchmen drew the wrong conclusions from Verdun, which resulted in the postwar Maginot Line of fortifications. Most disastrous of all was the effect of the Verdun experience on the three out of every four Frenchmen under arms who passed through it. Here was born that attitude of fatalism and defeatism which came to fruition in 1940, with Pétain as its tragically appropriate instrument.

Above: A German painting of the Somme battlefield as viewed from a balloon. **Left:** The devastation of the Somme created a crisis of morale in the Allied armies.

CHAPTER EIGHT
Eastern Tangled Webs

In the western world, recent history has provided for a variety of vaccination against the horrors of genocide. Within the span of a single generation, mankind has witnessed the ovens of Auschwitz, and the disasters of Biafra and Bangladesh. Yet man's existence is largely made up of dealing with a succession of ordinary problems and simple joys, and in contrast both the repetition and the sheer magnitude of such disasters has made genocide for many a matter to be put aside. Our minds are incapable of grasping the extent or significance of such tragedies.

The First World War has the unenviable distinction of being the scene of the first such holocaust of modern times. Its hapless victims were the Armenians, one of the numerous minorities within the polyglot Ottoman Empire. The first mark against them was that they were Christians within a largely Islamic autocracy; the second was that they were a relatively prosperous community surrounded by backwardness and sloth. Many Turks regarded this close-knit community of go-ahead infidels as a thorn in the side of the nation. Over the centuries, their numbers had been greatly reduced by slaughter, forced conversion to Islam, or emigration. More recently, pressure from European nations had caused the authorities to agree to instigate certain reforms. In practice, however, reform was never seriously attempted, and resentment of outside interference in these matters bred in the Turks a cruel determination to put an end to such complaints by a removal of the sources of the outcry.

In 1896 at least 80,000 Armenians had been slaughtered. This was a pale shadow of what was to come. With the outbreak of the Great War, chauvinist Young Turks saw their chance to annihilate the Armenian nation. Measure of strict internal control could be taken under the guise of wartime necessity, and thus the butchery could be disguised with relative ease until it was too late for others, even if willing, to intervene.

Carefully the Turks laid down their plans. First to be eliminated would be the 100,000 Armenian conscripts within the Ottoman armed forces. Next, Armenian community leaders throughout the empire would be arrested and silenced. Finally, the remaining Armenians would be taken from their homes and deported to die in the desert of thirst, sunstroke, or starvation. Implementation of this 'final solution' was entrusted to an assimilated Bulgarian gypsy, the Interior Minister, Talaat Bey, himself the descendant of a misunderstood and persecuted minority.

The Turco-Russian campaign in the Caucasus provided an additional pretext for persecution, for now the Turks alleged that a pro-Russian Armenian fifth column had conspired in Turkey's defeat. Consequently, in early 1915 the first part of the extermination campaign, that involving Armenian conscripts, was carried out successfully and secretly in an atmosphere white-hot with murderous fanaticism. Then in April one thousand leading Armenians in Constantinople were sent away and butchered.

It is human nature not to face the unendurable,

Left: Serbian refugees crowded the roads during the retreat of 1915. **Right:** A million and a half Armenians were exterminated by 1916. The world was largely indifferent to their fate.

Above: Turkish citizens view a few of the Armenians who were slaughtered. The genocide which began even before the war was given free rein once the war broke out. **Opposite top:** The Serbian retreat. **Opposite bottom:** German cavalry storm into Serbia.

and the Armenians were no exception. They were unable to visualize the extent of the intended infamy, and anyway could do little to help themselves against the operations of an efficient and merciless authority. In May the community leaders were murdered, and only large numbers of women and children remained, easy prey for their tormentors. Lest officialdom feel any wince of compassion, Talaat instructed that 'the Government . . . decided to destroy completely all Armenians living in Turkey . . . An end must be put to their existence, however criminal the measures taken may be, and no regard must be paid to either age or sex nor to conscientious scruples'.

Throughout the summer and autumn of 1915, mass deportations of Armenians proceeded apace. Arshag Sarkissian, most recent chronicler of the disaster, has described the scene: The people would be told to assemble in a central locale, and there they would learn that the government had decided to move them to 'better and safer areas'. Since (so they were told) the journey would be short, the Armenians need bring only a few of their possessions. The more infirm would be transported in ox-driven carts (probably for the sake of speed, and certainly not from compassion), while

the rest would go on foot. En route, many would be disposed of to hasten the journey, though time was always at hand for interruptions in the march for rape and orgies, corruption of young girls and boys alike. Finally, in the desert, the Armenians would be cut down or left to die except for those deemed attractive enough to grace a harem.

As in other infamous slaughters, heroic resistance took place, but in uncoordinated pockets, on a relatively small scale, and in an atmosphere of utter hopelessness against superior odds. In the summer of 1915 a quarter of a million Armenians managed to escape to Russia. These were exceptions. Of the two million Armenians within the Ottoman Empire in 1914, about one and a half million of them had disappeared from the face of the earth by 1916. German and other representations against the bloodbath were at first hotly denied; afterwards most protests were shunted aside with mutterings about other nations minding their own business. Later tyrants were to mark well the indifference with which the world as a whole greeted the Armenian tragedy. As Hitler remarked on the eve of the Second World War, 'After all, who remembers today the extermination of the Armenians'?

LA JOURNÉE SERBE
25 JUIN 1916
ANNIVERSAIRE DE LA BATAILLE DE KOSSOVO

The Serbian Débâcle

On the Serbian front, 1915 found the Balkan Kingdom in an appalling state. Serbia's armies had already been decimated by successive battles with Austria-Hungary. The soldiers had been ravaged by typhus, as indeed had much of the peasantry. After the Austrian-German Gorlice-Tarnów offensive, the Serbians required more assistance than ever but little was forthcoming. The British and French were preoccupied with the western front, and their efforts to persuade Bulgaria to remain neutral were unsuccessful. For their part, the Serbs had never believed much in the possibility of Bulgarian neutrality, for the enmity caused by the Second Balkan War of 1913 was too recent to have been assuaged. As for Bulgaria herself, she was infatuated with the idea of territorial gain, and believing Berlin and Vienna to be in a better position to fulfil their promises, she sided with the Central Powers. Probably only the fall of Constantinople could have persuaded her to do otherwise, since the Bulgars harboured the fiercest of irredentist ambitions against Serbian Macedonia, and the king was a Russophobe. Now plans were formulated for a coordinated German-Austrian-Bulgar attack on Serbia, and these were carried out when the last Bulgarian reservations disappeared with the Allied debacle at Gallipoli.

Falkenhayn's original interest in the subjection of Serbia was in order to utilize the Belgrade-Sofia section of the Constantinople railway which ran through the north east corner of the country. Germany felt that until all of the route to Constantinople lay under her control, the capacity of Turkey for remaining in the conflict was under constant threat. But Italy's entry into the war and her efforts to link up with Serbian forces persuaded Falkenhayn that Serbia was a threat to be stamped underfoot completely.

The armies of the Central Powers, though they held numerical superiority, expected difficulties in moving into Serbia. Communications in the region were primitive, and the barren and semi-mountainous terrain offered meagre comfort in the way of billets or supplies. Nevertheless, on 7 October 1915 the Austrians and Germans swarmed across the Sava and Danube rivers, and Belgrade fell to them two days later. On 11 October, by prearranged plan, the Bulgarian First Army moved against Serbia from the east. Yet subsequent progress was slow, and the Serbs retreated south and southeast out of the way of defeat. Meanwhile, Bulgarian forces cut off the Serbian escape-route to Salonika, and an Allied force arrived in the Vardar valley too late and too enfeebled to be of consequence. Yet despite the onset of winter snows, the lack of food and countless other privations, 150,000 men of the Serbian Army escaped to Albania in what Esposito rightly terms 'one of the most dramatic and difficult retreats in history'. In the process the Serbs were forced to discard much of their transport and artillery. But though they had suffered 100,000 casualties and lost 160,000 men as prisoners, the remaining Serbs had lived to fight another day. The furious Austrians salved their pride by swallowing fierce but tiny Montenegro.

In 1915 the Allies had embarked on their Macedonian adventure. The origins of the Salonika expedition were complex. In the winter of 1914–15 many had thought that relief might be brought to the western front by a northwestward thrust into Central Europe via the Danube, much as the Turks had done in earlier centuries, and in France a leading exponent of this idea was the Fifth Army commander, General Franchet d'Esperey. Then on 26 January 1915 the Greek Prime Minister, Eleutherios Venizelos, had offered to commit his country's forces to the Entente if Bulgarian or Rumanian aid were also secured. In particular Venizelos urged that if Bulgaria refused benevolent neutrality or alliance with the Entente, Allied troops should be sent to the Balkans to dissuade Bulgaria from siding with the Central Powers. At the same time Lloyd George favoured a display of force at the Greek Aegean port of Salonika in order to win the support of all the Balkan states and thereby crush Austria.

The practical difficulties were great. Salonika (Thessaloniki) was a port with limited facilities, and the railway northwards to the Serbian Danube positions was only a single-line track, which could not easily handle an army of any considerable size, yet which could be widened only with great difficulty and delay. On the other hand, the very inhospitality of the country was a factor in dissuading the Germans from attempts to corner the Allies. In the interim the Gallipoli campaign was occupying the forefront of attention, and the Macedonian issue temporarily receded into the background.

In June 1915, however, Joffre's sacking of General Maurice Sarrail because of the heavy losses in the west made it necessary to find the latter a new command. At the same time Paris had been actively considering the dispatch of further forces to the east, in addition to commitments at the Dardanelles. As the Gallipoli campaign turned into an obvious failure, the French persisted in their idea of a Salonika landing, and on 11 September the British agreed to contribute two divisions. A final decision on the worth of the Macedonian operation would be made after the Franco-British autumn campaigns in the west; but before this it became obvious that an attack by the Central Powers on Serbia was imminent. On 22 September the Serbs appealed for 150,000 Entente troops to be sent to her aid via Salonika. Three days later Bulgarian general mobilization persuaded the British to stand behind the Macedonian project, both in order to aid Serbia and in the hope that Greece could be persuaded to secure the Siberian flank against the Bulgars.

Greece, however, declined to fulfil her vaguely-worded obligations to her Serbian ally. Matters were further entangled by differing interpretations of the ill-defined commitments entered into in 1829 at the time of the creation of independent Greece. The British, French, and Russians argued that as protectors of the state under the 1829 agreement, they had the right to send troops to Greek territory. The Greek king, Constantine, and the army leaders denied this. Certainly in the course of the succeeding year the Allies made grave violations of Greek sovereignty, all of which the Entente excused to themselves under the formula 'reason of state'. As for Venizelos, his

position was supremely opportunistic. By co-operating with the Allies, he believed that Greece would gain territory at Turkish expense.

On 3 October one British and one French division arrived at Salonika from the Dardanelles. Venizelos had secretly consented to the landing, even though the Greek government felt obliged to issue a formal protest against this apparent assault on its neutral rights. However, by this time the whole atmosphere surrounding the Macedonian venture had become permeated with trickery and double-dealing, and the British began to have the gravest doubts concerning the project. Yet for the moment their support continued. Early in October the British and French agreed to send five further divisions to Macedonia; and by now Serbia had been invaded. A new crisis arose when, because of new disagreements with the Germanophile king, Venizelos again resigned as Greek prime minister. The air was electric with political uncertainty, when as we have seen, an Allied force was sent up the Vardar valley to aid the Serbs. But eventually the ambivalence of the Greek attitude, the Bulgarian threat (for Britain and France had declared war on Bulgaria on 14–15 October, and the increasingly wretched weather caused the Allies to withdraw).

Pressure now mounted once more for the abandonment of the Salonika project. The British General Staff had never been optimistic over its chances of success. Yet since the French seemed determined to treat the question as a test of British confidence in the Entente, the British could only grudgingly remain. Thus came about the vast Allied encampment at Salonika, which the Germans jeeringly referred to as a self-constructed Allied internment camp.

For their part, the Bulgars had been anxious to cross into Greece and drive the Allies into the sea. Falkenhayn forbade this, however, fearing that such a relentless pursuit would bring Greece into the Allied camp on a wave of popular sentiment against Bulgaria. There were, in addition, the considerations of poor physical communications and inhospitable terrain which applied to much of the fighting in southeast Europe. Moreover, the Germans were aware that both the Bulgars and the Austrians coveted Salonika for themselves. To avoid dissension among the Central Powers and a new extension of age-old Balkan feuds, it seemed best to do nothing. The decision was a fateful one, for at this moment the Bulgars could probably have annihilated the Allied armies and their Salonika base. Alternatively, Greek entry on the Allied side might have saved Serbia.

In the early spring of 1916, Macedonia was almost forgotten as the rival sets of belligerents carried out their main campaigns elsewhere. April, however, brought an extremely slow Allied advance from Salonika to the Greek frontier. Greek forces put up no opposition to this and in some cases cooperated in guard duties. Yet late in May, by secret agreement with Athens, a German-Bulgar force advanced some ten miles into Greece and took Fort Rupel, the major defensive position in this area. As a rejoinder the Allies made demands upon Greece, which included the establishment of a non-party government and the

Opposite top: After General Sarrail was sacked by Joffre on the Western Front, he was given a new opportunity to redeem himself in the Salonika campaign. **Opposite bottom:** The British contributed two divisions for the Salonika landing on the insistence of the French.

The many faces of
the Kaiser – a pastiche of
postcards.

demobilization of the armed forces. The first demand was evaded, but the second was followed. The gunboat diplomacy of the French in particular caused bitter resentment in Greece.

The French continued their strong support for an offensive in Macedonia as a prerequisite for Rumanian and possibly Greek participation on the Entente side. During May and June the British continued to oppose the idea, but in July gave way when it became clear that otherwise Rumania would refuse to join the Allies. On 27 August 1916, Rumania duly proclaimed her belligerency; but before this, emboldened by the ill-advised Greek demobilization, the Bulgars launched their own attack on the seventeenth. Though they gained considerable initial success, by the time of Rumania's entering the war the offensive had petered out.

On 12 September Serbian and French forces attacked west of the Vardar river. They were aided by Italian and Russian troops, for both these powers were conscious of considerations of prestige and future influence in the Balkans. The Serbs showed supreme resilience in the light of their earlier suffering. The British held fast to their positions on the Struma and carried out numerous small attacks.

Once more the wooded and mountainous terrain caused the Allied counteroffensive to move at a slow pace. At one point two days had to be spent in hacking a path through a beech forest by means of bayonets. After two months, however, the Allies had made a significant advance, and though by now the troops were suffering grievously from exhaustion and 50,000 casualties had been sustained, the Entente troops had pushed the

A French view of what was happening to Germans in the Carpathians.

The Allied advance to the Greek frontier was agonizingly slow.

Bulgars to breaking-point and the latter were saved only by the arrival of two improvised German divisions. Bulgarian and German casualties had risen to about 52,000, in addition to the loss of 8000 men as prisoners.

Yet for Sarrail none of this was enough. He had dreamed of some great stroke which would restore his reputation. At the very least he had wanted to drive Bulgaria to the negotiating table, but he had not succeeded, and neither had the offensive helped Rumania much. By this time trouble with Greece had again caused the Allies to threaten a blockade, and despite Athens' recalcitrance its imposition forced the Greeks to capitulate to Allied demands.

In May 1917 Sarrail essayed a new offensive, but the Serbs, still nursing the grudge that they had not been properly supported the previous year, made sure that the operation stalled. By the summer the Allies had completely lost patience with Greece. They forced Constantine to abdicate, Venizelos again became Prime Minister, and on 2 July 1917 Greece finally sided with the Entente.

In 1916 the hero of the eastern front was the Russian general, Alexei Brusilov. His name was given to the extraordinary initial success which the Russians were able to gain that year against the Central Powers. Later Brusilov himself maintained that if his early victories had been correctly exploited, the war in the east, and perhaps the whole war, could have been won that year. What seems almost certain is that Brusilov's victories at least prevented the Allies from losing in 1916 no mean achievement.

Westwood and other writers have emphasized

that the great Russian retreat of the previous autumn, successful as it was in avoiding destruction at the hands of the Central Powers, merely reinforced an already strong propensity in the minds of Russian generals to regard withdrawal as a means towards achieving victory itself. In this sense the lessons of 1812 had been learnt too well, or too much had been deduced from them.

By the spring of 1916, at least superficially, the major Russian deficiencies of the previous year were on their way to being repaired. Rifles and ammunition were now available in much greater supply, partly from increased home production and partly through imports; and the lull of winter had given the opportunity for improved training of recruits, though experienced officers were still in short supply. At the highest level, the machinations of the Germanophile Tsarina and her coterie, including the new Prime Minister, Sturmer, saw to it that the ablest and most independent-minded soldiers were passed over for promotion in favour of yes-men and sycophants.

In the winter of 1915, the Allied plans for a coordinated offensive had called for a relatively small Russian effort, due to her earlier extremely heavy losses. The bloodbath of Verdun necessitated a revision of this scheme, and now the French asked the Russians for action which would divert some German divisions eastwards.

The first and premature Russian effort in this direction, the battle of Lake Naroch (Narocz) on the Baltic flank, was highly inauspicious. Here, in March and April, Russian armies attacked with strong artillery support, but then, inexplicably, much of the artillery and aircraft cover was withdrawn. The Germans brought in heavy firepower and once more made use of gas, while the Russians, lacking the protection of gas masks, were thrown back with the loss of over 100,000 men, five times the German casualties.

On 14 April, however, the Tsar and his generals had concluded that a larger westward offensive should be undertaken shortly. Preparations were made at several different sites along the front, so that the Germans would be uncertain where the main attack was to take place. It would be necessary to push through a very well fortified Austro-Hungarian defence, but aerial reconnaissance was of tremendous help in enabling the Russians to anticipate the location of major hazards such as machine-gun nests and deep dugouts. In the interim, in mid-May the Italians appealed for Russian action to relieve Austro-Hungarian pressure in the Trentino.

The new Russian offensive was launched on 4 June, when three of Brusilov's four armies managed an immediate breakthrough. Once again an example of Habsburg internal weakness was provided when Czech troops surrendered to the Russians in droves and welcomed them as fellow Slavs and liberators. Soon Brusilov's troops punched yawning gaps in the Austrian lines, and the latter swiftly fell back. By 9 June Brusilov had taken over 70,000 prisoners. It was the greatest Russian victory of the war.

In the meantime Ludendorff was searching diligently for German units to reinforce the crumbling Austrians. Of even greater consequence was the fact that the attack, which Evert of the Russian West Front was to have undertaken in the direction of Wilno (Vilnius or Vilna) on 14 June, was cancelled because of bad weather and, some said, because of cowardice in the face of German (as opposed to Austrian) troops in this sector. As a substitute, a paltry and unsuccessful advance was essayed further south. Moreover, despite Brusilov's objections, Evert's troops were sent to Brusilov himself to strengthen his forces instead of mounting their own attack westwards. Now the Germans, aided by superior communications, switched their troops to the south and by August prevented further significant Russian advances. The main thrust of the Brusilov offensive came to an end about 10 August, though the campaign itself was not called off until October. Austria-Hungary and Germany had lost over 400,000 prisoners of war and over 340,000 casualties, while Russian losses exceeded 1,000,000. If Vienna tottered under the strain, so did Petrograd. This time the spirit of the Russian army was irreparably damaged.

If Evert had attacked towards the west as Brusilov had planned, it is possible that Austria-Hungary would have collapsed. This might have been enough to drive Germany to sue for peace by the year's end. Despite their own heavy toll, however, the Russians had forced the Central Powers to transfer troops eastwards from the western and Italian fronts. Cruttwell is of the opinion that the Brusilov offensive 'made inevitable' the breakup of the Habsburg Empire, while historians unite in emphasizing that the dynamism behind the campaign was uniquely that of General Brusilov himself. For this reason the Russian offensive of 1916 is the only campaign of the war to have been named for its commander.

On 27 August, as was noted earlier, Rumania declared war on the Central Powers. The Russians in particular had been angling for this event since the beginning of the war, but Brătianu, Rumania's Prime Minister, had bided his time to consider what was in the best interests of his nation. As it turned out, Rumania hesitated too long and was crushed, whereas her intervention even a few months earlier might have swung the balance against the Central Powers.

Bulgarian infantry advance toward the Allied position.

General Alexei Brusilov became the Russian hero of the Eastern Front.

Rumanians had grave doubts as to the wisdom of entering the war on either side; but if neutrality were to be abandoned, it was equally difficult to know for whom. Although she hankered after the border territory of Bessarabia, Rumania had many ties with her giant Russian neighbour. Rumania was also linked with Italy, from whose Roman legions a mixture of legend and fact holds the Rumanians to be descended, and with France, like Italy a 'Latin sister' and cultural mentor. Yet Rumania had also connections with Germany and Austria-Hungary, not least because of the abiding interest which these two powers had traditionally held in the Balkans. Public opinion was almost evenly divided in its preferences. Thus under the circumstances, a policy of prudent caution and self-interest seemed called for.

In 1916, however, the initial success of the Brusilov offensive emboldened the Russians to press the Rumanians much more firmly. On 17 August, having been promised large tracts of Magyar-controlled Transylvania and also the Banat and the Bulgarian Dobrudja as the spoils of victory, Rumania signed a military alliance with Britain and France. Yet to the disappointment of the Entente, Bucharest did not press south against Bulgaria and towards Salonika, since her most immediate ambitions against Bulgaria had already been satisfied three years earlier. Instead, when she entered the war (and the actual entry had been made only after the Russians had lost patience and threatened invasion unless Rumania took immediate action), Bucharest moved against Transylvania. The regional capital, Hermannstadt, fell on 6 September, due less to the valour of the pitiably equipped and disgracefully officered Rumanian army than to the fact that the Central Powers were, or had recently been, under severe pressure on several fronts.

The Germans, now deeply concerned, somehow scraped together enough forces under Falkenhayn and Mackensen to regain control of the situation. Though Russian troops caused Mackensen a temporary setback in the middle of September, towards the end of the month the Rumanians were driven back in north and south alike. After the fall of Rumania's chief port, Constanza,

The Russian armies achieved a major breakthrough in June 1916. It was the greatest Russian victory of the war.

on 23 October, the capitulation of Bucharest itself followed on 6 December. The Central Powers had now gained control of valuable resources of oil and wheat, and their links to Turkey were more secure than ever, though Bulgaria and Turkey soon engaged in a vicious quarrel over the fate of the Dobrudja. In addition, although their eastern front had been lengthened, the Central Powers surmised that the trouncing which they had given the new belligerent would cause other neutrals to think twice before abandoning their nonalignment.

The Mesopotamian Campaign

We should now consider events yet further east, in Mesopotamia or modern Iraq. There, on 11 March 1917, the British made their triumphal entry into Baghdad. After the earlier setbacks, the fall of this fabled city furnished welcome exotic interest to the headline writers. Here was a victory over the Turks which did something, at least, to assuage the festering wound of Gallipoli.

The campaign in Mesopotamia had begun early in the war, when the India Office had suggested a British demonstration at the head of the Persian Gulf to reinforce Arab tendencies to turn against their Ottoman overlords, if not actually to rally to the Allies. Thus it was hoped to dissuade the Turks from invading Egypt, since such an expedition was considered impossible without Arab support. At the same time, the war effort made it also necessary to secure the route of the Anglo-Persian oil pipeline.

After initial operations in November 1914, British Empire forces moved inland. Basra fell on 22 November; Qurna, junction of the Tigris and Euphrates rivers, on 9 December; and Amara on 3 June 1915. A determined Turkish offensive, ironically with extensive Arab support, had intervened around Basra on 11–13 April, but had been successfully fought off. Numerous other conquests were made, including that of Nasiriya on 25 July, but a high toll of troop strength was taken by sunstroke and the many diseases endemic to Mesopotamia.

Now General Sir John Nixon, leader of the Indian Expeditionary Force, decided that he could control the *vilayet* (province) of Basra more efficiently if he captured Kut-al-Amara, junction of the Tigris and the Shatt-al-Hai. By unspoken agreement, Kut was also considered the last stage before the capture of Baghdad, which some looked forward to as almost an *ersatz* Constantinople. Accordingly Major General Townshend of the Sixth Division was set the task of Kut's capture, and after a battle against the Turks outside, he entered Kut on 28 September. Now, especially as the Gallipoli campaign was obviously failing, 'a striking success in the East . . . to . . . win the Arabs' was considered vital. On 23 October, with Kitchener dissenting, the British cabinet authorized the over optimistic Nixon to attempt the capture of Baghdad itself. But after a ferocious clash in November at Ctesiphon, sixteen miles southeast of Baghdad, Townshend decided to fall back on Kut, which he reached on 3 December.

A decision to stand at Kut was taken in the knowledge that there were present enough supplies to last for at least two months in the event of

Far left: A Turkish siege forced a British surrender at Kut. **Left:** The Austrians attack.

Far left: Field Marshal August von Mackensen helped Hindenburg encircle the Russians at Tannenberg and later succeeded him as commander of the Ninth Army. In 1915 his new command, the joint Austro-German Eleventh Army, cleared the Russians from Galicia in a fortnight, a victory which won him a marshal's baton. In November 1915 his armies overran Serbia. **Left:** The Austrian Army on the march.

Far left: German aid to the Austrians helped to stop the Brusilov offensive just in time. **Centre left:** Rumania's doubts about entering the war were confirmed by the initial casualties which she suffered. **Left:** British gunboats helped the advance up the Tigris. This river gunboat of the Insect class saw service throughout the campaign. **Below:** The British march through Baghdad with Turkish prisoners in tow.

Above: General
Townshend, surrounded by
his staff at Kut. Townshend
must share the blame for
British losses at the hands
of the Turks. **Above right:**
The King of Montenegro
and General Allenby in
November 1916. Allenby's
successes later in the war
forced the Turks to
collapse.

siege, after which time relief would be likely. In
fact, the subsequent Turkish siege lasted almost
five months and caused much hardship. But if
the town could be held, it would provide a barrier
to further Turkish progress towards the Persian
Gulf. In any case, by the time they had fallen back
to Kut the British forces were probably too
exhausted to have travelled further. Townshend
must be blamed, however, for insufficient attempts
to ration food within the garrison or to search out
new supplies, and his appeals for relief caused a
premature and disastrous British attack which
was three times repulsed in January 1916, after
which a further opportunity for relief was
bungled. Finally, on 29 April, the beleaguered
British were forced to surrender unconditionally.
The Turks gained well over 10,000 British and
Indian prisoners, of whom the officers were
treated tolerably well, but the men were beaten,
murdered, sexually mutilated, or herded across
the desert like animals.

By this time the War Office (now in charge of

Mesopotamian operations) had decided that
neither Kut nor Baghdad was an important
British objective, even though 'as forward a position as can be made secure tactically' was to be
maintained. In September 1916 a complete withdrawal from Mesopotamia the following spring
was mooted, but later it was decided to advance to
the Shatt-al-Hai to free the right bank of the
Tigris of hostile forces. This was accomplished by
4 February 1917, and by the twenty-fourth Kut
was retaken, even though lack of supplies caused
the overall operation to be curtailed on 28
February. Nonetheless the troops were able to
move forward again on 5 March, and Baghdad
was occupied on the eleventh. The ancient city
had fallen to its thirtieth conqueror.

The Turks laid serious plans for the recapture
of Baghdad, but difficulties in Palestine caused
diversion of the necessary troops. In the autumn
of 1917 the British made further advances, though
the following spring the intense heat caused a
relative lull in operations. After Allenby's success
in Palestine in September 1918 at Megiddo (the
Biblical Armageddon), the British decided to
exploit their increased prestige by further operations in Mesopotamia, but events in the Turkish
theatre were now overtaken by Allenby's continued success. Turkey left the war under the
armistice of Mudros on 30 October.

The Mesopotamian campaign cost over 90,000
British Empire casualties, including nearly 29,000
dead. The Turks lost over 45,000 prisoners and un-
numbered dead and wounded. The siege of Kut
and Baghdad, although to a certain extent worthwhile, could certainly have been conducted with
less waste of human lives.

Right: The British swept
the Turks out of both
Palestine and Mesopotamia
by 1918. **Opposite left:**
Soldiers from different
areas of Rumania.
Opposite right: These
Turks were captured by
the 38th Lancashire
Brigade.

TURKEY

Baghdad

Landing of British troops
at Al Faw

→ Al Basrah
5.11.17

Advance and dates of capture
November 1914-October 1918

A
Khudhaira Bend taken
4 December1916-19 January
1917

B
Hai Salient taken
25 January -5 February
1917

C
Dahra Bend taken
9-16 February 1917

D
Shumran Bend taken
23-24 February 1917

Turkish counter-attacks

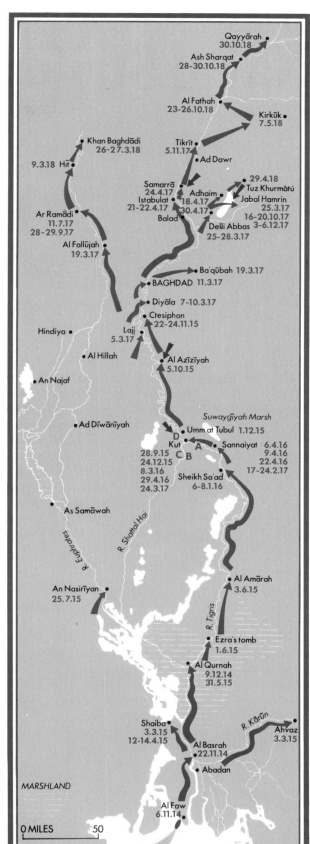

Qayyārah
30.10.18

Ash Sharqat
28-30.10.18

Al Fathah
23-26.10.18

Kirkūk
7.5.18

Tikrīt
5.11.17

Ad Dawr

Khan Baghdādi
26-27.3.18

9.3.18 Hit

29.4.18
Tuz Khurmātū

Samarrā
24.4.17
Istabulat
21-22.4.17

Adhaim
18.4.17
30.4.17

Jabal Hamrin
25.3.17

Ar Ramādi
11.7.17
28-29.9.17

Balad

Delli Abbas
25-28.3.17

16-20.10.17
3-6.12.17

Al Fallūjah
19.3.17

Ba'qūbah 19.3.17

BAGHDAD 11.3.17

Diyāla 7-10.3.17

Ctesiphon
22-24.11.15

Hindiya

Laji
5.3.17

Al Hillah

Al Azīzīyah
5.10.15

An Najaf

Ad Dīwāniyah

Suwaygīyah Marsh

Umm at Tubul 1.12.15

D

Kut
28.9.15
24.12.15
8.3.16
29.4.16
24.3.17

A

Sannaiyat   6.4.16
9.4.16
22.4.16
17-24.2.17

C B

Sheikh Sa'ad
6-8.1.16

As Samāwah

R. Shattal Hai

An Nasirīyan
25.7.15

Al Amārah
3.6.15

R. Euphrates

R. Tigris

Ezra's tomb
1.6.15

Al Qurnah
9.12.14
31.5.15

R. Kārūn

Ahvaz
3.3.15

Shaiba
3.3.15
12-14.4.15

Al Basrah
22.11.14

Abadan

MARSHLAND

Al Faw
6.11.14

0 MILES   50

W.THÖNY 16

149

CHAPTER NINE

Naval Strife and Peace Moves

The Battle of Jutland (or the Battle of Skaggerak) took place on the night of 31 May 1916, in a large area some seventy miles west of the North Jutland coast. For a generation both Britain and Germany had anticipated such a meeting, but so far each had failed to bring about conditions in which a vast naval encounter could be fought on favourable terms.

Conflict at sea was inevitable in 1916; the Allied blockade was affecting Germany, but Russia was suffering from German interference with her imports even more, making it necessary for the Allies to loosen the German stranglehold on the Baltic. The British Grand Fleet bases were in a good state of readiness, and the fleet itself was concentrated in the Orkney Islands at Scapa Flow; its commander, Admiral Sir John Jellicoe, was confident that he could deal with any German threat, either by closing off the northern exit from the North Sea, or by doing battle should England's coasts be threatened.

Admiral Reinhard Scheer, commander of the German High Seas Fleet, was also ready for the offensive. He and his colleagues had been deeply perturbed, first by the effects of the Allied blockade, and then by the curtailment of the German fleet's activities after the Battle of Dogger Bank in 1915. However, by the spring of 1916 the British fleet was almost twice as strong as that of Germany, so in an attempt to force some division of British strength, Scheer planned a series of raids to goad them into sending out small detachments which, he hoped, could then be destroyed by U-boats and surface vessels.

On 24–25 April, at a time when the British were under pressure because of the rebellion in Dublin, the Germans carried out a sortie in which they bombarded several towns along the east coast of England, including Norwich, Lowestoft,

Admiral Jellico boards HMS *Iron Duke*.

The British Fleet leaves Spithead in 1914.

Yarmouth, and Lincoln. A more extensive operation was planned for the second half of May. German battle cruisers were to bombard Sunderland, and when the British squadrons put out to sea in retaliation, twelve U-boats would move in for the kill. However, bad weather intervened and prevented reconnaissance by Zeppelin airships. Without prior information there was a danger that the High Seas Fleet might be cut off by British forces, and so an alternative plan had to be devised. The German battle cruiser force under Rear Admiral Franz von Hipper would proceed north from Heligoland Bight to the Norwegian coast, where it would demonstrate its presence. Scheer would follow from a distance, hoping that the British battle cruiser force under Vice Admiral Sir David Beatty would be tempted out of its base at Rosyth, near Edinburgh. Unfortunately, he did not realize that the British were able to decode German radio messages.

On the afternoon of 30 May the alternative scheme was approved. Although the British knew that a major action was to take place, the full meaning of the German messages was unclear. Still, Jellicoe decided to move the main portion of the Grand Fleet seawards from Scapa Flow. He was joined by a further force from Cromarty Firth and the base of Invergordon; the two contingents were to rendezvous ninety miles west of the southernmost tip of Norway on the morning of 31 May, their combined forces totalling twenty-four dreadnoughts, three battle cruisers, eight armoured cruisers, twelve light cruisers and fifty-one destroyers. Separately but simultaneously a scouting force of six battle cruisers, twelve light cruisers, four *Queen Elizabeth*-class battleships, twenty-eight destroyers and a seaplane carrier left Rosyth under Beatty's command. He was to be 120 miles west of Jutland Bank by 2:00 p.m. on

31 May, while Jellicoe would be fifty miles off the Norwegian coast. If by this time he had not sighted the enemy, he was to move northwards to meet Jellicoe.

Ironically, Scheer's U-boats had already failed him on two counts. They had not been able to successfully attack any of the British ships as they moved out; and their reconnaissance was incomplete – the Germans had no hint that their rival's main fleet was now at sea.

At 1:00 a.m. on 31 May, Hipper's force of five battle cruisers, five light cruisers, and thirty-three destroyers weighed anchor and headed into the North Sea. Behind them followed Scheer's fleet of sixteen dreadnoughts, six pre-dreadnought vessels, six light cruisers, and thirty-nine destroyers.

At 2:15 p.m. Beatty was changing course to join Jellicoe, when suddenly his light cruiser *Galatea* saw smoke to the east. On investigation the ship was found to be a Danish merchant steamer, as the German *Elbing* also discovered when it came on the scene. As the *Galatea* and the *Elbing* saw each other, the order was given to fire. The Battle of Jutland had begun, and this chance encounter with the Danish vessel may have cost the British a decisive victory; if the rival fleets had met an hour later further north the Germans would have been at an even greater distance from home and shelter.

When he learned what had happened, Beatty quickly turned southeast, hoping to place himself between the Germans and their home base, but the British battleships under Rear Admiral Evan-Thomas failed to read his signal to turn and fell behind. Meanwhile, Hipper had turned south, hoping to lead the British into the oncoming German battle squadrons.

At 3:48 p.m. each side opened fire. Six British ships faced five German vessels, and Beatty went

Top: The German fleet comes out to meet them, led by the armoured cruiser *Blücher*. **Above:** Admiral Sir David Beatty.

Below: Prince Henry of Prussia (with field glasses) and Admiral von Scheer, Commander-in-Chief, of the German High Seas Fleet at Jutland.

into action without waiting for the Fifth Battle Squadron to catch up with him. At 4:04 p.m. two salvoes from the *Von der Tann* caused the British *Indefatigable* to explode and capsize with the loss of one thousand men; this was closely followed by the blowing up of the *Queen Mary* under the impact of concentrated fire from *Derfflinger* and *Seydlitz*. Twelve hundred men went down with her, and a dark pillar of smoke estimated at a height of 800 to 2300 feet, rose above the spot. In the interim, the *Lion*'s turret had been removed by a shell from the *Lützow*, and the ship would have exploded but for the heroism of a dying man, Major Harvey, who ordered that its magazines be flooded. Several other British vessels were damaged; other German ships were similarly hit, and the *Seydlitz* lost a turret. In fact, the Fifth Battle Squadron, now finally in action, would have overwhelmed several enemy vessels had they not been issued defective shells which could not penetrate the German armour.

At 4:33, just as the tide seemed to be turning in Britain's favour, Commodore Goodenough of the Second Light Cruiser Squadron saw the German battle fleet on the horizon. Goodenough's sudden encounter gave Beatty a chance to escape the trap which Hipper had set for him. He turned northwards, but the Fifth Battle Squadron was still engaged in heavy fighting, during which the British *Nestor* was sunk and the *Barham* and *Malaya* damaged. The German *Lützow*, *Derfflinger* and *Seydlitz* were also hit.

In the interim Jellicoe's battleships were moving southeast; the battle cruisers under Rear Admiral Sir Horace Hood were farther east. In an attempt to get between the German fleet and the coast, Jellicoe moved his squadrons to the left, while Beatty's battle cruisers intersected with the battleships and took up new positions.

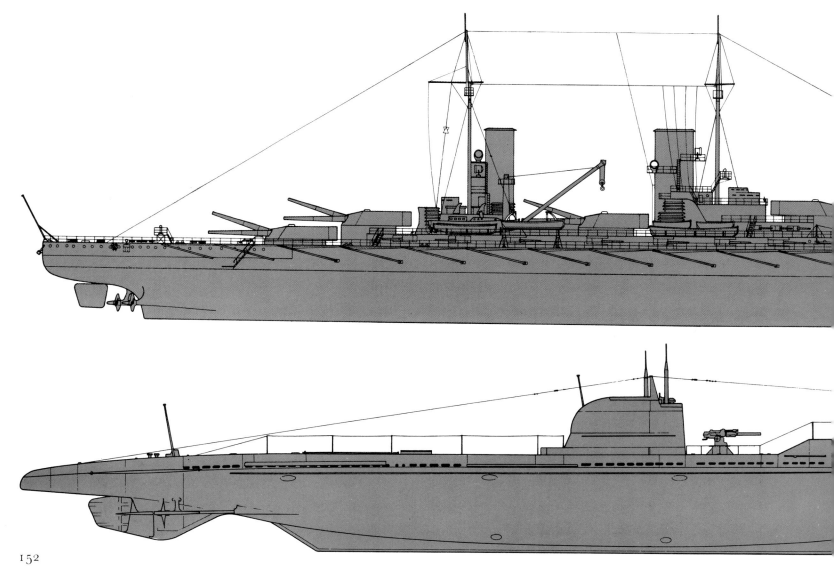

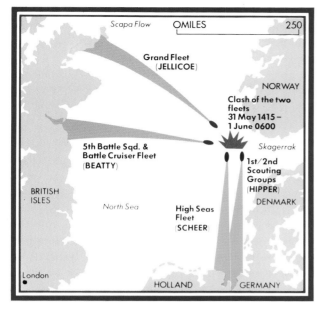

Opposite: The Grand Fleet opens fire at Jutland.

Hipper, who had turned north, suddenly sighted Beatty again at about 5:40. As he bore down on his adversary Jellicoe sent his left column on a south by southeast course. The German admiral was aghast when he saw this totally unexpected force come out of the mist, but he kept his wits and managed to execute a co-ordinated turnaway movement (*Gefechtskehrt-wendung*) to starboard. This superb somersaulting manoeuvre enabled the German ships to elude their foe in record time, if only temporarily.

The Germans had gained other impressive successes that afternoon. The British *Warspite* had been forced out of action, the *Defence* had been blown up, and the *Warrior* had to be abandoned next day because of the damage she sustained. In addition the *Derfflinger* had sunk the *Invincible*. The Germans had proved the excellence of their ship design and ammunition, even though the *Lützow*

was hit and disabled and the *Wiesbaden* wrecked. Nevertheless, Scheer was on the defensive. At 6:44 p.m., despite threatening mist and darkness, Jellicoe again turned southeast to move between the enemy fleet and their base. Scheer changed course, perhaps hoping to pass across the enemy's rear to safety, or perhaps thinking that the Grand Fleet was divided, but once more he was forced to retire in the face of the British dreadnoughts.

Meanwhile Scheer's destroyer flotillas launched twenty-eight torpedoes at the British fleet, to which Jellicoe's response was a simultaneous turning action of his own. None of the torpedoes found a target, but during the delay Jellicoe lost his chance to smash the German fleet. By 7:18 p.m. Scheer managed another turnaway, but the *Seydlitz* and the *Von der Tann* had been damaged and fire had broken out aboard the *Derfflinger*, which had lost three of its four heavy turrets. Jellicoe now decided against further interception of the enemy that night. This decision subsequently received much criticism, but visibility was failing and he no longer had accurate information on the German positions. Radar had not been invented, and he felt that further action would at best achieve uncertain results. Scheer still had to contend with a heavy enemy force between himself and home – unless he could slip through during the night. He decided to try, though fully conscious of the risks involved.

Though Jellicoe intended to renew the battle in daylight, he was hampered by inexact knowledge of German movements. Between 10:00 p.m. and 2:00 a.m., scarcely believing their good fortune, the Germans broke their way through the British line. The armoured cruiser *Black Prince* was eliminated, and their own *Pommern* was cut in half. Jellicoe had let several opportunities to cripple the enemy slip by, but many of his errors were the

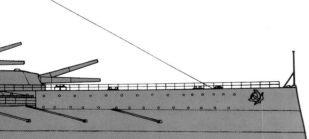

WHAT A RED RAG IS TO A BULL-

THE RED CROSS IS TO THE HUN.

To the already Long List of Outrages by the HUNS on The RED CROSS both on Land and Sea, there was added on January the 4th This Year, the Sinking without warning in the Bristol Channel of the Hospital Ship "REWA."—Fortunately owing to the Splendid Discipline and the Unselfish and Heroic Conduct of the Officers, Crew, and The Medical Staff, All the wounded, of whom there were over 700 on board were saved,—But three poor Lascar Firemen went down with the ship.

Opposite centre:
Grosser Kurfürst, 25m 391/28,148 tons. Length: 580ft. Beam: 97ft. Draft: 28ft 6in. Machinery: 3 shaft turbines, coal and oil fired, shaft hsp 35,000, Speed: 23 knots. Armament: 10 × 12in. guns, 14 × 5·9in. guns, 8 × 3·4in. A.A. guns, 5 × 20in. torpedo tubes (1 × Bow, 4 × Beam). Crew: 1,084. Armour: Main belt 14in.; midships 10in.; decks 4½in.; turrets and control tower 14in.
Opposite bottom:
UC 16 Sub, length: 173ft. Beam: 17ft. Displacement: 434/511 tons. Engine: 600 hp diesel, Speed: 12 knots surface, 714 knots submerged. Armament: 1 × 13·4in. gun, 3 × 19·7in. torpedo tubes and 18 mines.
Left: Anti-German propaganda ran riot during the period of unrestricted submarine warfare. The U-boat campaign was designed to break the increasingly effective Allied blockade of Germany.

Torpedoes began to take their toll.

result of misleading or incomplete information. Now there was nothing to do but follow the German example and head for home. At 11:00 a.m. on 1 June, the Grand Fleet set course for Scapa Flow.

British losses amounted to three battle cruisers, three cruisers, eight destroyers and over six thousand men. The figures for Germany were one battleship, one battle cruiser, four light cruisers, five destroyers and three thousand casualties. The loss of the three British battle cruisers was mainly the result of inadequate armour. Moreover, the powers of British guns was greatly diminished by the poor quality of their armour-piercing shells.

Such was the Battle of Jutland which in the end had involved over 250 ships, prompting Churchill to describe it as 'the culminating manifestation of naval force in the history of the world'. Both sides claimed to have won; in fact neither did so. Jutland was indecisive, and as Liddell Hart comments, its value as a battle was 'negligible'. If anything, the naval clash decreased British prestige in Allied eyes, for the British had failed to free the Baltic; as the noose around Russia tightened, that luckless nation lurched towards its rendezvous with destiny in 1917. British overall command of the sea, however, was unaffected.

Several historians have emphasized that Jellicoe's objective was less to insure a British victory than to forestall a German success, and in this he was successful. By the late summer of 1916 the German high command had decided that a further major naval battle involved unacceptable risks. The High Seas Fleet was placed on the defensive, and morale suffered badly, resulting in mutiny in August 1917 and a major revolt in 1918. Thus it may be said that this extraordinary battle had long-term consequences which far outweighed its immediate results.

America tries to Mediate
Since before the outbreak of war, Woodrow Wilson, the idealistic American President, had desperately tried first to avert and then to end a conflict which he thought would be the ruin of civilization and the rule of law. In the autumn of 1915 it seemed that the war was reaching a deadlock, and conditions for peace occupied his mind even more. Lacking a definite plan, however, he turned to his intimate friend, Colonel Edward House for advice.

House, always an Anglophile, believed that Imperial Germany was a diehard autocracy which would find no place in the new order following a peace settlement. In October 1915, he explained to the President that Britain and France should and could be convinced of the essential identity of interests between themselves and America; a tripartite understanding should be reached, according to which the United States would call for a peace conference. If the Germans cooperated, a compromise peace might yet be achieved without American belligerency, but if they proved recalcitrant, the United States could intervene on the Allied side under the banner of a moral crusade against the Kaiser.

Colonel House thought that the war could be ended on terms that would include the establishment of a League of Nations to monitor the peace settlement, universal disarmament, and a territorial settlement which would restore the pre-war frontiers. Wilson readily agreed to the scheme, though their views on the specifics of a peace settlement differed more than either man realized. For example, House already believed that American participation on the Allied side was all but inevitable, while Wilson still hoped to use moral rather than physical persuasion.

In January 1916 House was received in London with considerable scepticism and reserve. Grey, the Foreign Secretary and a close friend of House, and Balfour, First Lord of the Admiralty, pointed out that America's efforts to settle the conflict would meet entrenched resistance from Allied governments and peoples alike. The British were fully aware that German occupation of considerable French and Russian territory meant that a return to the 1914 *status quo* was the very most that could be expected. This boded ill for Allied war aims, which by now encompassed much in the way of revision of borders and redistribution of power. Above all, the Allies still believed that they could win, and this was infinitely preferable to a compromise arranged by a government which, however friendly, appeared increasingly interfering and naive.

In Berlin, House encountered similar obstinacy, though more subtle Germans tried to convince him that Allied obstructiveness was all that prevented peace, and that in consequence the United States ought to remain neutral. In Paris he was told bluntly that his efforts were coming at an entirely inappropriate time. Still, he left the impression both in Paris and London that America would back the Allies to the hilt.

On 22 February House and Grey produced a memorandum, agreeing that some time in the unspecified future the Allies would ask America to call a peace conference. The general feeling was that German non-cooperation would *probably* result in America's entering the war on the Allied side. (It is significant that the conditional 'probably' was omitted by House, but added by Wilson.) The terms which would be put to the Germans would include the restoration of Belgian and Serbian independence and sovereignty, the retrocession of Alsace-Lorraine to France, the cession of Constantinople to Russia, and the establishment of an independent Poland. Germany would receive extra colonies in compensation for these losses. A postwar security system would be established, including the abolition of competitive armaments, and guarantees against unprovoked aggression.

To London the signing of the memorandum meant a welcome postponement of American demands, but Washington was more optimistic. As it happened, however, the Allies never invited the President to issue his peace appeal.

German peace moves
With the collapse of Rumania at the end of 1916, the Germans saw an opportunity to propose a compromise peace from a position of apparent strength, and on 12 December the German government called publicly for peace negotiations, sternly declaring that otherwise the Fatherland in its 'indestructible strength' was prepared to fight on to a successful finish. The Central Powers hinted that they had their own plan to stem the flow of blood, but the terms were not disclosed.

In fact, the Central Powers envisaged the consolidation of German *Mittelafrika* by the acquisition of all or part of the immensely rich Belgian Congo. Germany would keep the important industrial resources of the French Briey-Longwy basin, while Belgium would come under German 'influence'; failing that, Germany would retain Liège. Austria was to benefit from adjustments along the Italian frontier, and Montenegro was to be split between Austria-Hungary and Albania. The Hungarian-Rumanian frontier was to be 'rectified', Serbia would be required to cede territory to both Austria-Hungary and Bulgaria, and the Straits question would be 'examined' at length.

These demands were put forward by German moderates who believed in the peace initiative for its own sake. Their more calculating colleagues hoped that the mere possibility of peace would

Below: The *Indomitable* and *Inflexible* move in for the kill. **Below centre:** The *Invincible* is hit. **Bottom:** The *Invincible* sinks. The torpedo boat *Badger* approaches to pick up the six survivors.

prevent or delay American participation on the Allied side. If peace on German terms was impossible, they reasoned, the gesture of negotiation might make the resumption of unrestricted submarine warfare by Germany more palatable. Also, many leading Germans feared that Austro-Hungarian morale would collapse without some gesture toward peace.

Just at this time, Wilson was preparing a further appeal for each side to state its minimum war aims, and on 18 December the American President called for 'soundings (to) be taken' to determine if mankind were within sight of that 'haven of peace' for which all yearned. But the Germans were reluctant to state their peace terms publicly, and the Entente, regarding German peace overtures as insincere, rejected them as lacking any positive indication that the Central Powers would return to the *status quo* of 1914 or guarantee their future non belligerency.

On 10 January 1917 the Entente replied at length to the American proposals. They claimed that Allied war aims implied:

Necessarily and first of all, the restoration of Belgium, Serbia, and Montenegro, with the compensation due to them; the evacuation of the invaded territories in France, in Russia, in Rumania, with just reparation; the reorganization of Europe guaranteed by a stable regime and based at once on respect for nationalities, and on the right to full security and liberty of economic development possessed by all peoples, small and great; and, at the same time, upon territorial conventions and international settlements such as to guarantee land

and sea frontiers against unjustified attack; the restoration of provinces formerly torn from the Allies by force or against the wish of their inhabitants; the liberation of the Italians, as also of the Slavs, Rumanians and Czechoslovaks from foreign domination; the setting free of the populations subject to the bloody tyranny of the Turks; and the turning out of Europe of the Ottoman Empire as decidedly foreign to Western Civilization.

In order to mollify Russia, the independence of Poland was not specifically referred to, and no mention was made of the future of the German colonies. As all but the most unrealistic must have known, these terms and the aggressive way in which they were stated had no chance of acceptance until Germany faced utter defeat.

At the end of January Count Bernstorff, the German ambassador in Washington, told Wilson of his government's decision to resume unrestricted submarine warfare. At the same time he informed Wilson privately that German peace demands included the restoration of Belgium 'under special guarantes for the safety of Germany' and the restitution of German-occupied parts of France 'under reservation of strategical and economic changes of the frontier, and financial compensations'. The French would keep that small part of Alsace which they had managed to occupy. Germany and the re-established Poland would redefine their eastern frontiers in order to secure themselves strategically and economically against Russia. Freedom of the seas was to be insured. Finally, Germany expected the return of her colonies and compensation for war damage.

Other attempts to end the war

In Vienna Emperor Karl succeeded the aged Franz Josef on the Habsburg throne, and immediately started to work for an early peace settlement, via his brother-in-law, Prince Sixtus (Sixte) of Bourbon. The Emperor's hope was that in return for a separate peace, the Western Allies would allow Austria-Hungary to remain more or less intact. The ensuing series of negotiations, however, proved fruitless, mainly because of the

irreconcilable nature of Austrian and Italian war aims. France made matters worse with demands that included a reversion to the French frontier of 1814 (i.e., including Alsace-Lorraine and the Saar and Landau territories), the restoration of Belgium and of Serbia with an Adriatic outlet, and the cession of Constantinople to Russia.

The Vatican's efforts to effect a compromise in the summer of 1917 were equally unsuccessful. The Pope called for the renunciation of reparations and territorial annexations, but neither side was prepared to agree.

In November 1917 the Marquis of Lansdowne published a memorandum which he had shown to the British cabinet a year previously. The document urged that, with absolute victory becoming increasingly unlikely, concrete proposals for a negotiated peace be drawn up. Earlier, the inclination of some cabinet members to negotiate had led to a major political crisis and to the formation of a new government under David Lloyd George, champion of the 'knockout blow'. In

1917 Lansdowne's views were simply ignored. Desperation had not reduced either side to breaking-point, so the war continued.

The Blockades

From the beginning, both Britain and Germany recognized the importance of trade warfare. In conducting this aspect of the war, each side reached for the weapons that were most readily available. Thus the main British device was the blockade of Germany and regulation of the trade of her neighbouring neutrals, the Netherlands, and the three Scandinavian countries. Germany's retaliation took the form of a hard-hitting submarine campaign which for a time threatened to cripple the import of goods vital to Britain.

Until America entered the war in April 1917, the established tenets of international law still influenced the conduct of the Allied blockade. The Entente knew that it could ill afford to offend the United States, the most powerful of the neutrals and a nation traditionally sensitive about its

Above left: The heir to the Habsburg throne, Karl, decorates his soldiers.
Above: The ageing Franz Josef, shortly before his death.

Opposite top: 'The Mighty German Fleet at Kiel' – Italian sarcasm about the inactivity of the German navy. After Jutland the High Seas Fleet never launched any serious threat to British naval supremacy. **Below left:** The Grand Fleet moves into line for the first barrage. **Below:** SMS *Thuringen* engaged a British cruiser during night action.

Above: A zig-zag sailing pattern was adopted to avoid direct submarine attack. **Far left:** Jutland during the height of battle. **Left:** The British cruiser *Queen Mary* is destroyed: 31 May 1916.

Right: The British lost more ships than the Germans at Jutland, but it is a matter of some controversy which side won the battle. **Below:** The German battle cruiser *Derfflinger* was heavily damaged.

maritime rights. However, with her participation, America's attitude changed to one of defending almost any measures deemed necessary.

Under international maritime law it was understood that a belligerent's rights included the capture of enemy merchantmen, the prevention of enemy trade in and out of its home ports by means of blockade, and the confiscation at sea of certain enemy war material. Ancillary rights included those of visit and search to determine a vessel's belligerency or otherwise and to inspect its cargo for contraband. In the latter case, goods might be subject to seizure upon their condemnation by a prize court.

Maritime law had been further codified in the sixty years preceding the war but since then the development of new weapons had drastically altered circumstances. For example, the 1856 Declaration of Paris had held that to be legal, a blockade had to be 'effective'; this was interpreted to mean that enforcement had to be at close range rather than on paper, but the use of undersea weapons and long-range guns made this sort of enforcement impossible, as well as affecting the practice of visit and search.

The British, therefore, decided to initiate their own system of controls; this was easy to do since Britain was in command of the sea and was also in a position geographically to control the entrances and exits to the North Sea and thus to Germany's ports. These controls gradually evolved into a system which was well-defined by the end of 1916.

Before the position was clarified, however, the rivals engaged in a series of moves and counter moves. A British declaration on 3 November 1914 stated that the North Sea was a military area in which ships would be exposed to mines and other hazards, and soon Britain had established contraband control stations in the Orkney Islands and near the Straits of Dover. Germany answered this on 4 February by declaring that the waters surrounding the British Isles formed a war zone in which any ship might be sunk without warning. This phase of unrestricted submarine warfare lasted only a few months, however, before it was shelved because of protests from neutral countries. The British replied in their turn on 11 March 1915 with an Order in Council declaring that goods bound for Germany might be seized even from a vessel sailing to a neutral port.

By late 1916 the Allied blockade was taking effect through the following channels:

1. Inspections in port. These replaced visit and search procedures. Besides the inspection of neutral merchantmen suspected of trade with the enemy, the ports handled a growing number of neutral vessels which called for examination voluntarily in order to keep in favour with the Allies.

2. Rationing. By means of a complex system, neutral nations bordering Germany were allowed imports sufficient only for their own needs. The aim obviously, was to prevent the re-exportation of goods to the Central Powers. In practice this measure had many loopholes and supplies did get through to Germany, but the system was still quite effective and was severely tightened after America joined the war. Although European neutrals resented British interference, more often than not it was in their interest to comply with the regulations lest they incur retaliatory measures such as confiscation of their goods.

3. Navicerts. These were letters of clearance issued for neutral cargoes, certifying their origin, contents, and destination in order to simplify subsequent processing.

4. Blacklists of firms known or suspected to be trading with the enemy. If neutrals continued dealing with them, the Allies retaliated by blacklisting the ships carrying such trade and denying them fuel facilities at sea.

5. Bunker control. Britain's coal exports and command of the major ocean routes and the coaling stations along them allowed her to regulate fuel for neutral vessels in transit.

6. Censorship and interception of neutral mails and cables.

7. Pre-emptive purchasing of neutral food surpluses to deny them to the enemy.

These and other Allied measures led Germany to revive unrestricted submarine warfare in February 1917, and this in turn led to American entry into the war. The blockade tightened still further, and as 1917 wore on very few imports were reaching the Central Powers. Many necessities of life disappeared altogether, civilian morale was undermined, and internal collapse was hastened. Several historians have concluded that without the blockade, the defeat of Germany would have been 'at least doubtful'. What is known is that widespread malnutrition, tuberculosis and other ailments resulted from the deprivations of its final eighteen months. An accurate calculation of resulting deaths is not possible, but estimates run as high as 750,000.

President Woodrow Wilson hoped for peace without victory in 1916.

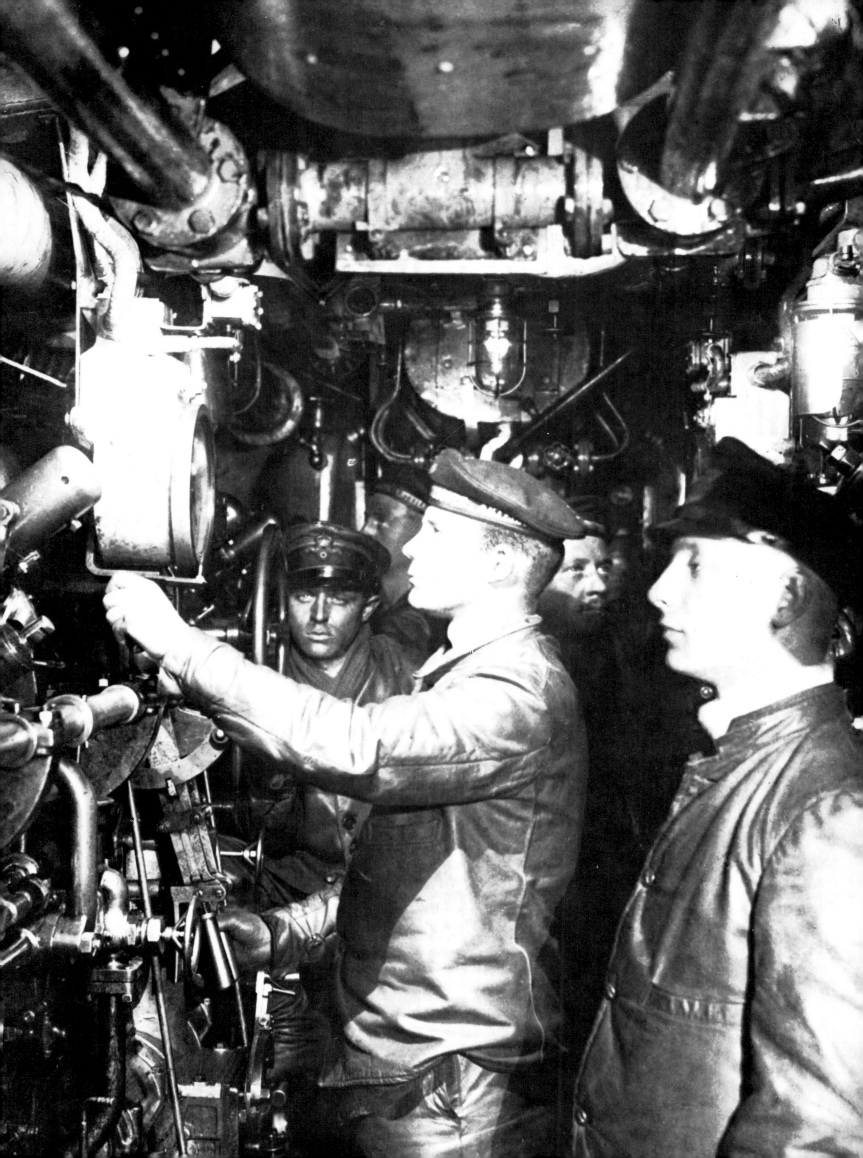

CHAPTER TEN

America Steps In

Germany's campaign of unrestricted submarine warfare was the most important immediate factor in America's decision for war. The additional and underlying causes of American belligerency were complex; but when the United States declared war against the Central Powers, the submarine issue weighed heavily on the scales.

The question of the use of submarines had become an important issue early in the conflict. It was obvious that German U-boats might have a disastrous effect against Great Britain in particular, for eighty per cent of British foodstuffs and most of her raw materials had to be imported by sea. Moreover, the Germans reasoned that unless their submarines did what they could to challenge British naval supremacy, the Grand Fleet would be able to deny the Reich access to American and other neutral resources. Then, in 1916, the Battle of Jutland had shown the great difficulties and high risks involved in challenging the British by conventional means alone. Finally, the Germans realized that their submarines were well fitted for the task of attacking shipping in the crowded sea lanes around the British Isles.

In September 1914 the German U-9 had effortlessly sunk three British cruisers. Despite this example of the submarine's efficiency, however, an all-out undersea campaign was postponed because of the possible political repercus-

sions. Yet by early 1915 it was clear that the war would be a protracted struggle, and in addition to the stalemate on the Western Front, the Allied blockade was already tightening. In these circumstances Germany undertook the initial phase of her intensive use of submarines on 18 February 1915.

The *Lusitania* disaster, described in an earlier chapter, emphasized the risk of adverse public opinion which an undersea campaign would involve. For although the Germans were correct in their assertion that the Allies had already bent the rules of international law to suit themselves, they failed to grasp that while British policy interfered with trade, German actions were leading directly to loss of life at sea among neutrals and belligerents alike.

America's moralistic attitude towards the conflict was given concrete expression in its outraged reaction to the sinking of the *Lusitania*. As we have seen, the Allies were quick to make the most of this tragedy, both in simplistic propaganda about 'the beastly Hun' as well as at a more sophisticated level. Furthermore, more realistic Americans were concerned that if Germany were to continue on the rampage at sea, America's growing and lucrative trade with the Allies in war matériel and other goods would be curtailed. At length, after three American notes on the subject of submarine

Far left: The engine room of a German submarine.
Left: A submarine takes on torpedoes.

Right: By 1916 British seaplanes helped escort convoys through the War Zone. **Opposite top:** Allied convoys were unable to stop the heavy attrition at sea caused by German submarines.

Opposite left and centre: Direct hit! A steamer is torpedoed by a German submarine . . . and sinks. **Opposite right:** The German submarine fleet became increasingly more effective against Allied shipping.

Admiral von Tirpitz, the creator of the German High Seas Fleet, resigned over the submarine issue in March 1916.

President Wilson addresses Congress advising the severance of diplomatic relations with Germany, April 1917.

depredations, the Germans realized that some concessions had to be made to public opinion in the United States lest that nation commit her power against them. After a further altercation over the sinking of the British liner *Arabic* in August 1915, with the loss of three American lives, orders were issued in Berlin severely restricting submarine activities. Yet American and other lives were once more sacrificed or endangered in March 1916, when the cross-Channel steamer *Sussex* was torpedoed. The United States then threatened to break diplomatic relations with Germany unless the latter promised that ships would no longer be sunk without warning and without provision for the safety of those aboard. Although the German government had to yield, stating that it would 'do its utmost to confine the operations of war . . . to the fighting forces of the belligerents . . .', it reminded Washington that Berlin expected action to induce the Allies to curb their violations of maritime law, failing which Germany would 'reserve to itself complete liberty of decision . . .'.

In the interim the entire submarine issue had become the subject of fierce controversy within German ruling circles, with an extremist position being taken by Admiral von Tirpitz until he resigned in disgust in March 1916. By early 1917, with the Allied blockade affecting the very fabric of German domestic life, and victory on land appearing increasingly unattainable, both Hindenburg and Ludendorff threw their weight

behind the faction advocating ruthless use of U-boats. Unrestricted submarine warfare was resumed on 1 February 1917, when Germany declared that the waters around the British Isles, western France, and the Mediterranean were an area of blockade in which Germany would sink at sight any vessel of any nationality. The calculation in Berlin was that as a result, the Allied war effort could be wrecked within six months and before possible American belligerency could materially aid the Entente.

Because of its previous stand and its increasing fury at German actions, the American government broke relations with Berlin on 3 February. In March German submarine attacks involved the sinking of seven American as well as countless other neutral and Allied vessels. Thus, in an atmosphere envenomed by the interception of the Zimmermann Telegram (in which Germany proposed to enter into an alliance with Mexico should the United States enter the war), America did go to war on 6 April.

Meanwhile German submarine attacks brought Britain within sight of defeat. From October to December 1916, U-boats sent to the bottom an average of over 300,000 tons of British shipping a month. The new year brought even more disastrous losses: 250,000 tons in the first ten days of April alone, and 875,000 tons for the whole month. No wonder Admiral Jellicoe admitted that if British tonnage continued to be crippled on such a scale, peace on German terms might be

"Disavowal? Disavowal? There Is No Such Word In the German Tongue!"

necessary by November 1917 or earlier. Yet eventually the point of crisis passed, for the convoy system, antisubmarine measures, provision of more cargo space, increased home production of foodstuffs, and an excess of confidence on the part of Germany all helped to stave off disaster. Thus was possible the transportation of two million fresh and eager American troops to France, an injection of adrenalin into the Allied system which tipped the scales in favour of victory.

On 2 April 1917 President Woodrow Wilson appeared before a special joint session of the Congress of the United States. Wilson had come to ask for a declaration of war against Germany. The House of Representatives, where the president was to speak, was filled to the brim with a tense and expectant audience. Congressmen and senators, members of the Supreme Court, cabinet colleagues, and a host of distinguished visitors were present.

How had events reached this point? How had the United States, the most powerful neutral and a nation by tradition wary of Old World entanglements, taken the decision to enter the stale and blood-soaked conflict which for nearly three years had already raged across Europe and the seas?

In his address President Wilson attempted to give a personal answer. He castigated the German submarine campaign as a wanton rampage against mankind. Armed neutrality, he continued, would not now be sufficient to protect American interests and lives. Thus the United States should 'accept the status of belligerency which has . . . been thrust upon it, by the actions of Imperial Germany and her associates'.

Wilson now believed – and did not hesitate to say so – that the present German government had to be brought to terms because it was the implacable foe of liberty. Thus the president had concluded with the utmost reluctance that in order to make the world 'safe for democracy', America must now play its full part in the conflict. 'The right is more precious than peace', Wilson declared. In sombre tones he continued:

We shall fight . . . for democracy, for the right of those who submit to authority to have a voice in their own governments, for the rights and liberties of small nations, for a universal dominion of right by such a concert of free peoples as shall bring peace and safety to all nations and make the world itself at last free . . . America is privileged to spend her blood and her might for the principles that gave her birth and happiness and the peace which she has treasured . . .

As the President reached the climax of his speech, the audience burst into wild and deafening applause. It seemed that only Wilson himself was solemn. As he later remarked sadly, his speech was 'a message of death for our young men'.

Carried away by their enthusiasm or idealism, both Houses of Congress voted for war by overwhelming majorities. The bulk of opinion throughout the country supported this decision. America had entered the fight.

Woodrow Wilson had greeted the outbreak of war in 1914 with shock and horror. During the July crisis he had been deeply involved in wrangling with the American Congress and distracted with worry over his wife's terminal illness. (Mrs. Wilson died on 6 August.) Then, once war had come, Wilson had to work within the limits set by American public opinion, which, though divided along ethnic and other lines in its preferences for the different belligerents, was basically thankful that the main theatre of war was likely to be far away, in the Old World whose intractable problems Americans had put behind them. The American people were basically agreed that Europe should settle its own squabbles; the United States would stand aloof from the fight. *The New York Times* spoke for many when it described the conflict as 'the least justified of all wars since man emerged from barbarism'.

On the other hand, as Wilson himself was

Above left: American public opinion became aroused against the destruction of neutral shipping by German submarines. **Above:** Wilson campaigned for a second term of office in 1916 under the slogan 'He Kept Us Out of War'.

167

aware, Americans were increasingly conscious of their growing importance on the international stage. Though they were extraordinarily reluctant to assume the status of world power to which destiny beckoned them, much less the consequences of the exercise of that power, the people of the United States would not tolerate repeated and naked violations of their rights. When such violations rose to a crescendo during the German U-boat campaign of early 1917, American opinion came to accept the necessity of military involvement to protect their national idealism.

As soon as the war began, the United States proclaimed its neutrality. Yet what did neutrality mean? Some historians have held that the overriding reason for American involvement on the Allied side was a desire to salvage or protect America's huge commercial interest in the Entente through her sales of munitions, raw materials, foodstuffs and other goods, and through huge loans. Such had been the quantity of this trade in goods and money that the United States had been pulled out of the recession of 1914–15. Yet it has been convincingly argued that the alternative, to have denied or severely restricted Allied access to American markets, would itself have been unneutral. It was not America's fault if the Allied blockade prevented the Germans from similar access. Arthur Link, a leading historian of American involvement in the war, writes that 'Only if Great Britain had been fighting for objectives that imperiled American security would Wilson have been justified in attempting to deny to the British advantages flowing from their control of the seas'. Besides, until the moment of its own belligerency the United States made frequent and to some extent effective protests whenever Britain trod too heavily on neutral rights in the course of administering her blockade of the Central Powers.

Whatever the rights and wrongs of the matter, trade statistics speak for themselves in showing the American economic involvement with the Entente. United States trade with the Central Powers, $169,000,000 in value in 1914, almost disappeared by 1916 to $1,159,000. Yet trade with the Allies, already high in 1914 at $824,000,000, rose by 1916 to $3,214,000,000.

As 1914 closed, Wilson still expected the war to end in an Allied vistory or, at worst, a stalemate. He viewed either prospect equally, though he hoped for a just peace of reconciliation after the conflict. Yet as we have seen, the German U-boat campaign of 1915 and especially the *Lusitania* incident brought German-American relations to a low point. After two earlier protests, Wilson

'A Fast Convoy'. War material and other goods could only be shipped across the Atlantic in convoy when the U-boat campaign was stepped up.

informed Berlin that America would consider further sinkings of ships without warning as 'deliberately unfriendly'. Such language had been too strong for William Jennings Bryan, Wilson's Secretary of State, and Bryan had resigned on 8 June 1915.

Ironically, the German submarine issue forced Wilson to discount the protests of Bryan and others at American lack of neutrality in acquiescing to several Allied measures to strengthen the economic blockade. The Entente argued with much plausibility that they had little alternative. Meanwhile American pressures and the dearth of German submarines caused the U-boat campaign to be modified. German-American relations improved to some extent. Then, in October 1915, Robert Lansing, Bryan's successor, transmitted to London a strongly-worded note which termed the spreading Allied blockade 'ineffective, illegal, and indefensible'. Thus American relations with the two warring sides were fairly if uneasily even-handed as 1916 began.

However, as Wilson knew, beneath the surface all was far from well. Since the Allies had begun to arm even merchant ships, pressures were mounting in Berlin for all-out submarine warfare. As a precaution against the unexpected, in the winter of 1915–16 Wilson himself advocated limited

Left: 'Drive the Ships Out!': German propaganda supporting the attempt to sweep Allied shipping from the seas.

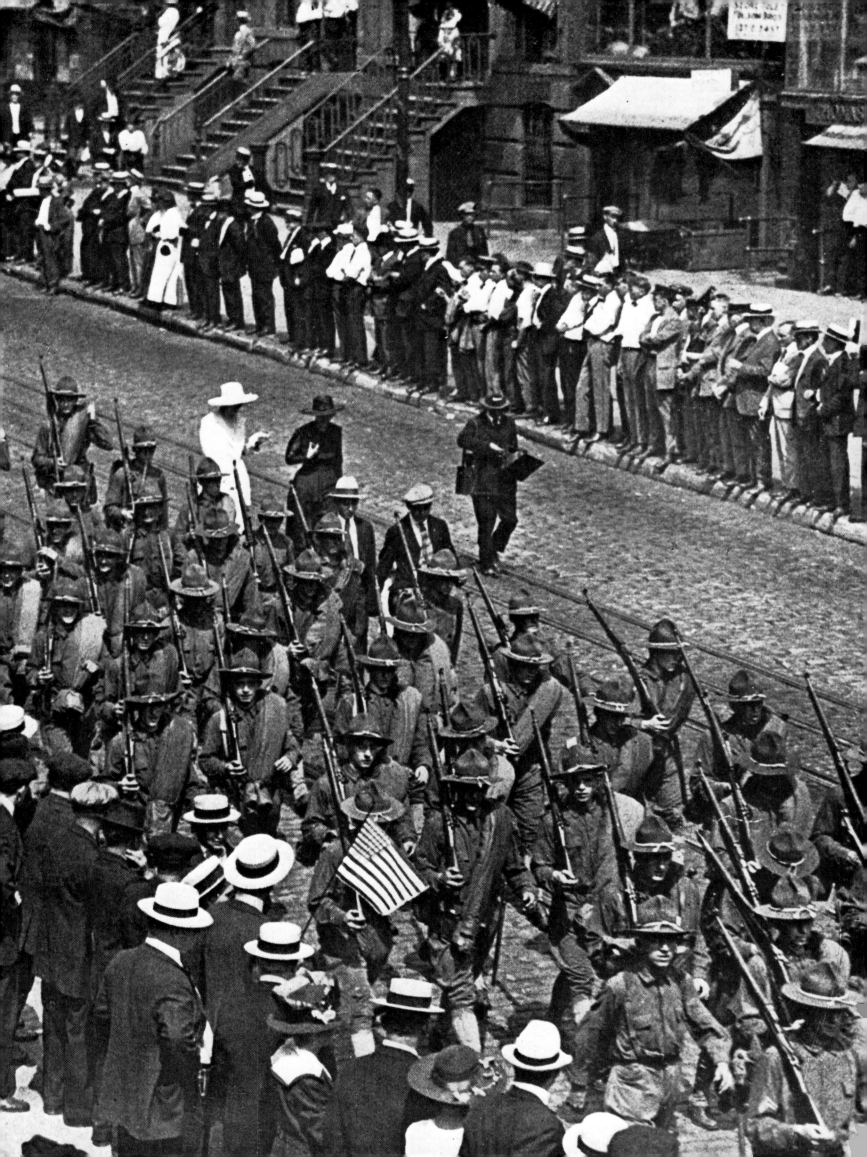

Previous page:
Conscripts and volunteers
answer the call in New
York. **Right:** So did
Tin Pan Alley.

measures to strengthen the American armed
forces. In the meantime, Colonel House was in
Europe on his latest peace mission, and in
February the House-Grey Memorandum was
initialled, only to be shelved. Indeed, the memorandum was partly undermined by British resentment at the American attitude on the question of
armed merchant ships, an issue which also led to
an American domestic crisis.

Originally the Germans had argued that since
the Allies had fitted a number of their merchant
vessels with large guns, which were to be used to
shoot on sight any enemy submarine, the Central
Powers could hardly be expected to adhere to the
traditional rules of visit and search. Seeing the
logic of the German position, in January 1916
Lansing had asked the Allies to consider a
modus vivendi under which the merchantmen would
be disarmed, and in return the Germans would
not sink any ship without first inspecting its cargo
and providing for the safety of those aboard. But

the Allies rejected this idea outright, and Washington fell back on its earlier position that despite
the dangers from Allied armed vessels, the Germans ought to refrain from sinkings without
warning. Berlin, however, thought the contrary
and announced the resumption of sinkings without warning as from the end of February.

Meanwhile the press had come to hear of the
modus vivendi proposals, and a faction in Congress
decided that, now that America's suggestions had
been spurned, she ought to stand aloof from the
defence of neutral rights. Thus the Gore-McLe-
more resolutions asked Congress to forbid American citizens to travel on belligerent ships in order
to minimize American involvement. Playing on
the fact that self-respect would not allow such an
abdication of American rights, Wilson managed to
oppose the resolutions successfully; but the affair
was indicative of the isolationist mood of a considerable section of the populace.

Soon afterwards, the *Sussex* crisis exploded. As
discussed earlier, the Germans yielded with
reservations to Wilson's ultimatum that he would
break relations if Germany did not abandon her
ruthless submarine operations. At the end of
May, Wilson announced that America would
participate in a postwar League of Nations, but
the announcement was tragically premature.

Despite heavy American pressures, neither
Britain nor France would agree to peace talks in
the uncertain state that the war had reached by
mid-1916. Americans viewed this as obstinacy,
and in the context of the post-*Sussex* relief of
tension in relations between Washington and
Berlin, Allied stock plummeted in American
estimation. In addition, America viewed with a
jaundiced eye Britain's fierce suppression of the
Irish Easter Rising and yet further measures in the
economic blockade. Wilson sent the Allies a
series of increasingly reproachful notes on the
latter issue. In September 1916 the President
obtained powers to restrict imports and deny
clearance to Allied ships, and he warned the
Entente that their continued recalcitrance could
force him to put these measures into practice. As
the Allies made no fundamental concessions, the
danger of serious friction with America grew.

Below: Wilson
campaigned for the victory
loans in 1917. **Below
right:** First American
conscripts were chosen in
this way.

Yet America was mainly held back by the increasing mood of extremism which a determination to settle the war in 1917 had bred within the dominant faction in Berlin. Moreover, 1916 was a presidential election year, and until his re-election in November, Wilson required a minimum of controversy while campaigning under the slogan 'He Kept Us Out of War'.

Once safely reconfirmed in the White House, however, Wilson launched his peace initiative of December 1916, attempting to settle the war before America was dragged in. Then February 1917 saw the commencement of an all-out German submarine campaign, despite the earlier *Sussex* pledge. At this time the majority of Americans still clung to the hope of peace, but events rapidly shattered their illusions. In late February, even as he was requesting Congress for defensive armament for American merchantmen and emphasizing that war would come only if Germany wanted it, Wilson learned of the sinking of the British liner *Laconia* with the loss of three American lives. Almost simultaneously, an outraged American public was informed of the existence of a telegram sent on 16 January by the German Foreign Secretary, Alfried Zimmermann, to the German Minister in Mexico City. The British had intercepted and decoded this, the famous Zimmermann Telegram. Zimmermann had proposed a German-Mexican alliance in the event of the now-expected American belligerency. Mexico would attack the United States 'to reconquer the lost territory in New Mexico, Texas and Arizona'. Germany further suggested that Mexico 'should communicate with Japan suggesting adherence to this plan'. Thus a far-reaching anti-American combination was envisaged.

As Arthur Link wrote, for Wilson the Zimmermann Telegram was the last straw which 'caused him to lose all faith in the German government and to believe that the unscrupulous military masters of the *Reich* would stop at nothing in their mad ambitions'. Now a significant part of the thunder-struck American populace supported any measures, including war, which the government might find necessary. Moreover, the Russian 'February' Revolution did a great deal to influence pro-Allied sentiment in the United States. A corrupt, victorious, and parasitical autocracy had been overthrown, and the new government appeared to harbour democratic aims. As the *Nation* commented, 'A German victory now would mean the collapse of free Russia'. By the end of March, demand for war was widespread across America, given impetus by the sinking of three American ships between 16 and 18 March, the last of them, the *Vigilancia*, with considerable loss of life.

Wilson still wanted to avoid war. He saw the danger that an injection of American strength might lead to an Allied victory sufficiently overwhelming to make for a contentious peace. He feared that Americans would be brutalized by their war experiences. But on 20 March the cabinet unanimously advised him to ask Congress for a declaration of war. Wilson took their advice in the belief that at least American entry would end a war already in its final agony, and reasoning (in partial contradiction to some of his other

BRINGING IT HOME.

PRESIDENT WILSON. "WHAT'S THAT? U-BOAT BLOCKADING NEW YORK? TUT! TUT! VERY INOPPORTUNE!"

Punch took a jaundiced view of American neutrality in 1916.

thoughts) that only as a belligerent could America strongly influence the subsequent peace settlement in the direction of Wilson's own high ideals. By now he was fairly realistic concerning the extent of Allied objectives. If left to their own devices, he concluded, the Europeans would never see justice done. America must step in to redress the moral balance. So, in fact, German actions triggered off a decision for war in which the motives far transcended the scope of the original provocations.

Was the entry of the United States into the First World War inevitable from the beginning? Almost certainly not. Despite the ties of blood, culture, and ideals which bound America, and especially its Establishment, to Britain, the Central Powers might have avoided American participation if they had played their hand with greater finesse. Stupid blunders like the *Lusitania* affair and the unrestricted submarine campaign slowly convinced leading American circles that the kind of world in which American democracy could thrive was incompatible with a German victory. Until 1917 at least, this sentiment was uncertain and reversible, and it is likely that an astute German statesman could have avoided the fatal parting of the ways. Indeed, there was every chance that America might at some stage have obtained a compromise peace not unfavourable to Germany itself. Yet Germany lacked a leader of Bismarckian stature, and German politicians (wrongly, as we now see) had little or no faith in Wilson's impartiality. Events outran the power of men to deal with them, and took on a momentum of their own. In a sense, even the United States slipped into war half-unknowingly, for if the American people had thought that the step they were taking would ultimately lead to a long-term involvement in world affairs, they would have drawn back in consternation. Rather, as a whole they believed with touching naïveté that the world could be put right by victory and justice, and then America could return to her own affairs. After all, this was a war to end wars.

CHAPTER ELEVEN
Upheaval and Chaos in Russia

Many would argue that the Russian Revolution was the greatest event since the fall of the Bastille. The importance of its impact on the structure of the international community, the distribution of power in the world, and the ideas by which men live, or profess to live, can hardly be over-estimated. Nineteen seventeen saw a fundamental upheaval in the world's largest state, a country which for all its backwardness and inefficiency corruption and sloth was potentially a giant among nations. The revolution also saw the rise to power of undoubtedly one of the most brilliant and formidable leaders in history: Vladimir Ulyanov, known to the world as Lenin.

The events of 1917 had roots which reached far back into the history of Russia itself. The intrigues at court and the military setbacks and hardships that accompanied the war have been frequently referred to in this narrative. No doubt this aspect of the fighting accelerated the process of internal disruption and disillusionment that led to revolution. For at least half a century, military reverses had intensified the undermining of the old order: the Crimean defeat led to the emancipation of the serfs in 1861; the Japanese victory of 1904–05 led to the 1905 revolution; and the disappointments and miseries of the Great War brought on the explosion of 1917. Yet other underlying and continuing factors had slowly but relentlessly done their work in tipping the balance against the status quo. Bad government existed independently of periodic fighting, as did agricultural penury, with millions of landless peasants, usurious landlords and profiteers, and gentry callously indifferent to the most elementary needs of those whom the system had placed at their mercy.

After the 1905 upheaval had subsided, the evils of the Tsarist regime actually increased. The decadence and obstinacy of the court completely separated it from the lives and interests of ordinary folk. In the succeeding decade, major and petty abuses of myriad varieties spread to such an extent that any incident could have sparked off an explosion whose final repercussions could not be perceived. The Duma (Parliament) was a mere travesty, its consultative powers flouted at will by the Tsar. At the end of 1916, there was still no end to the war in sight. A smouldering resentment spread inexorably throughout the land, a massive and largely inarticulate feeling which, searching in vain for an outlet, built up an inner tension comparable to the stresses beneath a geological fault which lead to an earthquake. Only a revolution from above could have staved off the revolu-

tion from below. None was forthcoming. Thus when the dam burst, the good in the system, what little there was, was swept away with the bad.

(Before discussing the revolution further, a note on dates should be added. Until the Bolshevik Revolution, the Russian calendar operated thirteen days behind that in use in the West; thus dates in the following chronicle of events will be given in both calendars.)

On the night of 17/30 to 18/31 December 1916, an extraordinary ritual was enacted. Some have called it the first concrete blow in the 1917 revolution; others have, perhaps more correctly, written that the happening only underlined for the last time the utter futility of trying to influence Tsar Nicholas in the direction of change. That evening, Prince Yussupov murdered the evil genius of the Tsarist regime, the lecherous 'monk' Grigory Rasputin, in a final effort to rid the court of the depravity and Germanophile influences which were alienating the population. Rasputin, a foul and semiliterate wolf in sheep's clothing, had become the power behind the throne through his autosuggestive treatment of the hereditary hemophilia which afflicted the young heir to the dynasty, the Tsarevich Alexei. In addition, Rasputin had spread his influence throughout the court by his assiduous cultivation of peasant manners and his equally shrewd seduction of the titled ladies of Petrograd. That day, as evening approached, Rasputin was tricked into accepting what he thought to be another assignation. Instead the witchdoctor was set upon, poisoned with cyanide, shot for good measure, and hurled

Opposite: Rasputin, the 'Mad Monk', surrounded by his admirers. It took cyanide, bullets, a knife and the icy waters of the river Neva to kill him.

Hunger was widespread before the revolution. It increased once the revolution began.

Front lines 1 July

Russian Advance by 16 July 1917

Counter-attack 19 July. Lost ground regained & further advance forced 3 August

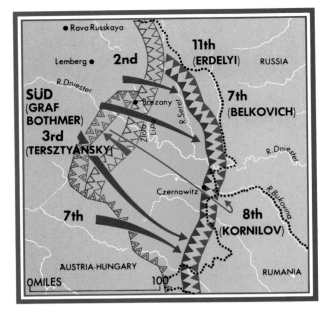

attempts at communicating with their recently departed 'holy friend' through seances.

In January, as conditions in Russia worsened and tension rose to still greater heights, a delegation from the Western Allies arrived to lay plans for a final and victorious military onslaught. During their discussions with the Russians, the French conspired to aim for the restoration of their 1814 frontiers, a measure which the British repudiated later when they learned what had happened. In any case, the whole discussion was academic. The old order was on its last legs.

People in the capital were still going about their business in an atmosphere of uneasy peace. Few indeed recognized that an irreversible change was imminent. Later, when the revolution had begun, only a small number understood its scope or significance. Proposals to shore up the monarchy were made even after the people had rejected the Romanovs and anyone to do with them.

As February wore on, food in the capital became increasingly scarce. The heavy snows of winter had damaged many transport vehicles and had led to a shortage of the fuel that was needed to bring in supplies from the countryside. Distribution of food was inefficient; profiteering was more shameless than ever. On 23 February/8 March there were widespread strikes and food riots, and far from dying down, the strikes continued next day. The popular outburst apparently had no preconceived, detailed aims or central coordination; yet before police dispersed the demonstrators, the cry, 'Down with autocracy'! was heard. The 'February' Revolution had begun.

By 25 February/10 March the strikes had spread to include a quarter of a million workers. Factories and industries ground to a halt. Although troops and police were sent to break up demonstrations, and certain police opened fire indiscriminately on defenceless crowds, many army units refused to take part in the slaughter. Instead their members defected to the populace in their tens of thousands, many regiments butchering those officers who stood behind the old regime. Unseeing to the end, on 26 February/11 March the Tsar answered urgent appeals for reform from Rodzianko, President of the Duma, by ordering that body to disband. Yet the Duma remained assembled unofficially in Petrograd.

On 27 February/12 March, events moved to a climax. More and more soldiers joined the tide of revolt. The Tsar had ordered up troops from the front to crush the workers, but these soldiers too were either prevented from reaching the capital or were persuaded to throw in their lot with the revolution. In the afternoon, factory delegates, socialists of varying shades, and strike committee leaders formed the Petrograd Soviet (Council of Workers' Deputies). Subsequently the name was embellished to Council of Workers' and Soldiers' Deputies. On 1/14 March the Duma elected its own Provisional Committee, and a Provisional Government was nominated under Prince Lvov. Thereafter authority was divided between the Soviet and the Provisional Government; and this division of power proved to be one of the weaknesses of the first revolution.

Swiftly the rest of the country followed the lead of Petrograd. Although the overthrow of the

Lenin exhorts the colonial people of the world to follow the Soviet path to freedom from the imperialists.

beneath the ice of the river Neva. Yussupov and his fellow conspirators had hoped that the Tsar would be frightened into moderate reforms, which would permit the essential structure of autocracy to be maintained. Instead, however, the Tsar and Tsarina retreated behind a veil of resentful obduracy and devoted themselves to

Romanovs was an accomplished fact, attempts were at first made to persuade Tsar Nicholas to abdicate in favour of his son Alexei, while the Tsar himself favored his brother, the Grand Duke Mikhail, as successor. With the situation still unresolved, on 2/15 March, Nicholas abdicated. Afterwards he and the other members of the royal family were arrested and, according to the accepted version, were eliminated in the Ural town of Ekaterinburg. However, certain doubts remain concerning the authenticity of this story.

The Provisional Government still made no decision either for or against the monarchy. It did not matter. The Duma whence it came was itself unrepresentative of popular forces, and instead served the interests of upper- and middle-class elements who were no match for the militantly organized workers and soldiers. Thus, because their own social and political ideas differed from those of the proletariat, the Duma and the Provisional Government were only partially effective.

At this point the German government hesitated – and lost. In the heady aftermath of liberation, confusion reigned over widespread areas of Russia. Much of the armed forces, not including those who had already left the front to work for the revolution, were demoralized by the sufferings of the war and influenced by the propaganda of the Petrograd Soviet. Under the circumstances, a German move against Russia would have had a high probability of success. Then Germany would have been free to move all her forces westwards, and might well have knocked the Entente out of the war before American help arrived. On the other hand, Berlin was anxious over events on the Western Front, and moreover thought that a hard bargain might be struck with the new Russian regime if internal chaos were allowed to progress undisturbed. Some thought that, alternatively, the warring forces might be immediately united in the face of an external threat from Germany. In any case, the Reich attempted further disruption by facilitating the entry of potential troublemakers into Russia – most significantly Lenin. The Germans allowed Lenin to pass through Germany from exile in Switzerland in a sealed train. Had those Germans who let Lenin through have imagined the successes which he would achieve in Russia and

almost in Germany itself, they might have had second thoughts.

Meanwhile the Provisional Government, egged on by Allied pressure, determined on a renewed military offensive. Dreams of the Balkans and Constantinople (Tsargrad, as Russians had once thought of it) also lured them on. Yet Lenin, leading the Bolshevik extreme left-wing revolutionaries, opposed continuance of the war; and many voices on all sides supported him. But by now, the Petrograd Soviet was being swept away by the power of the revolution. Throughout the period leading to the 'October' Revolution, the Petrograd Soviet and the Provisional Government, though they grappled for the reins of power, made repeated attempts to resolve their differences. Indeed, until May the Petrograd Soviet more or less accepted the authority of the Provisional Government; and in the matter of resuming the war, the radicals lost. Earlier the Petrograd Soviet had appealed to the belligerents for peace and the renunciation of chauvinistic war aims. Similarly, the Provisional Government had proclaimed that it desired 'not the forcible seizure of foreign territories, but the establishment of a stable peace on the basis of the self-determination of peoples'. Nevertheless the Provisional Government promised to continue the fight and respect existing Russian obligations.

On 18 June/1 July a strong Russian offensive was launched in two places, using many Siberian troops thought to have been protected by distance from revolutionary doctrines. In fact, Bolshevik propaganda and German fraternization had already effectively undermined military morale, and when the Russians attacked, their paucity of reserves quickly became evident. Meanwhile the Germans had brought in four divisions from the west in readiness for a counteroffensive. First, however, the Russian offensive of 22 June/5 July under Kornilov succeeded in pulverizing the defences of Tersztyansky's Austrian Third Army and made a considerable advance before suddenly faltering and then being stopped short by the German reserves.

After some delays and prevarications, the German counter-assault began on 6/19 July. One of its outstanding features was the brilliant use of artillery bombardment by Colonel Bruchmüller,

Above left: All the people had to do was kick in the door, and the whole House of Romanov came crashing down. **Above:** The Duma controlled events now. News sheets distributed by the Duma were issued on a regular basis to the people of Petrograd.

Grand Duke Nicholas briefly controlled the Provisional Government.

Above and right: General Kornilov, whose rivalry with Kerensky assumed the dimensions of a revolt

Below: The leadership of Kerensky (left) was ineffectual.

РАЙОННЫМЪ
Совѣтамъ Рабочихъ Депутатовъ Фабрично-Заводскимъ Комитетамъ

ПРИКАЗЪ.

Корниловскія банды Керенскаго угрожаютъ подступамъ къ столицѣ. Отданы всѣ необходимыя распоряженія для того, чтобы безпощадно раздавить контръ-революціонное покушеніе противъ народа и его завоеваній.

Армія и Красная Гвардія революціи нуждаются въ немедленной поддержкѣ рабочихъ.

Приказываемъ районнымъ Совѣтамъ и фабр.-зав. комитетамъ:

1) выдвинуть наибольшее количество рабочихъ для рытья окоповъ, воздвиганія баррикадъ и укрѣпленія проволочныхъ загражденій;

2) гдѣ для этого потребуется прекращеніе работъ на фабрикахъ и заводахъ, немедленно исполнить;

3) собрать всю имѣющуюся въ запасѣ колючую и простую проволоку, а равно всѣ орудія, необходимыя для рытья окоповъ и возведенія баррикадъ;

4) все имѣющееся оружіе имѣть при себѣ;

5) соблюдать строжайшую дисциплину и быть готовыми поддержать армію революціи всѣми средствами.

Предсѣдатель Петроградскаго Совѣта Раб. и Солд. Депутатовъ
Народный Комиссаръ ЛЕВЪ ТРОЦКІЙ.

Предсѣдатель Военно-Революціоннаго Комитета
Главнокомандующій ПОДВОЙСКІЙ.

120

TO THE DISTRICT
SOVIETS OF WORKER'S DEPUTIES AND SHOP-FACTORY COMMITTEES

ORDER

THE KORNILOV BANDS OF KERENSKY ARE THREATENING THE OUTSKIRTS OF OUR CAPITAL. ALL NECESSARY ORDERS HAVE BEEN GIVEN TO CRUSH MERCILESSLY EVERY COUNTER-REVOLUTIONARY ATTEMPT AGAINST THE PEOPLE AND ITS CONQUESTS.

THE ARMY AND THE RED GUARD OF THE REVOLUTION ARE IN NEED OF IMMEDIATE SUPPORT OF THE WORKERS.

THE DISTRICT SOVIETS AND SHOP-FACTORY COMMITTEES ARE ORDERED:

1) To bring forward the largest possible number of workers to dig trenches, erect barricades and set up wire defenses;

2) Wherever necessary for this purpose to SUSPEND WORK in shops and factories, it must be done IMMEDIATELY.

3) To collect all available plain and barbed wire, as well as all tools FOR DIGGING TRENCHES AND ERECTING BARRICADES;

4) ALL AVAILABLE ARMS TO BE CARRIED ON PERSONS;

5) Strictest discipline must be preserved and all must be ready to support the Army of the Revolution to the utmost.

President of the Petrograd Soviet of Workers & Soldiers Deputies
People's Commissar LEV TROTSKY.

President of the Military-Revolutionary Committee
Chief Commander PODVOISKY.

[*Reproduction in English of the Russian text on opposite page.*]

121

later nicknamed 'Breakthrough' (*Durchbruch*) Müller because of the devastating effect of his weaponry on the Russian morale. As the Germans poured along the front, the Russian troops retreated in droves. Discipline and command-structure were wrecked, and the Russians' pell-mell flight through Galicia was marked by hideous assaults on the local populace. Soon all the gains of the so-called Kerensky offensive had been eliminated.

Further south, on 9/22 July, the Rumanians, their army now reorganized by the French, had launched an attack in the Carpathians, aided by the Russian Fourth Army. Though the Rumanian offensive won success at first, it was pushed back by Mackensen on 23 July/6 August and after, in a series of fights known as the Battle of Maraseti. Then this front again fell silent.

Soon after the renewed fighting on the Eastern Front, the events known as the 'July Days' took place. By this time the Bolsheviks already had strong support in Petrograd, but in the provinces the moderate socialists still prevailed. While this situation lasted, Lenin was eager to avoid a trial of strength; but the workers in Petrograd got out of hand and unsuccessfully attempted a *coup d'état*.

On 3/16 July soldiers and workers demanded that the reins of power be yielded to the Petrograd Soviet, but the Provisional Government brought in troops and put down the revolt. Now the Provisional Government turned on the Bolsheviks, accusing them of undermining tactics which were leading to the defeat of the Russian armies in the field. It denounced the Bolsheviks as traitors and Lenin in particular as a German agent. On 6/19 July Lenin fled into hiding as a warrant for his arrest was issued.

The Provisional Government never recovered

from the blows to its prestige caused by the 'July Days'. The forces represented by the Petrograd and other soviets began to assert their strength. On 24 July/6 August they demanded constitutional and land reforms, and when the government of Prince Lvov refused, it was swept away. Kerensky formed a moderate but hopelessly indecisive coalition. Soon rivalry surfaced between Kerensky and Kornilov, the new Russian commander-in-chief. First, however, the fall of Riga intervened.

Ludendorff had decided that if the Russians could be driven out of their Baltic bridgehead at Riga, the Latvian capital, Petrograd would be unnerved. Bruchmüller and his men once more put their artillery to good use, but the retreating Russian Twelfth Army managed to get away with all but nine thousand of its men. Yet on 21 August/3 September, Riga fell without noticeable effort, and afterwards the Germans occupied several islands at the mouth of the Gulf of Riga, from where, if necessary, it would be relatively easy to strike at the Russian naval base of Kronstadt and also at Helsinki (Helsingfors).

By this time the Western Allies had reluctantly concluded that Russia, awash in its own troubles, would either leave the war or cease to play any important role in its conduct. Lloyd George commented that he had, 'lost all interest in Russia as a working factor in the success of the Allies'.

In the interim, Kornilov seized on the fall of Riga to withdraw his support from the government. The details behind this incident are still far from clear, but the rivalry between Kerensky and Kornilov now assumed the dimensions of a revolt. On 25 August/7 September Kornilov ordered a march on Petrograd, but this was nullified with Bolshevik help.

The position of the moderate socialists weak-

ened yet further, as it became increasingly obvious that the Provisional Government was proving itself incompetent. The coalition government collapsed, and on 1/14 September Kerensky formed a Directory marked, as Deutscher tartly remarks, by his 'personal incapacity to rule'. Soon the Bolsheviks had obtained majorities on the soviets of both Petrograd and Moscow, as well as in most of the provinces. Thence their influence in the country as a whole mounted rapidly.

In this situation, Lenin decided that the time for the major Bolshevik Revolution was ripe. The 'bourgeois-democratic' phase of the political transformation of the country had proceeded and had served its purpose, and it was time to move on. On 10/23 October the Bolshevik Central Committee took a definite decision to prepare for revolution, despite the opposition of Zinoviev and Kamenev, two of its members.

How had conditions riped for the final cataclysm? The Provisional Government, for all its liberal measures in certain spheres, hung back in the face of the many and difficult social problems of the country. Its determination to continue the war had meant that there was less time, energy, and funds to instigate quickly a broad measure of needed reforms. The Bolsheviks were perfectly suited to exploit the situation, for they were ruthless and dynamic, with a gift for appealing to the unsatisfied hopes and needs of the general population. Above all, their guiding light, Lenin, and their organizational genius, Trotsky, towered like giants over mediocrities like Kerensky.

With supreme irony, Kerensky's final miscalculation was that he vastly underestimated the Bolsheviks' strength and looked forward to an insurrection as a chance to repress them. He had not long to wait – but his plans went awry.

Late in October (or early in November, accord-

Mutiny within the army was rife. Attempts to prevent soldiers from going home, as in this case, were futile.

Lenin seized control of the state after the Bolsheviks achieved their easy coup.

Leon Trotsky organized the Red Army and became the People's Commissar for Foreign Affairs.

ing to the Julian calendar) Kerensky decided to secure his position by sending the more revolutionary armed contingents to the front, and thus away from the capital, where they might cause trouble. The Revolutionary Military Committee of the Petrograd Soviet vehemently objected. Stung into action, on 23 October/5 November Kerensky ordered the arrest of several Bolshevik leaders. It was too late. His actions had given the revolutionaries the pretext they needed. Castigating 'counterrevolutionary conspirators' who were plotting against it, the Revolutionary Military Committee moved swiftly. On the night of 24–25 October/6–7 November the Bolsheviks took over key points throughout the capital. By morning Kerensky had fled to the front in a vain endeavour to round up support. Almost effortlessly and with little bloodshed, the initial aims of the revolution had been achieved; and though three years of bloody civil war were needed to consolidate their control, the Bolsheviks could rejoice that the world's first Marxist state had come into existence.

On the evening of 25 October/7 November, Lenin called for 'a just, democratic peace . . . without annexations . . . and . . . indemnities'. In another momentous decree, he declared that 'landlord property is abolished forthwith without compensation'. Next day a Council of People's Commissars was formed with Lenin as chairman. The establishment of the dictatorship of the proletariat, to be followed by peace, was proclaimed. Indeed, not only in the first heady moments of their success, but for long afterwards, the Bolsheviks hoped that the world revolution was at hand, and that afterwards peace would spontaneously occur as proletarian governments took power in every country.

The story of the many internal developments which took place as a result of the 'October' Revolution lies beyond the scope of this narrative. It is sufficient to say that the two major problems of the new regime were the consolidation of its power throughout the vast Russian territories and the establishment of some kind of relationship between Soviet Russia and the non-revolutionary world outside. In this sphere the first priority was some arrangement by which Russia might leave the war. To the general embarrassment of the Bolsheviks, the hoped-for immediate world revolution had not yet occurred, and Britain and France had made no response to the Soviet call for a general peace. It seemed that there was no alternative but to ask the Central Powers for a separate peace, despite the violent ideological objections of many Bolsheviks to this measure. It did not matter that under the 1914 Pact of London, the Tsarist regime had promised Britain and France not to make a separate peace; The Bolsheviks repudiated past obligations en masse, and as if to rub this in they published the texts of the Allied secret treaties, which had been concluded earlier in the war. This underlined the Marxist feeling that the war was a struggle between rival and equally loathsome imperialisms in which the working people in every country had no interest and, indeed, no place.

Eventually the Allies made known their own position. Having agreed that Russia was still bound by the Treaty of London, Britain and France declared that although there would be no separate peace, they 'would proceed to a revision of war aims together with Russia' as soon as that country was ruled by 'a government aware of its duties to the country and defending the interests of the country and not of the enemy'. The Bolshevik mood was hardly improved by this slap in the face, and arrangements to negotiate with the Central Powers proceeded.

Sir John Wheeler-Bennett, the historian of the Treaty of Brest-Litovsk (as the separate peace was called) has declared that for Russia, the capitulation was 'the greatest humiliation in her diplomatic and military history' because of the Draconian terms of the settlement.

Brest-Litovsk: A Separate Peace

Preliminary conversations between the Bolsheviks and the Central Powers had begun on 3 December at the Polish town of Brest-Litovsk, German headquarters for the Eastern Front. On 15 December agreement was reached for a twenty-eight-day truce from 17 December, during which negotiations for a settlement would be concluded. The Germans' wish for a quiet Eastern Front in order to turn westwards had overcome their distaste for negotiating with men whom they considered to be guttersnipes. However, the severity of the terms which the Central Powers demanded was partly conditioned by their realization that the Bolsheviks as yet had no indisputable claim to the right to speak for Russians as a whole, let alone the non-Russian nationalities of the former empire. In addition, there were difficulties peculiar to negotiations with the new Russian regime. Unlike governments bound by bourgeois conventions, the Communists were willing to use a remarkable array of tactical weaponry in the furtherance of their aims. For example, they would temporarily yield whole provinces at a time if by so doing they thought they could arouse the class solidarity of the working masses of the Central Powers.

Left: The revolt of the Bolsheviks was well-organized and effective.
Below: Strong points were taken throughout the capital.

Above: German cavalry march in triumph through a Ukrainian town. Helpless against the German invader, the Soviet government decided to make a separate peace.
Opposite: Joffe, Karakhan and Trotsky formed the Russian delegation which is greeted by the Germans in Brest-Litovsk.

German troops pursued bands of Bolsheviks in the Ukraine when Russian lines cracked.

On the German side, Hindenburg and Ludendorff were anxious to exploit the opportunity of confrontation with an enemy at bay by annexing the Russian Baltic regions of Estonia, Livonia, Courland (Kurland) and Lithuania. Centuries ago these areas had been penetrated by the Teutonic Knights, and much of their aristocracy and bourgeoisie was of German origin. In addition, Germany needed the 'breadbasket' of the Ukraine to feed its people, by now in great distress because of the Allied blockade. Moreover, the more amputations of provinces from the sick and wounded body of Russia proper, the weaker Germany's opponent would be left, reasoned many of the German general staff. The Germans clearly held the upper hand; and if the Bolsheviks

proved recalcitrant at Brest-Litovsk, the German armies would drive forward to Petrograd itself to dictate terms.

The German foreign secretary, Baron Richard von Kühlmann, disagreed with the 'politics of illusion' of the German general staff. Kühlmann was less confident of Germany's ability to force a military victory; a shrewd negotiated peace with the Entente was, he felt, a better bet. Moreover, whereas Ludendorff wanted territorial and strategic gains in the east in order, as he bluntly put it, to help 'the manoeuvring of my left wing in the next war', Kühlmann wanted to obtain large territories in the east in order to use them as bargaining counters at the peace table vis-à-vis the lands which Germany had conquered in the west. Eventually, however, when it became clear that the British and French had no intention of coming to Brest-Litovsk for a general settlement, in Berlin imperialist designs carried the day.

For their part, the Bolsheviks had to weigh their desire for immediate peace against their wish to use the peace conference as a showcase for propaganda designed to undermine the will to war of the ordinary people among the other belligerents. A headlong clash of wills took place between Kühlmann and Trotsky, now People's Commissar for Foreign Affairs. Meanwhile the Austrian foreign minister, Count Ottokar von Czernin, stood by helplessly in the knowledge that the Emperor had told him that in no cir-

cumstances must he return home without that peace which, it was thought, alone could save the dying Habsburg Empire.

After weeks of negotiations, prevarications, and interminable delays, on 9 February 1918 the Central Powers reached a separate agreement with the Ukraine, which had previously broken away from Russia itself. The Ukraine became a *de facto* protectorate of Germany, while an agreement was reached for the export of a million tons of foodstuffs to the Central Powers.

Now the Bolsheviks realized that they needed peace even more than they needed propagandistic ferment. Counter-revolutionary forces were rapidly organizing on all sides. Swiftly abandoning his policy of delay, on 10 February Trotsky declared a state of 'no war, no peace' and returned to Petrograd in the belief that the opposing side would accept the situation. But instead the Germans resumed the offensive and struck within eighty miles of Petrograd, meeting hardly any resistance from the bewildered and demoralized populace or the remnants of the military. The Bolsheviks had no option but to cave in.

On 3 March the Treaty of Brest-Litovsk was signed. In tandem with later agreements, the Russians were forced to yield Russian Poland, Estonia, Litvonia, Courland, Lithuania, and certain small islands to Germany and Austria-Hungary, and to surrender Kars, Ardahan, and Batum to Turkey. Finnish independence was to be recog-

nized, in addition to that of the Ukraine and Georgia. Massive reparations payments in money and goods were to be undertaken. This amounted to a Carthaginian peace, since under its terms Russia was almost cut off from the Baltic, was entirely landlocked to the south, and lost 34 percent of her population, 32 percent of her agricultural land and 89 percent of her coal resources. Despite the harshness of these terms, Russia had no option but to ratify the treaty on 29 March.

Meanwhile, after concluding an armistice on 9 December, the Rumanians encountered the full wrath of the Central Powers. Bucharest now paid dearly for her abandonment of that grouping in favour of the Entente. In March she was forced to yield the entire Dobrudja for future partitioning among Germany, Austria-Hungary, Bulgaria, and Turkey. Austria-Hungary was to receive substantial territory on the Rumanian side of the Carpathians. The Rumanian Army was to be reduced almost to nothing, and odious economic measures against Rumania were discussed. Even worse was to follow, for in the final settlement, signed 7 May, Rumania was cut off from the sea entirely, with the use of Constanza as a free port. Her vast oil resources fell prey to Germany, and several other onerous conditions were to be enforced by an army of occupation which would leave only at a time 'to be agreed upon'. Through Rumania was to be encouraged to gain Bessarabia from Russia, this measure was evidently a further move to weaken Russia rather than one motivated by any regard for Russia's smaller neighbour. Rumania was saved only by an Allied vistory in which she theoretically participated by resuming war against the Central Powers just before the armistice of November 1918.

The Bolsheviks had signed at Brest-Litovsk with gritted teeth. Yet had they not capitulated and gained time to organize the Red Army and reinforce their power base, they might well have been destroyed by Germans or dissident internal forces separately or in collusion. Moreover, the irony of Brest-Litovsk was that far from liberating German forces for use in the west, the extent of the Central Powers' gains caused a million men to remain committed in the east in a holding-down operation. Who knows what might have been achieved in the spring of 1918 if these forces had streamed westwards?

The Allies learned one major lesson from Brest-Litovsk. Here they saw the full extent of German territorial ambition, and the experience was salutary in silencing those who still pressed for a compromise peace in the west. The effect on the United States was even greater. In April 1918 President Wilson declared that the German eastern treaties had shown that Germany demanded as arbiter 'force, and force alone'; America would reply with '. . . but one response . . .: Force, Force to the utmost . . .'. The Allied and Associated Powers closed ranks as never before. Furthermore, in 1919 the German socialists were persuaded to accept the Versailles *diktat* partly in the belief that its injustices would be fought against by a world public opinion as outraged as it was by the Peace of Brest-Litovsk. Truly the repercussions of the peace negotiations of the winter and spring of 1918 were endless.

Opposite top: General von Hoffmann (with cane) helped form part of the German delegation which won so many concessions from the Bolsheviks at Brest-Litovsk. **Far left:** Stormtroops advance after a smoke bomb attack on the Rumanian Front. **Left:** Rumania was bombarded into submission by the Central Powers.

CHAPTER TWELVE
Ideals–and Continued War

In 1917, even as momentous events were taking place in the East, the Western Front was also very active.

The Allies met at Chantilly in November 1916 to plan their strategy for the year ahead. Joffre and Haig, the French and British supremos, both realized that Verdun and the Somme had worn the German armies to a thread. On the other hand, the French in particular were reaching the end of their own tether, especially psychologically. Now Joffre believed that his men had the stamina and *élan* for one more great battle. This must be decisive. Joffre looked forward to spring as the occasion for this offensive, but in the interim he was replaced by the young General Robert Nivelle. In the meantime, bad weather prevented any large-scale concerted action during the winter, though in February a somewhat larger campaign took place on the Ancre.

Nivelle was bursting with confidence. His optimism proved both infectious and misplaced. Somehow he convinced both the French and British Prime Ministers – Briand and Lloyd George – that he could break through in the west in a mere two days – although this was the key to victory sought in vain for two and a half years!

Nonetheless, Nivelle's boldness was undiminished. Relying on the twin tactics of speed and surprise, the French would mount a large-scale offensive on the Aisne, while the British would make their major diversionary attack near Arras. Before this could happen, however, several things went wrong. The Germans pulled back to strong defensive positions (the Hindenburg Line), yet Nivelle continued with his plans much as if nothing untoward had occurred. Then his security proved unreliable, and exact information as to Allied movements reached the Germans. Nonetheless the Second Battle of the Aisne, otherwise called the Nivelle Offensive, began on 16 April.

Above: General Nivelle aged twenty years in the five months he commanded French troops on the Western Front. **Opposite:** View of Oosttaverne Wood, showing trenches taken by the British in the Battle of Messines.

Below left: Dozens of French tanks were destroyed on the first day of the Second Battle of the Aisne. **Below:** The French advance under fire. **Below right:** German machine guns help to stop the French advance.

Nivelle exhorted his troops with typical verve: *L'heure est venue!* (The hour has come!) *Confiance! Courage! Vive la France!*

The attack on the Aisne was certainly not without its successes, except that, measured against the overweening confidence of its commander it was judged a failure. As had happened before, German machine guns wreaked havoc among the advancing French, and a large number of the French tank force of two hundred was destroyed on the first day. Yet on 17 April Mangin's French Sixth Army advanced two and a half miles and captured a large quantity of German artillery. As later gains became increasingly unimpressive, further efforts at progress were postponed until May, when they were unsuccessful.

On 15 May Pétain in turn had replaced Nivelle. As at Verdun, his influence quickly had a calming effect. Calm could not have been more desperately needed, for their exhaustion and frustration had resulted in widespread mutinies among the French armies. As the ill-starred Nivelle Offensive had cost the French an additional hundred thousand or more casualties, it became increasingly obvious that the tattered Gallic armies would have to stand on the defensive until American forces at last arrived on the Continent. Meanwhile the Germans had hardly escaped unscathed: their toll of dead and wounded was one hundred and sixty-three thousand.

Thus, pending the arrival of 'Uncle Sam', the British were left with almost the full burden of Allied fighting in the West. On 9 April the attack at Arras had begun, and north of the Scarpe river the troops, urged on by their own high morale, made the deepest advance achieved in a single day since trench warfare had stabilized the front. However, tanks were employed to very poor effect. By 11 April, full realization was dawning that the Germans had brought in fresh troops for which

the increasingly weary British were no match. Still, in the second phase of the battle, on 23–24 April, in the midst of particularly ferocious fighting, the British gained the upper hand. However, this achieved little long-term result, and further efforts concentrated mainly around a renewed offensive undertaken on 3 May in order to encourage and shield the French. Final casualties for Arras were 150,000 British and perhaps nearly as many Germans (though statistics for this battle are unreliable).

The British were now faced with the need for a move in Flanders. Like Sir John French before him, Haig had long sought the opportunity to clear the Belgian coast of the enemy. Indeed, he had wanted to attack in this direction instead of on the Somme or later at Arras, but various factors had contributed to his being overruled. Now, considering Nivelle's failure and events in Russia, the Germans, even though many of their troops were worn out, had somehow to be prevented from dealing a hammer-blow at either Italy or the possibly disintegrating former Tsarist empire. Attrition in the west seemed the answer. Moreover, the British Admiralty, and in particular Jellicoe, the First Sea Lord, was anxious to cripple the German submarines, some of which operated from Ostend and Zeebrugge, and to do this the British would have to break through to the coast. Subsequently it was learned that the Admiralty had exaggerated the importance of the Belgian submarine bases and that the main U-boat campaign was conducted from German ports. It is uncertain how much Haig himself believed in Jellicoe's alarmism, but the latter's arguments tied in neatly with Haig's ideas on a Flanders offensive. In any case, in a final bitter irony, by the time the attempted breakthrough was launched, the adoption of the convoy system for merchant vessels had mitigated the worst of the submarine damage.

Haig knew that it would be necessary first to secure the southern approach by capturing the strategically vital Messines Ridge, whence he hoped to break through at Ypres and proceed northeast. An advance along the coast and an amphibious landing near Ostend would also be required for this plan to achieve maximum effect. Control of the coast would outflank the German northern line before Berlin could transfer more troops from the East; and the new Allied flank would itself be protected by its contiguity to neutral Holland. On the other hand, the actual staging of the operation became increasingly difficult in the absence of French support except for an elite force of six divisions. Still, Haig remained confident, despite the warnings of Robertson and the scepticism of Lloyd George. Haig seems to have been motivated by a wish to continue to protect the tottering French, but more importantly, by a desire to make his mark with a great victory in Flanders that would bring the British into clear pre-eminence in the Allied coalition and push Germany over the brink into defeat. The French, in fact, thought very little of Haig's projected clearing operation, and Foch, their chief of the general staff, sneered that the campaign would become 'a duck's march'.

The Battle of Messines took place on 7–8 June.

Top: Canadian troops of the 19th Infantry Battalion consolidate their positions. Above: An eight-inch Mark V howitzer in action near Arras. Left: Scottish troops advance to the attack. Opposite: British soldiers regroup near an abandoned tank.

Its most interesting and memorable aspect was the detonation of almost a million pounds of explosive, which had previously been placed under the German positions. Nineteen mines were fired simultaneously, and the entire top of the hill was blown away. The explosion could be heard across the Channel. Then a tremendous artillery barrage began, under cover of which Plumer's Second Army advanced across the crest of Messines, and the Germans pulled back to positions behind the Ypres-Comines (Komen) Canal, where they found themselves too debilitated to counterattack. Their morale, not to mention their health, had been further undermined in the interim by gas and boiling oil. At the cost of at least 17,000 casualties, the British had succeeded in closing the salient south of Ypres. German losses were 25,000, including 7,500 prisoners.

After a delay of over seven weeks, caused among other things by cabinet debates as to the advisability of the Flanders project, at the end of July the new offensive began. The Third Battle of Ypres, also known collectively and inaccurately as 'Passchendaele' (after a village near Ypres), began after an Allied air offensive commencing 11 July and involving 700 aircraft.

Lasting until 6 November, Third Ypres was plagued with inordinate bad luck. The fatal delay between the Messines and Ypres operations had given the Germans the chance to bring up reinforcements and provide a new and efficient system of defences. Nevertheless, in fact Haig had himself planned a considerable delay between the two battles.

Third Ypres saw the German use of mustard gas, the effect of which was to create on all parts of the body burns and huge blisters which were slow to heal. In July 1918 the French in turn made use of this atrocious weapon, and no doubt would have done so earlier if they had had the means to produce it.

To return to the battle itself: the preliminary bombardment of a fortnight's duration was counterproductive, for its 65,000 tons of shells destroyed the surface drainage of the area and turned the soil into a sticky, soggy entrapment which badly hindered the Allied advance. In fact, the entire area was unsuitable for fighting purposes, because a level plain stretching for twenty miles made all the British preparations obvious to the enemy and made excellent targets of both men and supplies after the battle had begun.

Above left: An eighteen-pounder is pulled out of the mud. The territory around Passchendaele became an unspeakable quagmire.
Above right: A wounded Canadian being carried to a dressing station on the back of a comrade, followed by two German prisoners.
Opposite top left: Grenades were taken to German soldiers on the front by messenger dog.
Opposite top right: Slaughtered Germans; Third Battle of Ypres, 31 July 1917. **Opposite bottom:** Near 'Clapham Junction', looking towards Sanctuary Wood: 23 September 1917.

Haig's original plan had been for the Fifth Army under General Sir Hubert Gough to advance fifteen miles and seize control of strategic communications in the region, after which the Fourth Army would attack on the coast with the aid of troop landings. The British Second Army would move northeast to gain control of Passchendaele. However, the actual outcome was quite different. Third Ypres became essentially a battle for control of a vital plateau, and no breakthrough to the sea occurred.

Despite all setbacks, the first day's fighting was marked by British successes. But the previously balmy weather broke, and heavy rains added the finishing touches to the developing quagmire. Thousands of shell craters filled to the brim with mud and water. Earlier warnings that this would happen were made in plenty – but ignored. The Royal Engineers worked magnificently, constructing roads of planks and boards over which men and matériel had to travel. Often, however, all but the most surefooted found themselves up to their waists in mud and slime, and many men drowned.

The first part of Third Ypres involved the Fifth Army primarily, and was marked by the opening Battle of Pilckem Ridge, as well as those of Gheluvelt Plateau (10 August) and Langemarck (16 August), in both of which the Germans fiercely and successfully counterattacked. Already Gough had concluded that no worthwhile success could be achieved, and he so informed Haig. But Haig refused to call off the battle, not only on account of his wish to aid the French, but because otherwise his forces might have been diverted to the Italian Front and the Allied lines might have collapsed in the West.

At the end of August Haig transferred the main burden of operations from Gough to the more cautious Plumer. Yet Plumer spent too much time in September carefully preparing his next moves. In this he failed to take advantage of a period of relatively more favourable weather. Finally, however, the second phase of Third Ypres opened with the Battle of Menin (Menen) Road Ridge on 20 September. Brilliant use of artillery contributed greatly to the British Empire forces' success. Six days later, the battle fought at Polygon Wood was a similar triumph, as was Broodseinde (4 October), even though the troops were plagued with dust clouds of sandstorm-like intensity. By October, in fact, the weather had worsened again;

casualties were somewhere between 175,000 and 400,000. In contrast, the small French army under Antoine suffered less than 9000 dead and wounded. The campaign had continued beyond all usefulness because of Haig's obstinate belief that Germany was near to collapse. He was sustained in this illusion by the sycophancy of many of his staff. Thus it was that Third Ypres came to epitomize the tragedy and waste of heroic effort for indifferent strategic results, and in retrospect its importance has been denigrated and its short-term successes eclipsed by the accompanying suffering and misery.

British reserves were now virtually nonexistent; thus the subsequent Battle of Cambrai was doomed before it began. Moreover, Lloyd George began to distrust both Haig and Robertson, and concentrated more on his pet diversion of a brilliant victory to be gained in Palestine.

The Fourteen Points

In January 1918, Woodrow Wilson made his first definitive statement of war aims. For some time, various sources had been urging the American president to clarify the ideals and objectives for which Americans, at least, were fighting. After consultations with Colonel House and certain experts known as The Inquiry, Wilson enunciated his famous Fourteen Points.

Wilson spoke at a crucial moment for the Allied cause. The Bolshevik Revolution in Russia, its leaders' call for a peace based on neither annexations nor indemnities, and its publication of the Allied secret treaties all caused grave embarrassment to the Allied and Associated Powers (as the Western coalition was known after American entry into the war, the United States being an 'associate' rather than an ally of the others). The need was urgent for a high-minded formulation of war aims, not only to counteract the Soviets and their accusations as to Allied cunning and duplicity, but to still the strident objections to the secret treaties which liberal and progressive opinion made within the Allied camp itself. On the other hand, Wilson was temperamentally inclined to excessive idealism, whereas the Allies themselves never had any intention of renouncing those territorial acquisitions which they felt vital, and for which their populations clamoured as a reward for the misery and destruction of the war. To complicate matters further, in late December 1917 the pronouncements of Czernin, the Austro-Hungarian Foreign Minister, led to speculation that a renewed peace initiative by the Central Powers was in the offing. It was now clear that Russia needed immediate encouragement if she were not to sign a separate peace with Germany and Austria (which, as we have seen, is what subsequently took place at Brest-Litovsk).

In drafting the Fourteen Points, as well as to consider Russian susceptibilities two other major considerations were kept in mind. On the subject of Alsace-Lorraine, the former French province which the Second Reich had annexed as a result of the Franco-Prussian War, Wilson was determined to make a statement. The President favoured restoration of Alsace-Lorraine to France, although the case for doing so was not clear-cut; a large part of the population was ethnically and linguistically

and despite all tactical successes, there was no strategic innovation. Furthermore, the amphibious coastal operation had by now been given up.

The third and final phase of the campaign centred around control of the village of Passchendaele, which finally fell on 6 November. Pouring rain drenched everything in sight. Ludendorff called the living and fighting conditions 'mere unspeakable suffering'. Indeed, the Passchendaele phase of Third Ypres became an exercise in futility. Passchendaele neither prevented the Russian collapse, nor the Central Powers' victory at Caporetto. Attrition was severe – but it affected both sides.

Casualties for Third Ypres are difficult to estimate. Beyond doubt, the cost was horrifying; the question is only one of the quantitative extent of the slaughter. British losses were certainly 245,000, but may have been up to 300,000. German

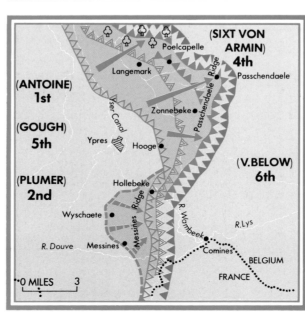

(ANTOINE)
1st

(GOUGH)
5th

(PLUMER)
2nd

(SIXT VON ARMIN)
4th

(V. BELOW)
6th

Poelcapelle
Langemark
Passchendaele
Yser Canal
Zonnebeke
Passchendaele Ridge
Ypres
Hooge
Hollebeke
Messines Ridge
Wyschaete
R. Wambeek
R. Lys
R. Douve
Messines
Comines
BELGIUM
FRANCE

0 MILES 3

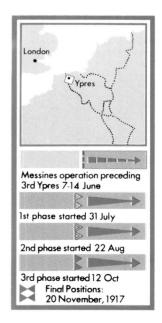

London
Ypres

Messines operation preceding
3rd Ypres 7-14 June

1st phase started 31 July

2nd phase started 22 Aug

3rd phase started 12 Oct
Final Positions:
20 November, 1917

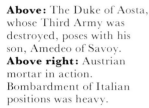

German, although the great majority of the people spoke French as well and had close ties to France (except for the considerable number of immigrants imported by the Germans since 1871 in an attempt to consolidate their claim to the province). At first, Wilson decided that after the return of Alsace-Lorraine to the French, the Germans ought to be allowed 'the use of the economic resources' of the region, resources which were particularly important for minerals. Later he changed his mind and omitted the above reference to German rights. Regarding freedom of the seas, Wilson had to be careful not to offend Great Britain, and rather than deal with specific points at issue, the President decided on a fair but firm statement.

Just before the Fourteen Points were announced, Washington received news of Lloyd George's personal statement of British aims. Britain, the Prime Minister declared, was not involved in an aggressive war or a vendetta against the German nation. The peace settlement ought to be based on the principle of 'government with the consent of the governed', he continued. However, Britain expected Belgium to be restored and Alsace-Lorraine to be given up. Germany was not to receive back her colonies. The legitimate claims of the Poles for independence and the Italians for 'unredeemed' compatriots should be met; indeed, all the minorities of the Habsburg Empire had a right to 'genuine' and 'democratic' self-government. Some kind of postwar international organization was essential to preserve peace without an armaments race.

After an initial reaction of some consternation, Wilson persuaded himself that Lloyd George's statement was sufficiently close to his own to make it all the more necessary to speak out. A few finishing touches were added to the President's speech, including a modifying clause in Point 2 (see below) which sought to make it more acceptable to the British, and the omission of reference to German economic interests in Point 8.

On 8 January 1918, Woodrow Wilson delivered his Fourteen Points before a joint session of Congress. On Points 6 and 7, no compromise would be possible; however, Points 8–13 inclusive were, it seems, negotiable, for the President declared that they 'should' rather than 'must' be realized. Point 14, Wilson's prescription for a League of Nations, was the most important of all, and it was his personal tragedy that the United States turned her back on this experiment in international organizations.

President Wilson's Fourteen Points were as follows:

1. 'Open covenants of peace, openly arrived at . . . diplomacy shall proceed always frankly and in the public view.

2. 'Absolute freedom of navigation upon the seas, . . . in peace and in war . . .

3. 'The removal, so far as possible, of all economic barriers and the establishment of an equality of trade conditions among all the nations . . .

4. 'Adequate guarantees given and taken that national armaments will be reduced to the lowest point consistent with domestic safety.

5. 'A free, open-minded, and absolutely impartial adjustment of all colonial claims, based upon a strict observance of the principle that . . . the interests of the populations concerned must have equal weight with the equitable claims of the government whose title is to be determined.

6. 'The evacuation of all Russian territory . . .

7. 'Belgium . . . must be evacuated and restored. . .

8. 'All French territory should be freed and the invaded portions restored, and the wrong done to France by Prussia in 1871 in the matter of Alsace-Lorraine . . . should be righted . . .

9. 'A readjustment of the frontiers of Italy should be effected along clearly recognizable lines of nationality.

10. 'The peoples of Austria-Hungary . . . should be accorded the freest opportunity of autonomous development.

11. 'Rumania, Serbia and Montenegro should be evacuated; occupied territories restored; Serbia accorded free and secure access to the sea; and the relations of the several Balkan states to one another determined by friendly counsel along historically established lines of allegiance and nationality; and international guarantees of the political and economic independence and territorial integrity of the several Balkan states should be entered into.

12. 'The Turkish portions of the present Ottoman Empire should be assured a secure sovereignty, but the other nationalities which are now under Turkish rule should be assured an undoubted security of life and an absolutely unmolested opportunity of autonomous development, and the Dardanelles should be permanently opened as a free passage to the ships and commerce of all nations under international guarantees.

13. 'An independent Polish state should be erected which should include the territories inhabited by indisputably Polish populations, which should be assured a free and secure access to the sea . . .

14. 'A general association of nations must be formed under specific covenants for the purpose of affording mutual guarantees of political independence and territorial integrity to great and small states alike.'

Arthur Link, historian of the Wilsonian era, describes the Fourteen Points as 'incomparably the greatest liberal manifesto of the war'. American opinion was overwhelmingly behind the President. British and French left-wing support was assured.

However, those who thought in a less lofty and more realistic vein soon pointed out the flaws in the President's declaration. In Germany, opinion on the Fourteen Points was generally unfavourable at the time; only later, when the war was clearly lost, did moderates and left-wing thinkers support Wilson's plan. By the time the Treaty of Brest-Litovsk was signed on 3 March, it was clear to Wilson and most others that the war would continue to the bitter end. There would not, indeed could not, they realized, be a negotiated peace because of the irreconcilable aims of the opposing sides. Bitter but unshakeable in his beliefs, Wilson determined to fight on with all of America's might until victory was won. His last hope was that justice and reason would prevail at the postwar peace conference.

In retrospect we see that the Fourteen Points were loaded with anomalies and contradictions. For example, it was simply unrealistic to declare, in the middle of a war replete with detailed and secret Allied commitments such as the Treaty of London with Italy in 1915, that semipublic diplomacy ought to be the rule in future, as was implied in Point 1. Point 5, calling for colonial justice, ran counter to British, French, and Japanese intentions to retain the ex-German colonies which they had occupied during the war. Similarly, Point 9 was in opposition to Italy's grotesquely inflated territorial ambitions. Point 10 was, in a sense, an exercise in naïveté. One example will suffice: a fair and democratic case could be made out for Czechoslovak independence, but it proved impossible to establish the

Above left: Italian soldiers desert to the enemy at Caporetto. **Above:** Austrian reserves press forward when Italian morale collapsed.

state with viable borders and yet exlude a huge German minority and smaller minorities of Hungarians, Poles, and Ruthenians. Central Europe was too much a patchwork quilt of nationalities for it to be possible to draw any new borders with anything approaching complete fairness. Point 13 was used as the point of departure for the establishment of a Polish state whose chauvinism and intolerance towards all minorities verged on lunacy. Such were some of the inconsistencies and distortions which emerged from Wilson's well-meaning efforts.

Showdown in Italy

In 1915, as we saw earlier, the Italian Isonzo offensives achieved indifferent results. Little further was gained in the six subsequent battles of 1916–17, although in the Eleventh Battle of the Isonzo (19 August–12 September 1917), staged to coordinate with Third Ypres in the West, General Luigi Capello's Italian Second Army broke through to the Bainsizza Plateau and rendered the Austrian positions precarious. The Italian success was only limited, however, since among other reversals the Duke of Aosta's Third Army was vanquished. Yet the Austrians doubted that they could withstand a Twelfth Isonzo, and thus they decided to forestall this by attacking the Italians themselves.

Above: Gas masks were used by the French in the trenches throughout most of the war.
Right: The Austrians won their greatest victory in what they called 'The Miracle' of Caporetto.
Opposite top: A Canadian six-inch howitzer.
Opposite bottom: The Austrians constructed their defences by night on the Italian Front. **Below right:** Mark IV Tank (Male). Crew: 8. Overall length: 26ft. 5in. Height: 8ft. 2in. Width: 12ft. 10in. Armament: 2 ×6pdr., 4 ×Lewis 303 machine guns. Maximum armor: 12mm. Engine: Daimler 6 cylinder, 105 b.h.p. Performance: 3·7 m.p.h. Range: 35 miles.

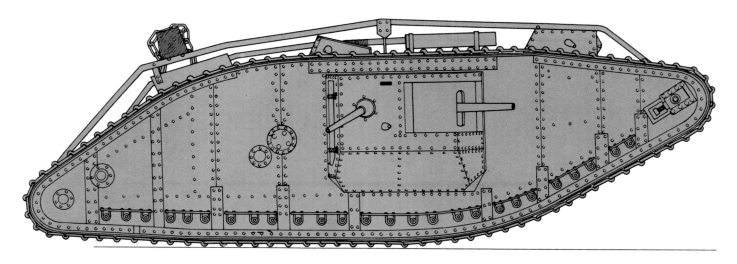

While he was chief of the Austrian general staff, Conrad had been obsessed with dealing a knock-out blow against Italy. In early 1917, Conrad was replaced and sent to command the Trentino sector of the Italian Front. Here he reflected further on his plan for an Austrian attack on the Caporetto (Karfreit; now Kobarid) sector of the Isonzo region, where, it seemed, the Italian lines were least ably defended. At the end of August Conrad sought German assistance for this move. Austrian motives were complicated, and they did not seek inordinate help from their ally, since they feared that as a result, Italy might gain equivalent Anglo-French support. Escalation of the conflict might then shatter Vienna's hopes of a compromise peace. Yet on the recommendation of Lieutenant General Krafft von Dellmensingen, the Germans finally decided that since 'success lies only just on the border of possibility', they would assume direction of a limited offensive in the Caporetto area, keeping largely clear of what Ludendorff in particular considered to be Austria's bungling methods.

In September 1917 six German and nine Austrian divisions, newly grouped into the German Fourteenth Army, assembled some sixty miles east of Caporetto. The equipment and the troops themselves were of generally high quality. Three more Austrian formations and six additional German divisions were also available.

Krafft von Dellmensingen, now chief of staff of the Fourteenth Army, reasoned that two simultaneous thrusts meeting near Caporetto would isolate a contingent of Italians, and allow the Germans and Austrians to advance to the Stol and Colovrat ridges and beyond, thus taking in flank much of the Italian Second Army and leading to a general enemy retreat. Meanwhile Cadorna, the Italian commander, heard rumours of an enemy offensive and ordered defensive preparations in depth, though actually such precautions as were finally taken were rather

haphazard. Later Czech and Transylvanian deserters from the Austrian forces gave the Italians more detailed news. Ironically, Cadorna himself had abandoned for the moment that Twelfth Isonzo which the Austrians feared, for he was short of ammunition.

Cadorna has been characterized as an autocrat and a bully, and military historians agree on his lack of empathy with his troops. Certainly neither he nor Capello took sufficient note of low morale among their men. Rather, Capello had spent too much time dreaming of an Italian counter-offensive in the Tolmino (Tolmein) area, an idea that Cadorna rejected.

On 24 October, under cover of misty, rainy weather, the Austrian bombardment opened on a vast scale. Thus began Caporetto (the Twelfth Battle of the Isonzo). The Austro-Germans used gas and high explosive shells, and panic spread as the Italians found that their gas masks were ineffective. For the most part the Central Powers were able to push forward with little difficulty, their success increased by bad leadership in the Italian ranks. The Austrians, somewhat astonished at their own prowess, now referred to *Das Wunder von Karfreit*. Many Italians simply deserted and ran, due to a mixture of fear of German military might and apathy or active hostility towards the war itself. The Italian troops were also influenced by the opposition of the Vatican to the conflict, the example of Bolshevism in Russia, and resentment at the deprived conditions under which they had to live as soldiers. Moreover, not until Caporetto did the enemy invade Italian soil; thus previously an important ingredient in patriotic appeals to fight had been missing.

By the morning of 25 October the Italian situation was poor. In the previous afternoon the enemy had made a fifteen-mile breach in the Italian line; by the evening of the twenty-fifth a retreat to the Tagliamento River became necessary. Everywhere Italian morale had caved in, and Capello was desperately ill and thus unable to use much influence to exhort his troops to greater efforts.

Throughout 26 October, as the Germans and Austrians continued to press forward, Cadorna was the victim of garbled information and mismanaged reports. Early on the twenty-seventh, however, the orders for retreat at last went out – not that the disorganized troops had bothered to wait for them. As they streamed away in their hundreds of thousands, the Italians stopped to enjoy themselves en route, eating, drinking, and carousing. The roads were cluttered with fleeing civilians, and any reinforcements of men or supplies were hopelessly entangled by this mass defection.

By the night of 2–3 November, despite confusion and indecision in the Austrian command structure, the Central Powers had made a passage north of the Tagliamento, across which Cadorna and his troops had retreated by 31 October. On 4 November Cadorna ordered a further pullback to the River Piave, behind which his armies stood by 9 November. Paradoxically, morale and discipline were already beginning to improve, and this process was accelerated by General Armando Diaz, who now replaced Cadorna as commander

Below: Men of the 11th Royal Irish Fusiliers with German prisoners.
Opposite Top: British machine gunners operate out of a captured second-line trench.
Opposite bottom: French tank passing captured German guns in the Battle of Cambrai.

and whose beneficial effect on his troops was similar to that of Pétain in France.

Caporetto was over. The Italians had lost 10,000 killed, 30,000 wounded and up to 293,000 prisoners, in addition to the countless numbers of deserters. Strangely, the realization of the dimensions of this disaster pulled the Italians together as never before. In a concerted drive to support the war effort, artillery and munitions were manufactured in vast quantities. Finally, in October 1918, Caporetto was avenged in the victory of Vittorio Veneto.

Tank Warfare

Our attention must now return briefly to the Western Front. Here, between 20 November and 3 December 1917, was fought the Battle of Cambrai, most remembered for a British dawn attack on the opening day of battle, which used almost four hundred tanks in a bold attempt to seize the initiative in the West before the arrival of German reinforcements from the Russian Front.

As the battle was originally conceived, tanks were to be used to 'demoralize and disorganize' the enemy 'and not to capture ground'. A tank raid of eight to twelve hours' duration would be completed before the Germans had time to group for counterattack. However, the Third Army commander, General Sir Julian Byng, was inclined to escalate the project into a large-scale offensive which aimed at a breakthrough to Cambrai and thrusts beyond to Valenciennes. Yet the objections of General Kiggell, Haig's chief of staff, were sufficient to persuade the British supremo to delay the Cambrai project pending the outcome of the Third Battle of Ypres, by which time British reserves had been wiped out in the Passchendaele slaughterhouse and decisive results were no longer feasible. Under the circumstances, by the time the Cambrai action was approved, Byng's objectives were over-ambitious.

At 6:20 a.m. on 20 November, without the customary warning of a preliminary bombardment and with the added advantage of concealment in heavy mist, the British tanks rolled forward. For the first time, tanks were being employed as their architects had intended: in conditions of surprise and in large numbers. On the first day of battle alone, the tanks advanced over three miles. Next day, bells pealed in London in anticipation of a great triumph. Although, as it turned out, the self-congratulation was premature, the new tactics used at Cambrai were employed to good effect the following year and again in the Second World War.

The British had calculated that their tanks could surmount the formidable barriers of the Hindenburg Line by flattening its massive barbed-wire defences instead of taking time to cut through them by means of artillery fire. In addition, brushwood would be dropped from the front of each tank and laid across the massive trenches to provide ersatz bridges. The success of these ploys changed the conduct of trench warfare.

In the early stages the British received an unpleasant setback. At Flesquieres, three German batteries wreaked havoc among the advancing tanks; one alone destroyed sixteen of the new weapons. This had the effect of delaying the

Above: 'Howitzer Firing' by Paul Nash. **Above centre:** General Cadorna, Chief of Staff of the Italian army. **Top right:** An Italian bomb thrower. **Far right:** An Italian poster portrays a light infantryman with one of his most important defences – the shovel.

Right: Ordnance BL 9·2 Howitzer Mark II. Total weight of gun and carriage: 16·4 tons (it must have 11 tons of earth). Maximum elevation: 50°. Minimum angle: 15°. Height: 8ft 1in. (loading position). Overall length in working position: 17ft. 6in. Crew: 14. Performance: maximum range 13,935yds. **Right centre:** Ordnance QF 4·5 Howitzer Mark 1. Total weight of gun and carriage: 1·33 tons. Maximum elevation: 45°. Maximum depression:—45° Height: 5ft. 9in. Overall length in working position: 13ft. 6in. Performance: maximum range 7,300 yds. crew: 10.

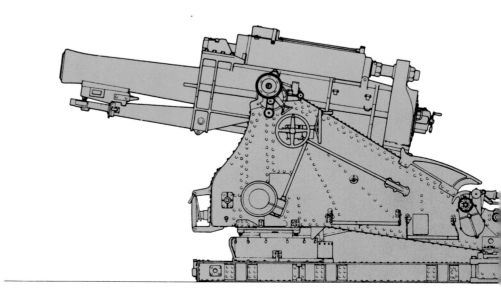

advance of the infantry, which had been utilizing the tanks as an essential advance auxiliary.

On the evening of the twenty-first, only inconclusive results had been achieved, whereas by this time Haig had hoped to have won the battle. Unwilling to give up, he spent the next week pursuing limited objectives, handicapped by the dearth of his reserves and the weariness of his men.

After the initial fighting, the most important clash of Cambrai took place on 30 November. In a clever counterstroke, which employed their skill and enthusiasm to the utmost, the Germans pounded away with gas and smoke shells; then their aircraft, flying low, riddled the exhausted British with machine-gun fire. Meanwhile the German infantry was brought forward. For a time the issue seemed in doubt, but soon the Germans were able to continue their advance. Tired and inexperienced troops and, more importantly, overcautious senior commanders accounted for much of the British losses, which amounted to 37,000 men, besides 6000 prisoners. German casualties numbered 30,000, in addition to the loss of 11,000 prisoners; but Berlin was satisfied, feeling that it was regaining the initiative.

CHAPTER THIRTEEN

Each Side Bids to Win

Top left: Germans march forward as the Kaiserschlacht opens. **Top centre:** Middlesex men hold a street barricade in Bailleul, 15 April 1918. **Top:** A German mortar position. **Above:** Ludendorff, who hoped to break through in the West before the Americans arrived. **Left:** German tactics were successful, but a terrible price was paid.

Below: General (later Marshal) Foch, who became overall commander-in-chief of the Entente forces on 26 March 1918. On his left is General Weygand, who held the same position on the Western Front in the disastrous spring of 1940. **Far right:** General von Hutier, who attacked and faltered south of the Somme.

The war was now three and a half years old. It had taken a frightful toll in human lives, reflected in the acute shortage of skilled and experienced fighting men from which the British and French Empire forces were suffering by early 1918. Moreover, bleak despondency and frustration gripped and numbed the many who asked: when and how would the carnage end?

As if there were not enough difficulties on the Western Front, in the autumn of 1917 the Italian rout at Caporetto had made it necessary for the Western Allies to send eleven divisions to prop up their crumbling colleague. Furthermore, the long-awaited injection of new American blood at the front was proving slow to materialize, for by March 1918 only six rather inexperienced divisions had arrived in France. The battered armies resolved to cling to their present positions somehow until 'the Yanks' arrived in sufficient numbers to make a fresh offensive possible.

Meanwhile, the Allies braced themselves for a renewed German offensive, although, the plight of the Germans was hardly much better than that of the Entente. On the German home front, cynicism grew apace with the desperate lack of food. Politically, the situation was equally grim. Bulgaria was exhausted; and Austria-Hungary and Turkey, surviving only by a miracle, lurched on from crisis to crisis. However, by the summer of 1918 German troops were being transferred in large numbers from the East, and had the Americans not arrived in force by then, the Germans would have been at a distinct advantage.

Yet earlier, Ludendorff, by now the kingmaker in German life, had concluded that a spring offensive was vital to pre-empt American gains and encourage Germany's reeling allies. After being tempted to attack in Flanders, where a break-through to the sea would cut off the British from the Channel ports, Ludendorff decided that the rain-soaked terrain precluded the quick success for which he strove, and instead determined to thrust into the lightly-defended region of the Somme.

Once again Ludendorff concentrated on tactics which had proved their worth the previous year at Riga and Caporetto. These included a short preliminary bombardment of gas and smoke shells, to be followed by a strong artillery barrage. The difficulty was, however, that whereas in the above-mentioned battles the Germans faced opponents of very low morale in operations on a restricted scale, in the West a huge offensive would be needed against troops of greater resilience.

The German Somme offensive (referred to as the *Kaiserschlacht* or 'Emperor Battle') opened on 21 March 1918. Its ultimate objective was to separate the British from the French and to corner the British on the coast. Some thought Ludendorff's fatal mistake was to become obsessed with the fate of the British instead of concentrating against the weaker French in the sector farthest from the British lines. However this may be, under cover of thick fog, the Somme attack commenced with a fantastically powerful artillery barrage from 6000 guns, the greatest bombardment yet seen by history. On the first day of battle the Germans scored heavy successes. By 23 March Gough was forced to pull back his British Fifth Army behind the Somme; Byng's Third Army, though heavily pressed, did not fare as badly. A few days later, land communications between the British and French were in danger, but fortunately for the Allies, when the Germans moved towards Arras they were thrown back and the British lines held.

South of the Somme, though Hutier's German Eighteenth Army took Montdidier on 27 March, both his men and supplies were beginning to falter. Subsequently several German attacks proved futile, and on 4 April, despite the tremendous tactical success achieved, Ludendorff called off the offensive.

The Allies had sustained almost 200,000 casualties and had lost up to 90,000 prisoners. Their consolation was that their armies had neither been separated nor destroyed. German losses were approximately 200,000, but from now on they could ill afford casualties which were even remotely equal to those of the Entente, for the Americans were beginning to arrive in even greater numbers.

By this time the Allies had felt the situation sufficiently serious to create a long-overdue uni-

Right: General Sir Hubert Gough, Commander of the Fifth Army, which covered much of the Allied sector of the front. **Below:** The Yanks arrive! The march through Paris on the way to the front. **Below right:** One of the 305,000 British casualities. **Opposite top:** The Americans at Chateau-Thierry. **Opposite bottom:** A street barricade at Chateau-Thierry. The arrival of fresh American soldiers was an incalculable boost to the morale of the Allies.

fied command. Thus on 26 March General Foch had become overall commander-in-chief of the Entente forces.

In the interim Ludendorff made one more effort to smash the BEF once and for all. This, the Lys offensive, lasted from 9 to 29 April, but although the German tactics were brilliantly successful, strategic gains were once more non-existent. Both sides paid a terrible price for these three weeks of battle: 350,000 German and 305,000 British casualties. The Germans were gambling for high stakes; they could not possibly afford to sustain losses on this scale. Meanwhile American troops continued to pour into France, bringing new hope. Foch, as usual, remained buoyantly optimistic, exclaiming *Bon!* whenever he was told of news from the front, whether good, bad, or indifferent.

Despite the realities facing him, Ludendorff doggedly maintained that 'one more' blow would wipe out the British. With this in mind, on the morning of 27 May his First and Seventh Armies attacked on the Aisne at the oddly-named location of Chemin des Dames. Smashing through the Allied defenses, by the end of May the Germans had reached the Marne. In desperation Pétain called on General John Pershing for an American division to stem the German onslaught. The American Third Division reached Château-Thierry by 1 June, and their efforts enabled the Allies to meet and withstand repeated enemy thrusts. Similarly the American Second Division held back the Germans further west. Bitterly disappointed, Ludendorff called off the Aisne offensive on 6 June.

Ludendorff had manoeuvred himself into an unfavourable position. His troops were located in a salient which was vulnerable to counterattacks, yet if he withdrew, his soldiers' morale would undoubtedly suffer. Searching around for a means of deliverance, Ludendorff determined to make two further thrusts against the Noyon-Montdidier and Soissons sectors, in this way exposing Paris itself to danger. He calculated that the threat to the French capital would induce the latter to pull back and leave Flanders less adequately defended. This, he reasoned, would give him a chance to pulverize the British. However, between 9 and 13 June the French under Fayolle

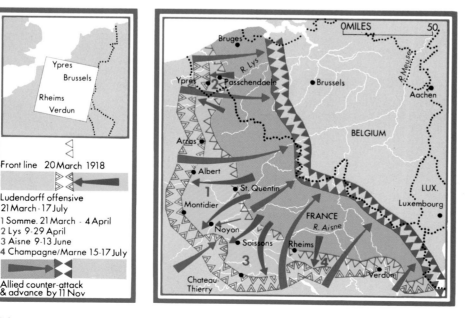

Front line 20 March 1918

Ludendorff offensive
21 March - 17 July
1 Somme. 21 March - 4 April
2 Lys 9-29 April
3 Aisne 9-13 June
4 Champagne/Marne 15-17 July

Allied counter-attack
& advance by 11 Nov

foiled this scheme. Once more the Germans suffered heavy casualties to little effect, whereas the French got away lightly.

Champagne–Marne offensive

In the succeeding month, while Foch laid his plans for a counter-offensive, German morale weakened and discipline suffered dramatically. By now many of Ludendorff's crack troops were dead, and in their place to a large extent stood men past their prime, inexperienced youths, or those at best marginally fit for battle. Yet Ludendorff managed to strike once more, in the Champagne-Marne offensive of 15–17 July. Foch, having gained advance information as to Ludendorff's plans, was well placed to inflict a heavy setback. The German *Friedensturm* (peace offensive) was finally checked, for after the loss of 800,000 men in a period of four months, Ludendorff was in no position to launch further attacks, for Germany the war was already lost.

Above: Bridge across the Marne blown up by the French. **Right:** Kansas troops in a tight spot.

Below: A French mess near the front lines. Rolling kitchens such as these provided the only hot meals available to front line troops . . . except for a tin heated by matches in a trench.

The Second Marne

The Allied Aisne-Marne counteroffensive of 18 July–6 August, which together with the preceding German drive is commonly known as Second Marne now took place. Foch's objective was to reduce the German salients of Marne and Amiens, created during the previous enemy offensives, and that of Saint-Mihiel, which had remained quiescent since the first autumn of the war.

First to be dealt with was the Marne salient. The Allied attacking force consisted of the French Fifth, Sixth, Ninth, and Tenth Armies, in which were already incorporated four British, two Italian, and eight American divisions. The initial day of the assault, 18 July, proved highly successful, outstandingly so for the French tank force. Next day Mangin's Tenth Army raced on towards Soissons, and the Germans found themselves obliged to conduct a fighting withdrawal. Thus the Marne salient was eliminated – an extraordinary victory for the Allies and the French in particular, and the first major Allied success that year. Foch, meanwhile, had received his just reward, having been created *Maréchal de France*.

By now the Americans were playing a truly vital role on the Western Front. In the Aisne-Marne offensive they had fielded eight divisions, whose value was tremendously enhanced by their containing twice the infantry strength of either Allied or German divisions. By this time, although the Germans had not been annihilated, they had definitely lost the psychological initiative. The American performance, exceeding British and French expectations, spurred the Entente on to greater efforts, tired and exhausted though they were.

Meanwhile an Allied operation against the Amiens salient was in preparation. Rawlinson underlined the secrecy which was vital to the offensive by having included in the soldiers' pay-

books a small notice which stated baldly: 'Keep Your Mouth Shut.' The most elaborate precautions enabled secrecy to be maintained up to the opening of battle.

The Battle of Amiens (or, as the French called it, Montdidier) was of tremendous importance. Fuller called it 'the most decisive . . . of the First

Above: General Pershing receives an honour guard upon his arrival in Boulogne.

World War', while Liddell Hart praised Amiens as 'the most brilliant (victory) ever gained by British arms' during the war. The German official history admits that the battle was 'the greatest defeat which the German army . . . suffered' in the Great War. Moreover, such a gain was achieved with relative economy: British casualties numbered under 9,000 on the first day's fighting. Whereas, after Second Marne, the German armies had not yet lost hope, after Amiens they were in a state of psychological collapse. The long Western stalemate had been broken, and the Germans gave up hope of a renewed offensive.

In the early hours of 8 August, in conditions of zero visibility due to a dense mist, Rawlinson's British Fourth Army moved against the enemy, employing the tactics earlier proved at Cambrai and using a formidable array of weaponry which included hundreds of tanks, many of the latest type. Without a preliminary bombardment, suddenly the tank armada struck. Two thousand guns pounded and hammered in unison against the German defences. Soon the British Empire forces, in which Canadian and Australian troops formed a *corps d'élite*, were joined in the affray by the French First Army under Debeney. The Third Army (Humbert) was also to be included. Facing them were von der Marwitz's Second Army and Hutier's Eighteenth Army.

As the British tanks rolled effortlessly forward, the German infantry proved unable to defend

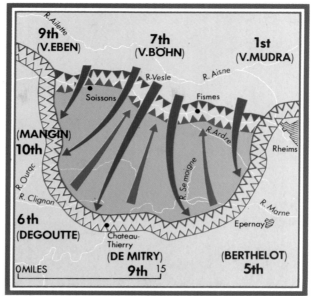

Salient forced by Germany's last offensive 15-18 July, 1918

Allied counter-attack (French, American & British), returning to the original line by 7 August, 1918

themselves against these behemoths. Not that the tanks were responsible for mass slaughter; rather, the suddenness of their appearance and the scale of the attack led to a kind of moral caving-in. Many men simply took to their heels. Almost immediately the British captured 16,000 prisoners, while the French made good progress.

As whole units at a time disintegrated, Ludendorff was moved to call 8 August 1918 'The black day of the German Army in the history of this war'. Even though artillery fire managed to cripple 109

Opposite top left: General John J. ('Black Jack') Pershing, the American Commander-in-Chief. **Opposite top right:** Manfred von Richthofen, the Red Baron, Germany's greatest air ace. **Far left:** Dog fight in the skies. Air warfare made a significant impact on the Western Front in the latter stages of the war. **Left:** 'The Blind Spot.' by N. G. Arnold. A Sopwith Camel closes in under a German tailplane.

Far left: S.E.5a. Engine: 200 hp Wolseley W4a Viper. Span: 26ft. 7.5in. Length: 20ft. 11in. Armament: one fixed ·303 in. Vickers machine gun, one ·303in. Lewis machine gun on Foster mounting. Maximum speed: 130 mph at 10,000 feet. **Left:** Spad XIII. Engine: 220 hp Hispano-Suiza 8BA.

Span: 26ft. 3.75in. Length: 20ft. 4in. Armament: two fixed, ·303 Vickers machine guns. Maximum speed: 133·5 mph at 622 ft. **Right:** Fokker DVII. Engine: 175 hp Mercedes D3. Span: 29ft. 3·5in. Length: 22ft. 11·5in. Armament: two 7.92mm Spandau machine guns. Maximum speed: 118·1 mph at 6549ft.

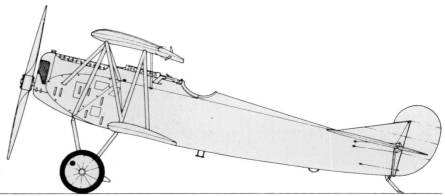

British tanks on the first day, Amiens was the greatest Allied triumph since the Marne in 1914, although neither Foch nor Haig was aware of this at the time. However, as the attack reached the scarred battlefields of the Somme, it faltered in a welter of derelict impediments; and, as earlier at Cambrai, lack of reserves began to tell. By 11 August, the first phase of the offensive was over. French casualties were over 24,000; those of the British were 22,000; and German losses were 75,000, including prisoners, of which the French took over 11,000 and the British over 18,000.

After lengthy argument between Haig and Foch over how best to exploit an extremely favourable situation, Haig got his own way, and on 21 August his armies once more thrust forward. At first the Germans retreated under the impact of Byng's Third Army, but by 22 August they were counterattacking, without greatly disrupting the Allied progress. By the end of August the Germans had been forced to evacuate their previously strong position at Roye-Chaulnes, Mont-Saint-Quentin had been taken, and the enemy had retreated to its spring positions on the Hindenburg line (*Siegfried Stellung*). Such was the German despair that at a Crown Council on 14 August the Kaiser said that 'a suitable time must be chosen to come to an understanding with the enemy'. If possible, negotiations with the Entente would be initiated through the mediation of the Queen of Holland and the King of Spain. As for Ludendorff, he stated simply: 'The war must be ended.' Meanwhile the Reich forces would attempt to stage a fighting retreat and to remain on French soil as long as possible. In practical terms, however, the German lack of strategy devolved into mere passive resistance. At the same time the Austrians' almost blind belief in German military supremacy had been dealt an irremediable body blow. Seeing the psychological results of their offensive, Haig and Foch came to the conclusion that the war could be won in 1918 after all.

What had led to *Der Schwarze Tag*, to Germany's 'Black Day'? Undoubtedly the brilliant employment of tanks and the exploitation of the element of surprise had played an important role in events. Yet military success alone is insufficient to explain the disproportion of the German inner collapse. Perhaps the foremost additional reason for the Reich's collective nervous breakdown was the throttling effect of the Allied economic blockade. Even with massive imports of food from the Ukraine and Rumania, Germany was living at the borderline of starvation. Already depressed by tales of woe from home, the German soldier saw that the costly 1918 offensives had

Left: The Big Parade . . . forward. **Above:** Another parade . . . back; 750 German prisoners go into French custody.

Bottom right: French tanks move up to stem the German tide. **Opposite top:** 'The Red Door' on 'The Black Day'. **Opposite bottom:** A French armoured car moves forward to the front.

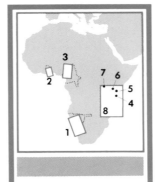

Territory owned by Allies

Territory owned by Central powers, subsequently lost to the Allies
Maps 1-7

Allied attack from the sea   25.4.15

Allied attacks and dates of victory   3.11.14

Central powers movements and dates of positions

1st phase of battle

2nd phase of battle
Map 8

Allied attack and Central powers retreat 1918

Allied attack and Central powers retreat 1918

1 Invasion of German SW Africa begun August 1914, completed July 1915
2 Successfully invaded & gained by August 1914
3 Easy success in Togoland was not to be repeated in the Cameroons invasion, begun in 1914; was not to be successful until February 1916
4 Fiasco at Tanga. British sustained a decisive defeat
5, 6, 7 Opening phases of the German E. Africa campaigns
8 Three years of campaigning with heavy losses due to climactic conditions; battle ending with Central Powers surrender, November 1918

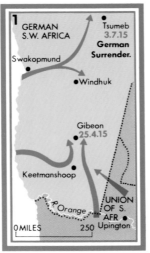

1
GERMAN S.W. AFRICA
Tsumeb 3.7.15 German Surrender.
Swakopmund
Windhuk
Gibeon 25.4.15
Keetmanshoop
R. Orange
UNION OF S. AFR.
Upington
0 MILES 250

2
Gold Coast Constab.
French irregular Cav. & Inf.
R. Oti
DAHOMÉ
R. Oaka
R. Mo
Sakodé
TOGOLAND
Bismarkburg 7.8.14
German Defence (MAROIX)
(ELGEE)
Kpandu 22.8.14
GOLD COAST
(MARCHAND) 7.8.14
R. Volta Lomé 13.8.14 (BRYANT)
0 MILES 50

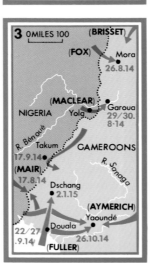

3 0 MILES 100 (BRISSET)
(FOX)
Mora 26.8.14
(MACLEAR)
Garoua 29/30. 8-14
NIGERIA Yola
R. Bénoué GAMEROONS
Takum 17.9.14
R. Sanaga
(MAIR) 17.8.14
Dschang 2.1.15
(AYMERICH)
Yaoundé
22/27 .9.14 Douala 26.10.14
(FULLER)

4
Tanga Island
0 ½ MILE
Tanga Bay
GERMAN E. AFRICA TANGA
4.11.14 3.11.14

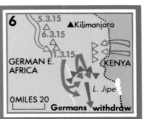

5
R. Suba R. Umba
18.1.15
KENYA
Yasini
0 MILES 3
GERMAN E. AFRICA

6
5.3.15 ▲Kilimanjaro
6.3.15
11.3.15
GERMAN E. AFRICA KENYA
L. Jipe
0 MILES 20 Germans withdraw

7
L. Victoria
24.6.15
GERMAN E. AFRICA
23.6.15
Bukoba
0 MILES 7
Germans withdraw

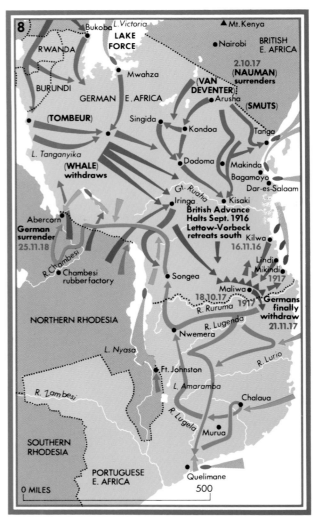

8
Bukoba L. Victoria ▲Mt. Kenya
LAKE FORCE Nairobi BRITISH E. AFRICA
RWANDA Mwahza
BURUNDI GERMAN E. AFRICA 2.10.17 (NAUMAN) surrenders
(VAN DEVENTER) Arusha (SMUTS)
(TOMBEUR) Singida Kondoa Tanga
L. Tanganyika Dodoma Makinda
(WHALE) withdraws Bagamoyo
Gt. Ruaha Dar-es-Salaam
Iringa Kisaki
Abercorn British Advance Halts Sept. 1916 Lettow-Vorbeck retreats south Kilwa
German surrender 25.11.18 16.11.16
R. Chambesi Chambesi rubber factory Songea Lindi Mikindi 1917
NORTHERN RHODESIA 18.10.17 1917
R. Ruruma Maliwa Germans finally withdraw 21.11.17
Nwemera R. Lugenda
L. Nyasa R. Lurio
R. Zambesi Ft. Johnston L. Amaramba Chalaua
SOUTHERN RHODESIA R. Lugela
Murua
PORTUGUESE E. AFRICA Quelimane
0 MILES 500

212

merely led him into a hopeless position, a defensive blind alley. Several sources including Ludendorff have recorded that as German reinforcements arrived at the front, those whom they replaced abused them with catcalls and cries of 'Blacklegs, you're prolonging the war!' It was a far cry from the glorious and unsullied days of the summer of 1914.

Influenza

One of the most self-evident observations concerning the First World War is that it is a tale of unrelieved military casualties. Less well known is the fact that, even as the war was drawing to a close at last, a worldwide influenza pandemic infected and in many cases killed countless civilians and soldiers alike. Indeed, it is thought that at least twenty-seven million people died of virulent influenza in 1918–19; and in India alone, deaths from the flu exceeded the total casualty lists for 1914–18.

The great influenza pandemic may have originated in Spain or France in early 1918; other theories hold that *la grippe* began its journey of devastation in places as far apart as China and Kansas. Possibly the disease had been germinating in several areas simultaneously, and rose to epidemic proportions when the deprivations of war had caused a widespread decline in health. Certainly the pandemic found a comfortable breeding-ground in the unsanitary trenches of northern France and the crowded metropolises of Europe, Asia, and America.

The course of the disease ran approximately from the spring of 1918 until the following year, reaching its height in the last autumn of the war. In its wake the influenza carried complications such as pneumonia, and its debilitating effects led or contributed to tuberculosis, heart disease, miscarriages and other complaints; thus the true total of its casualties is impossible to estimate. Everywhere a large percentage of the population contracted the illness; at least twenty million in the United States alone.

Countless pathetic tales of misery accumulated as the pandemic took its course. ANZAC troops in Britain were decimated by its effects, and special cemeteries on Salisbury Plain were laid out to accommodate the fatalities. In the second and most severe wave of the 'flu, six to eight per cent of the population was wiped out.

Perhaps the most saddening aspect of the pandemic was its high incidence among youth.

Right: A captured German tank, Elfriede. The first major tank battles took place during the spring and summer of 1918. **Far right:** Americans move through Chateau-Thierry.

Left: A contemporary painting shows horses killed by battery fire. Millions of animals were slaughtered on all fronts during the course of the war.

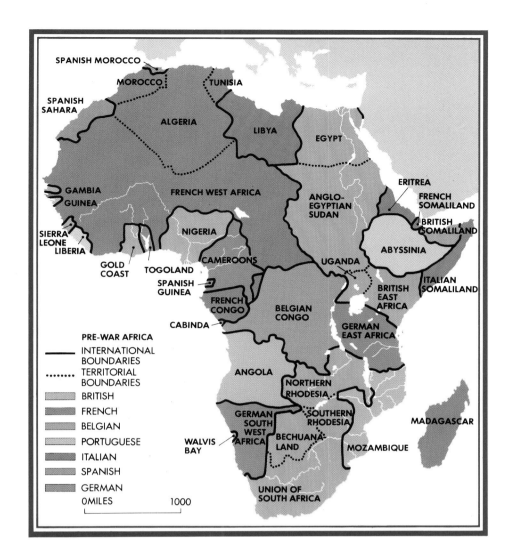

SPANISH MOROCCO
MOROCCO
TUNISIA
SPANISH SAHARA
ALGERIA
LIBYA
EGYPT
GAMBIA
GUINEA
FRENCH WEST AFRICA
ANGLO-EGYPTIAN SUDAN
ERITREA
FRENCH SOMALILAND
SIERRA LEONE
LIBERIA
NIGERIA
BRITISH SOMALILAND
GOLD COAST
TOGOLAND
CAMEROONS
UGANDA
ABYSSINIA
SPANISH GUINEA
FRENCH CONGO
BELGIAN CONGO
BRITISH EAST AFRICA
ITALIAN SOMALILAND
CABINDA
GERMAN EAST AFRICA
ANGOLA
NORTHERN RHODESIA
GERMAN SOUTH WEST AFRICA
SOUTHERN RHODESIA
MADAGASCAR
WALVIS BAY
BECHUANA-LAND
MOZAMBIQUE
UNION OF SOUTH AFRICA

PRE-WAR AFRICA
INTERNATIONAL BOUNDARIES
TERRITORIAL BOUNDARIES
BRITISH
FRENCH
BELGIAN
PORTUGUESE
ITALIAN
SPANISH
GERMAN
0 MILES   1000

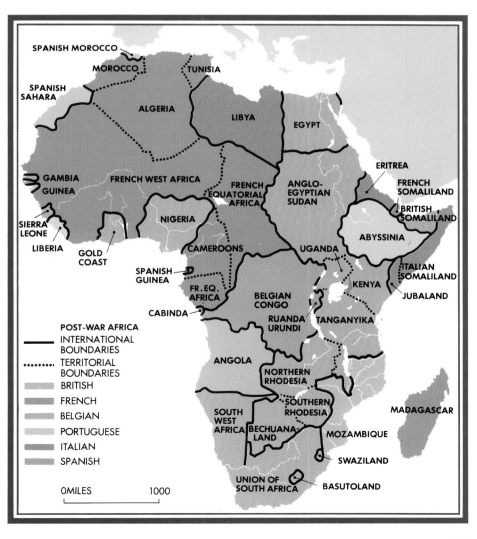

SPANISH MOROCCO
MOROCCO
TUNISIA
SPANISH SAHARA
ALGERIA
LIBYA
EGYPT
GAMBIA
GUINEA
FRENCH WEST AFRICA
FRENCH EQUATORIAL AFRICA
ANGLO-EGYPTIAN SUDAN
ERITREA
FRENCH SOMALILAND
SIERRA LEONE
LIBERIA
NIGERIA
BRITISH SOMALILAND
GOLD COAST
CAMEROONS
UGANDA
ABYSSINIA
SPANISH GUINEA
FR. EQ. AFRICA
ITALIAN SOMALILAND
CABINDA
BELGIAN CONGO
KENYA
JUBALAND
RUANDA URUNDI
TANGANYIKA
ANGOLA
NORTHERN RHODESIA
SOUTH WEST AFRICA
SOUTHERN RHODESIA
MADAGASCAR
BECHUANA-LAND
MOZAMBIQUE
SWAZILAND
UNION OF SOUTH AFRICA
BASUTOLAND

POST-WAR AFRICA
INTERNATIONAL BOUNDARIES
TERRITORIAL BOUNDARIES
BRITISH
FRENCH
BELGIAN
PORTUGUESE
ITALIAN
SPANISH
0 MILES   1000

The flower of European manhood had already been killed or maimed at the battlefront; now, on top of this 45 per cent of influenza fatalities occurred among the 15–35 age group. One doctor commented fatalistically: 'The disease simply had its way. It came like a thief in the night and stole treasure.' It was an undeserved end to more than four years of worldwide suffering and carnage.

The German Colonies

As mentioned earlier in this narrative, in the course of the World War, the German colonies in Africa and the Pacific fell to the Allies. Though the final fate of these possessions was not yet to be determined, the Entente quickly saw the necessity for eliminating the excellent German naval and communications bases; besides, Britain, France, and Japan in particular coveted several of these colonies for themselves.

In Africa, the German colony of Togoland fell to a combined Anglo-French attack in the first few weeks of the war. The Allied objective, the destruction of the radio communications complex at Kamina, was quickly achieved.

Kamerun (the Cameroons) was considerably harder to capture. In early September 1914, the British attacking mission failed completely, and though an amphibious Anglo-French expedition met with some success, it was hampered by difficult terrain and intense heat. Eventually, in February 1916, the last of the German opposition was worn down, and, as in Togoland, a joint British-French administration was set up.

Farther south lay the large colony of German Southwest Africa. Besides its mineral resources, the territory was important for the radio station at the capital of Windhoek. South African troops bore responsibility for operations in this theatre, but the project was impeded by disaffection on the part of two South African military leaders. In January 1915, however, operations recommenced, and by July South Africa was in control of its northwestern neighbour.

To the east lay the largest and richest of Germany's colonies: Tanganyika or German East Africa. Here the Allied forces encountered their most determined colonial opposition under the leadership of the legendary Lieutenant Colonel (later Major General) Paul von Lettow-Vorbeck. By a combination of wiliness and military skill, Lettow-Vorbeck held out against his opponents throughout the war. By this means he bottled up 300,000 Allied troops who were needed elsewhere. Only on 25 November 1918 did Lettow-Vorbeck accept the *fait accompli* of the armistice.

In the Far East Kiaochow and the German Pacific Islands, including the Carolines and the Marshalls, fell to various Allied forces, among them troops of Japan, Australia, and New Zealand.

After the war, when the Treaty of Versailles deprived Germany of her former colonies, France and Great Britain reached an arrangement over division of the Togoland and Cameroons mandates. Britain also received Tanganyika, Belgium gained Ruanda and Urundi, while South Africa retained control of Southwest Africa; and the Pacific Islands were divided by the equator between Japan in the north and Australia and New Zealand to the south.

Right: Thousands of German prisoners were taken after the 'Black Day'.

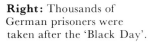

CHAPTER FOURTEEN

The Bitter End:
The Central Powers Cave In

In addition to the Mesopotamia campaign described earlier in this narrative, important operations also took place elsewhere in the Middle East, notably in Egypt and Palestine.

In December 1914 Britain had proclaimed a protectorate over Egypt, which in theory had previously been under Turkish suzerainty. London had gained a wide degree of political manoeuvre by deposing the Khedive, Abbas II Hilmi, and replacing him by his more moderate uncle, Sultan (later King) Husain Kamil. During 1915 the British took further steps to extend their influence in this strategically and geopolitically vital region by concluding agreements with the Sharif of Mecca and with Ibn Saud, whom London now recognized as ruler of Nejd. Having established this wide sphere of influence, however, London thought it advisable to compensate its Entente allies. Accordingly, in May 1916, the Sykes-Picot Agreement recognized Russian claims to the border territories of Turkish Armenia and northern Kurdistan, and French pre-eminence in western Syria and the Lebanon to the Damascus-Homs-Hama-Aleppo line. Britain was to be pre-eminent in the coastal region of Palestine and in the Mesopotamian areas of Basra and Baghdad. An intermediate zone was to be divided into a French sphere in northern Syria and the rest of Mesopotamia, and a British sphere in the rest of Arabia and what is today Jordan.

These power political arrangements were extremely difficult to reconcile with London's previous commitments to the Sharif of Mecca. To some extent the British negotiators on the spot may have exceeded their brief from Whitehall, given the wish of many for a vast British Arab Empire.

The Sykes-Picot Agreement contained one source of particular controversy. It was decided that the province of Jerusalem should be under international administration. Not only was this considered a useful buffer between two potentially predatory allies, London and Paris; the British were also influenced by the fundamentalist religious veneration of the Holy Land common to Lloyd George, Balfour, Smuts and others; a wish to place the region holy to Judaism, Islam, and Christianity alike in a special category; and the Zionist sympathies of several influential men in British life.

By early 1917, however, the new government of Lloyd George had become increasingly dissatisfied with the future of British interests in Palestine as defined by the Sykes-Picot agreement.

The movement to establish a Jewish homeland in Palestine had been gaining in strength since the Russian pogroms of the 1880s, and at this point Chaim Weizmann, a brilliant chemist and states-man-diplomat who later became first president of Israel, took up the cause of Zionism in Britain. He produced telling arguments that a favourable British attitude would influence American Jewish sentiment in a pro-Allied direction. In addition, the time for Zionism was ripe in 1917.

The British campaign in Palestine was moving to a climax, and on 2 November 1917, Arthur Balfour, British foreign secretary, wrote a letter subsequently known as the Balfour Declaration, to the president of the British Zionist Federation, Lord Rothschild, stating that:

'His Majesty's Government views with favour the establishment in Palestine of a national home for the Jewish people, and will use their best endeavours to facilitate the achievement of this object, it being clearly understood that nothing shall be done which may prejudice the civil and religious rights of existing non-Jewish communities in Palestine, or the rights and political status enjoyed by Jews in any other country.'

As a result of this policy, when Britain was granted a mandate over Palestine in the postwar peace settlement, Jewish emigration proceeded apace. Later, even when the British washed their hands of the matter and the Arabs looked on with hostility, The Jews continued to stream back to their ancient home, to emerge at last as a sovereign nation.

The campaign in Egypt and Palestine opened early in the war. In February 1915 a Turkish force of 20,000 under the German Colonel (subsequently General) Baron Kress von Kressenstein attacked the Suez Canal, the vital lifeline of the British Empire, after a march across the Sinai Peninsula. Fire from British and French warships foiled the Turks' attempt to cross the canal itself, though the British were as yet unable to follow the enemy's retreat because of lack of sufficient camel transports and fears that an insufficiently planned attack would result in a reverse, which would lower British prestige throughout Islam. In any event, the Turks had shown that a large number of troops could cross the practically waterless Sinai despite the obstacles.

Fears that the failure of the Allied campaign at Gallipoli would leave Egypt increasingly vulnerable were widely entertained, though they proved exaggerated. In 1915 and 1916, however, the British were harassed by raids on the part of the

Opposite: British transport crossing the Sakultutan Pass, December 1917.

Chaim Weizmann at a banquet of the Zionist Commission in Palestine.

Advanced headquarters of the 1st Corps and the 7th Division among captured trenches on the Palestine Front. On the left is Captain Kermit Roosevelt, the son of Teddy, who later joined the American army in France.

wandering Senussi sect. Perhaps the most important effect of this was that Kitchener worried over the Senussi revolt to the point of pre-occupation. Eventually, nonetheless, the tribal uprising was put down.

The western border of Egypt thus secured, the British were free to advance across Sinai into Palestine. It was hoped thereby that the Arab revolt initiated under the Hashemite Sharif Husain in the Hejaz would spread, and that Husain's bid for independence would be backed by an advance on the Hejaz Railway. On 10 June 1916, although Mecca, the Muslim holy city, was captured, Feisal, one of Husain's sons, failed in his attempt to take the venerated city of Medina, which was also the chief Turkish garrison.

As the British advanced, Kress and his Turkish forces once more gave trouble, but in spite of this by 9 January 1917 the British forces had reached Rafah, on the then Palestine-Egyptian frontier. Now they prepared to attack Gaza, the historic gateway into Palestine itself. In March British Empire forces under Lieutenant General Sir Archibald Murray's deputy, Major General Sir Charles Dobell, were committed against the Turkish garrison town. In this as in other desert campaigns, water supply was a major problem, and access to the wells of Gaza thus became vital.

On 26 March, in thick sea-fog, the British surrounded Gaza. The later progress of the fight for the town was marred by much bungling. A ridge south of Gaza itself, captured at high cost, was abandoned by mistake. Other errors abounded. A second attack in mid-April failed completely, and because of the latter debacle, General Sir Edmund (later Viscount) 'the Bull' Allenby replaced Murray as commander of forces in the area. Allenby, the ebullient hero of Arras, soon raised the flagging British morale, and with his reinforced divisions planned to attack along the Turkish fortified areas extending from Beersheba, a railhead and gateway to what is now the Negev Desert, to Gaza and the coast. A seaborne landing was considered unsuitable because of the unfriendly coastal terrain and the turbulence of the waters just offshore; in any case, losses elsewhere from German U-boats meant that ships could not be spared for such a task.

The Gaza operation went unexpectedly well for the British. It was notable for the eight tanks used, the only ones thus employed outside the Western Front during the war. Beersheba fell on the first

day of fighting to mounted Australians with bayonets drawn. For some reason the defending Turks failed to destroy Beersheba's wells, which they might have known were indispensable to their enemy. After the fall of Gaza on 7 November, Allenby struck north, his forces reaching the middle of the Palestinian coast on 16 November, where they occupied the important town of Jaffa.

Next Allenby moved eastwards into the Judaean Hills, the time-honoured protectors of Jerusalem. There he ran into considerable opposition from troops under Falkenhayn. Despite all setbacks, the British superiority in strength proved itself. After assaults around Nebi-Samweil (Samuel) to the northwest and Bethlehem to the south, Jerusalem received the latest of its conquerors on 9 December. In this, Allenby was fulfilling the Prime Minister's wish of having 'Jerusalem as a Christmas present to the British nation', one which Lloyd George calculated would impress other belligerents and neutrals alike.

As he entered Jerusalem, Allenby surrendered to the invisible and enchanted spell which surrounds the Holy City. He had tried his best to direct fighting away from Jerusalem's priceless treasures of three faiths. The conquering general entered the Holy Land's eternal capital on foot, for Lloyd George had particularly instructed that Jerusalem be occupied with reverent if impressive humility. At the end of December Falkenhayn made a costly attempt to retake the city, but he was unsuccessful.

Soon afterwards Lloyd George urged a blow that would drive Turkey to sue for peace, believing that this could be done by means of the Palestine campaign. Yet Allenby and his advisers doubted that Turkey would capitulate without a German cave-in in the West.

Early in 1918 considerable flooding caused a hitch in Allenby's plans. By March, however, he was able to move against Amman, later the capital of Transjordan and subsequently Jordan, where his objective was the destruction of the Hejaz Railway. Yet lack of sufficient striking strength vitiated the project, and a further attack on 11 April was beaten off by the enemy. Now, despite Lloyd George's hopes, more than 60,000 British Empire troops had to be recalled from Palestine to meet the needs of the Western Front, where the German spring offensive was under way. In the meantime the Turkish troops, in contrast to British soldiers, became increasingly ragged and laid low by typhus and malaria. In Constantinople, Enver and his Young Turk party had completely lost interest in Palestine because of the opportunities for Pan-Turanian aggrandizement which the Brest-Litovsk settlement had provided.

The next major battle in Palestine was that at Megiddo, not far from Haifa, on 19 September. Allenby's planned 'battle of annihilation' was given an eerie quality by being staged on the site of the Biblical Armageddon, where according to Revelations 16:16 armies from all five continents would foregather at the end of the world in an apocalyptic clash. Once Megiddo had fallen, the British struck out across the Plain of Esdraelon and the Jezreel Valley to the River Jordan, while other British troops took Nazareth and almost captured the German commander, Liman von Sanders, who had replaced Falkenhayn in March 1918.

The Turks had for a long while been harassed

Turkish machine-gunners strike back in Palestine.

223

Left: Lawrence of Arabia. **Bottom left:** General Allenby enters Jerusalem, December 1917. **Right:** The charge of El Maghar before the fall of Jerusalem.

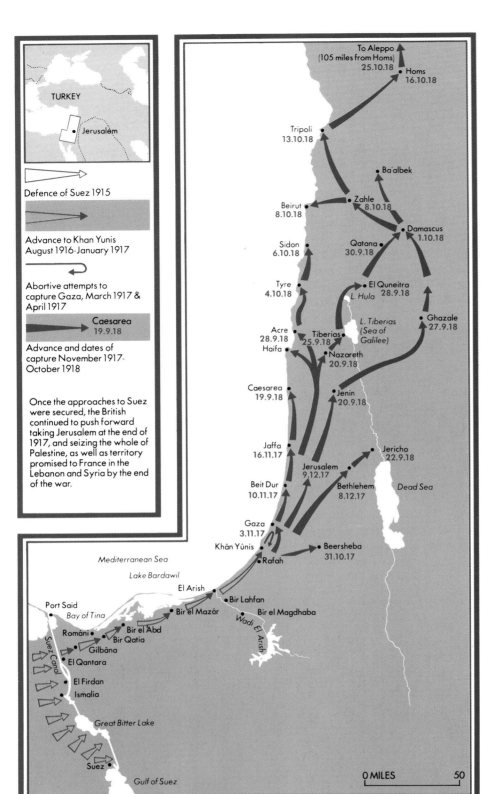

TURKEY

Jerusalem

Defence of Suez 1915

Advance to Khan Yunis August 1916-January 1917

Abortive attempts to capture Gaza, March 1917 & April 1917

Caesarea 19.9.18

Advance and dates of capture November 1917-October 1918

Once the approaches to Suez were secured, the British continued to push forward taking Jerusalem at the end of 1917, and seizing the whole of Palestine, as well as territory promised to France in the Lebanon and Syria by the end of the war.

To Aleppo (105 miles from Homs) 25.10.18

Homs 16.10.18

Tripoli 13.10.18

Ba'albek

Zahle 8.10.18

Beirut 8.10.18

Damascus 1.10.18

Sidon 6.10.18

Qatana 30.9.18

Tyre 4.10.18

El Quneitra 28.9.18

L. Hula

Ghazale 27.9.18

L. Tiberias (Sea of Galilee)

Acre 28.9.18

Tiberias 25.9.18

Haifa

Nazareth 20.9.18

Caesarea 19.9.18

Jenin 20.9.18

Jaffa 16.11.17

Jericho 22.9.18

Jerusalem 9.12.17

Beit Dur 10.11.17

Bethlehem 8.12.17

Dead Sea

Gaza 3.11.17

Khân Yûnis

Beersheba 31.10.17

Rafah

Mediterranean Sea

Lake Bardawil

El Arish

Port Said
Bay of Tina

Bir Lahfan

Bir el Mazâr

Bir el Magdhaba

Români

Bir el Abd

Wadi El Arish

Bir Qatia

Gilbâna

Suez Canal

El Qantara

El Firdan

Ismalia

Great Bitter Lake

Suez

Gulf of Suez

0 MILES 50

by blows to their communications from forces under the legendary T. E. Lawrence. These included raids on the Hejaz Railway in order to disrupt the line and tie down as many Turks as possible to defend it. Lawrence's Arabs had also staged an important diversionary attack on Deraa, a major railway junction, prior to Megiddo.

By late September the destruction of the Turkish armies in Palestine proper was complete. Now, moving north into Syria, the victorious forces effortlessly captured Damascus on 1 October, and Homs fell some sixteen days later. Aleppo fell on 26 October. In any case the Ottomans' death knell had sounded with the collapse of Bulgaria on 30 September, for thenceforth the Turks were cut off from their German ally and became susceptible to Allied attacks on Turkey-in-Europe. On 30 October, at Mudros, an armistice with Turkey was reached. The Turkish campaign was over, at a cost of 92,500 British Empire battle casualties in Mesopotamia alone.

Collapse in the West

After 'Germany's Black Day' on 8 August, the German position, as we have seen, went from bad to worse. To the dispassionate onlooker, it was only a question of time before the Reich gave in. Indeed, among the Central Powers themselves, Emperor Karl of Austria-Hungary recognized this instinctively when he said that *Der Schwarze Tag* had disturbed Vienna far more than the earlier Austrian defeat on the Piave – for the latter had been expected; a major reversal for the mighty German Army was another matter. Yet Ludendorff's last hope was that he might stand behind the Hindenburg Line with its complex of trenches, tunnels, and wire-tangled obstacles to afford him a breathing-space.

At the same time American troops continued to arrive in France in droves; and soon the fresh-faced youths were given the task of reducing the Saint-Mihiel salient, which had been created four years earlier during the initial German offensive.

The United States First Army under General

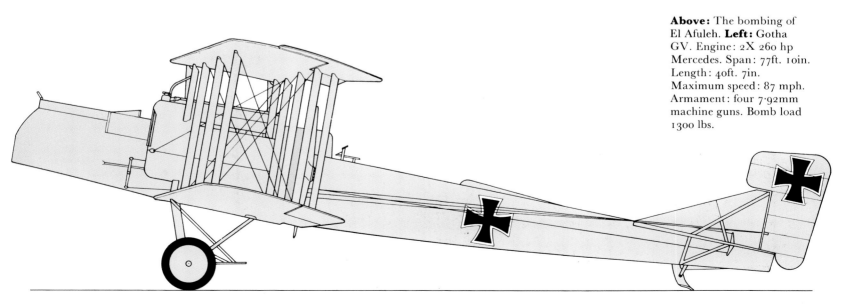

Above: The bombing of
El Afuleh. **Left:** Gotha
GV. Engine: 2X 260 hp
Mercedes. Span: 77ft. 10in.
Length: 40ft. 7in.
Maximum speed: 87 mph.
Armament: four 7·92mm
machine guns. Bomb load
1300 lbs.

John Pershing was quick to rise to the occasion. The importance of the operation was obvious, since the salient stood in the path of the main rail communications between Paris and the French eastern border. In addition, the area included important iron resources at Briey and Metz.

Although they did their best, by this time the Germans were too exhausted to defend Saint-Mihiel properly; in any case, as a defensive position it was valueless. Previous to the American attack on 12 September, Berlin had ordered a withdrawal from the salient and the removal of whatever heavy materials and equipment could be taken along. After a dispute between Foch and Pershing as to the details of deployment of the American forces, it was decided that the Saint-Mihiel operation would have the limited objective of taking the base of the salient, from which the Americans would move into the Meuse-Argonne region for the final offensive against Germany.

On 12 September the Battle of Saint-Mihiel began. The First Army under Pershing was joined by the French Second Colonial Corps and British, Italian and Portuguese units. While the Americans broke through from the south, the French struck repeated blows at the tip of the salient; and by the end of the second day the troops' mission had been accomplished in the face of patchy resistance. Luck was against the Germans, for the Allies had even been aided initially by fog. On 16 September the operation ended, the Allies having taken 15,000 prisoners and 450 guns at a cost of barely 7000 casualties.

By this time the British cabinet, hitherto dubious of Foch's view that the war could be ended in 1918, and remembering the disastrous effects of Haig's hyper-optimism at Passchendaele, was now won over by the continuing Allied run of successes. Even so, the cabinet warned Haig that further heavy British casualties 'would have grave effects' on public opinion, for British losses in the last three weeks of August alone had been about 115,000.

Now, as Foch once more took the offensive, he was anxious to prevent as far as possible an orderly German retreat and especially a 'scorched earth' policy with regard to communications – for if this occurred the resultant chaos would certainly delay an Allied victory. Thus Foch concentrated on capturing the vital railway junctions of Aulnoye and Mézières, for if these could be taken the German retreat might well degenerate into confusion. To gain this objective, Foch decided to deploy a mainly British force eastwards to Aulnoye, and a chiefly American force north to Mézières. It was considered easier to take Mézières than Metz, which was the strongest fortress in Europe.

The Allies were full of that confidence which flows from superiority in men and the scent of victory. Two hundred and twenty Allied divisions faced 197 German divisions, but whereas all the German units were under strength and only a quarter were effective fighting units, the 42 American units were at full strength and contained twice the infantry of other divisions.

Under the rallying-cry *Tout le monde à la bataille* ('Everyone in the fight'), the Allied advance to the Rhine began on 26 September, when Pershing's

Left: On the road to Damascus. The Allied conquest of Syria was a walk-over. **Right:** American troops move in caution near St. Mihiel. **Far right:** US phosphorous bombs in action. **Below:** One of Lawrence's Arab patrols on the march.

Left: A sixty-pounder in a barrage at dawn. Right: Mule just hit by a shell splinter. Opposite left: German flame-throwers could only stop the tanks temporarily. Opposite right: A 340mm rail gun in action. Rail guns were one of the most destructively powerful and mobile weapons of the war. Opposite bottom: An advanced dressing station near Cambrai.

Below: A French truck brings back wounded.

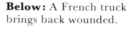

First Army drove towards Mézières. Next day the British First and Third Armies entered the affray and pushed towards Aulnoye. Further British and French units came in on the twenty-ninth, while the previous day the Belgian armies thrust towards Ghent. A massive and co-ordinated Allied drive was under way, to the accompaniment of the feeling that soon, despite the misery of succeeding years, all would once again be well.

The final Allied offensive can be classified into four groupings: the operation in Flanders, that in Cambrai-Saint-Quentin (western pincers movement), that of the French centre sector, and the Meuse-Argonne (southern pincers) operation. The first part of this plan was effected by the end of October; the second in the first eleven days of November.

In the Meuse-Argonne sector the American First and French Fourth Armies, the latter commanded by General Gouraud, went into action after a mass northward movement of 500,000 men fifty miles from Saint-Mihiel had been carried out smoothly. The Germans had taken care to fortify the region with innumerable strong defences in depth. An additional defensive protection was the Argonne Forest itself.

The initial Franco-American penetration was quite successful, though in places the advance bogged down amid strong German resistance characterized by merciless bursts of machine-gun fire from snipers in thickets. The Allies were further delayed by the terrain, scarred and pitted as it was from previous battles. Thus the operation became increasingly difficult and costly as October wore on, and the Americans were cramped by their hasty preparations, difficulties in communications, and by sheer congestion from their own numbers of troops in the field. However, an offensive on the Méuse by Bullard's American Second Army was helpful, and at the end of the month the Argonne Forest had been cleared and the French had pushed forward to the Aisne.

On the Cambrai-Saint-Quentin front the British and French were faced with overcoming a series of strong defensive positions in the path of their objective, Aulnoye. For example, there existed deep canal entrenchments which could

not be bridged by tanks, in addition to mazes of barbed wire cluttered about the region. Yet, even though the Anglo-French attacks were slower than anticipated, by the twenty-eighth the German lines had broken. At this point Ludendorff, his nerve collapsing, advised Hindenburg that Germany had definitely lost the war. As he pointed out, even if the Western Front held by some miracle, the Bulgarian collapse had made possible an eventual Entente invasion from the southeast. Thus Hindenburg had to tell Berlin that 'an immediate armistice' was necessary 'in order to avert a catastrophe', and on 4 October Berlin and Vienna sent notes to President Wilson suggesting an armistice.

Ludendorff in particular seems to have held to a naïve and utterly misplaced faith in Wilson's willingness and ability to influence the Entente into peace negotiations on the basis of Wilson's Fourteen Points. (It appears that Ludendorff had never read these!) In any case, the new and more representative German government formed on 3 October with Prince Max of Baden as Chancellor was maintained only by the support of the Centre (men such as Erzberger), Progressives, and Majority Socialists (Scheidemann and others), all of whom were insisting on ending the war on practically any terms. Although Ludendorff raged that Germany's quagmire of troubles was all the fault of the Left, he was shrewd enough to ask the Kaiser to include in the new government 'those circles . . . to whom we owe chiefly our present position . . .'. The Left was thus to bear the onus of peace-making with Germany's unbending opponents; and in future this section of German political opinion was to be pilloried collectively as 'the November criminals'. The forces of reaction had nothing to lose, as it was obvious that the Allies would not negotiate with a militarist clique. Rather, Ludendorff and his coterie would bide their time, and await the aftermath of disillusionment with the peace settlement.

We must now return to the chronicle of military events. In the western pincers operation, an extensive artillery bombardment had been needed to weaken the German defences. In the Saint-Quentin sector, 25,000 tons of metal spewed

forth in the form of a million shells. A side effect was that supplies of food and ammunition to the German troops were interrupted, and among the inexperienced troops who were of necessity now being used, morale was wrecked. As the Allied forces swarmed across the Saint-Quentin Canal, the shattered Germans took to their heels; then the Allies pushed forward once again. Between 27 September and 9 October, a desperate battle ensued for Cambrai, and by the latter date the Germans had been driven from the town. The Hindenburg Line cracked definitively on 5 October, and Ludendorff hastily fell back to the Selle River.

From 17–20 October the British and French attacked the new German lines, but met the kind of stubborn resistance put up by a cornered animal. Despite this, the Germans were overcome and the Allied drive moved inexorably forward.

In Flanders the Belgian offensive, commanded by King Albert, opened in pouring rain; yet despite the hampering effect on communications, Ypres Ridge had fallen by 1 October. Moreover, Ludendorff had had to withdraw large numbers of troops from the area because they were needed more desperately further south, and by the end of the month King Albert's forces stood on the Schelde. Belgian revenge for the humiliation of 1914 was at hand.

In the French centre sector, the main objective was passive: the prevention of German withdrawal to the remaining fronts. All went rather well, and the close of October saw the Germans losing everywhere. By now German morale was at vanishing point, for besides the collapse of the other Central Powers, Germany herself was in turmoil. On 3 November sections of the fleet mutinied at Kiel. Meanwhile workers' uprisings broke out in a number of places, in the hope that if the war were ended by revolutionary upheaval, some kind of socialist democracy would be established. At the same time the Establishment propaganda machine continued to acclaim German retreats as withdrawals to improved defences, though Ludendorff, of course, knew the stark truth. He had decided that his best course

Left: An American company moves up for the kill. **Above:** Men of the 20th Manchesters resting by tank which slipped down a railway embankment near Cambrai.

231

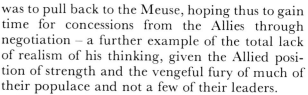

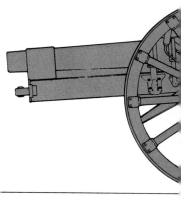

was to pull back to the Meuse, hoping thus to gain time for concessions from the Allies through negotiation – a further example of the total lack of realism of his thinking, given the Allied position of strength and the vengeful fury of much of their populace and not a few of their leaders.

In the meantime, by 12 October Berlin had been driven by its dire circumstances to accept that the detailed meaning and interpretation of the Fourteen Points as a basis for an armistice was to be left to the enemy. On 14 October, after a German submarine had sunk the *Leinster* with the loss of four hundred aboard, Wilson sent a fierce note to Berlin railing against German 'acts of inhumanity, spoilation and desolation'. In desperation to secure some kind of settlement before internal social revolution got out of hand completely, on 20 October Berlin assured Wilson

that Germany had rid herself of that 'arbitrary power' against which the American president had preached.

On 25 October Ludendorff suddenly decided that conciliation had gone too far. He denounced the negotiations with America as taking place in intolerable conditions. The only result was that next day he was replaced by Gröner. Then, on 27 October, came news that Vienna intended to sue for peace. It seemed that Germany's position was now hopeless enough for her to take what terms she could get. As Scheidemann of the MSPD (Majority Socialists) put it: 'Better a terrible end than terror without end.' However, this cut both ways, for the slogan was also used by those who called for a *Götterdämmerung*-like apocalypse rather than submission to dishonourable defeat.

By now the decline in morale and the resent-

Opposite top: British awaiting attack. Opposite centre: Attack on the Aisne. Left: The German Crown Prince flees from Germany on a Dutch steamer: 10th November 1918. Below: Armistice 1918.

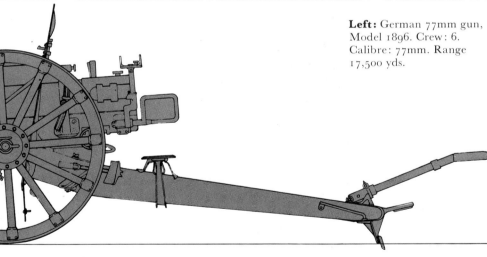

Left: German 77mm gun, Model 1896. Crew: 6. Calibre: 77mm. Range 17,500 yds.

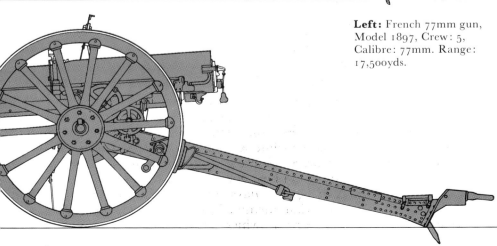

Left: French 77mm gun, Model 1897, Crew: 5, Calibre: 77mm. Range: 17,500yds.

ment of the German population against continued fighting had reached their peak. The Kaiser became a scapegoat for the general feeling of impotent fury at the course of events, and the feeling grew that only by ridding themselves of the Kaiser and his concomitant autocracy could the German people hope for justice at Allied hands. In consequence, on 9 November Wilhelm II was forced to abdicate, though he signed the formal instrument of abdication only in exile on the twenty-eighth, and Prince Max was succeeded as Chancellor by Friedrich Ebert, the SPD leader. Thus the son of a saddler presided over the demise of the Hohenzollern dynasty. At 2:00 p.m. on the ninth a republic was proclaimed. On the advice of Hindenburg, next day the ex-Kaiser slipped away to refuge in neutral Holland, to the chagrin of the many among the Allies who wanted to try Wilhelm II as a war criminal.

In the meantime the last phase of the Allied offensive had swung into operation. It was marked by an American and French push to the Meuse and the Mézières-Sedan positions, by 7 and 10 November respectively. In the west, British forces attacked south of Valenciennes, seeking to break the Germans on the Schelde. After fierce fighting the Germans caved in; indeed, their collapse soon spread throughout the line. Just before the armistice of 11 November, Canadian forces reoccupied Mons, the scene of so much action in 1914.

Armistice 1918

The armistice with Germany had not been easy to arrange. The Allies had objected to peace with Berlin on the basis of the Fourteen Points, in the formulation of which they had not been consulted, and the meaning of which was unclear and confusing in several places. Colonel House finally provided an authoritative commentary on the meaning of Wilson's declaration, and at length the Allies agreed to the Fourteen Points as a basis of negotiation subject to two reservations: Point 2, relating to freedom of the seas, 'is open to various interpretations, some of which they could not accept.' Thus the Allies, led in this instance by Lloyd George, reserved to themselves 'complete freedom' of action in this regard. Moreover, they argued that the clauses dealing with the restoration of the territories which Germany had invaded must be interpreted to mean that Germany would pay compensation for damage to Allied civilians and their property.

After much additional haggling over details, the armistice terms were prepared and made ready for signature. On the evening of 7 November Matthias Erzberger, the German Secretary of State, arrived at Marshal Foch's headquarters at Rethondes in the forest of Compiègne to sign for Germany. Accompanying him were Count von Oberndorff, Major General von Winterfeldt, and Captain Vanselow of the German Navy. The Allied signatories were to be Foch and Admiral Sir Rosslyn Wemsyss, the British First Sea Lord.

As he faced the German delegation, Foch was at his most adamant. Quickly he intimated that he would not argue about terms. As he stated baldly: 'Do you ask for an armistice? If so I will make known to you the conditions on which it may be

Above: The German navy, now in Allied hands, enters Scapa Flow. **Above right:** The High Seas Fleet, like the battleship *Bayern* here, was scuttled by the Germans in 1919. They preffered to destroy their navy rather than to let it fall permanently into Allied hands. **Opposite top left:** Captured Italians on the Piave. **Opposite top centre:** German troops cross the Rhine at Koblenz after the Armistice. **Opposite top right:** British tanks and troops follow them into Cologne to begin a long occupation. **Opposite bottom:** The Bulgarians surrendered early . . . in September.

obtained.' Then, in reply to a formal German request, General Weygand, Foch's Chief of Staff, read out the armistice terms. The Germans were to have seventy-two hours in which to accept or reject them. Erzberger wanted fighting to cease immediately because, he explained, continued chaos in Germany would merely feed the appetites of Bolshevism. Foch refused. He also rejected Germany's request that the Allied blockade be raised, while the promise nevertheless to allow Germany supplies was very badly kept until the following spring, when goods arrived in quantity after the vehement humanitarian protests of the British General Plumer.

At 4:05 a.m. on 11 November, Germany signed an armistice which the Allies thought would render impossible further hostilities even after a period of retrenchment. Erzberger said that some parts of the agreement were impracticable, and stated, 'A nation of seventy millions suffers but does not die.' Foch replied curtly and enigmatically: '*Très bien.*'

At 11:00 a.m. a general cease-fire was sounded. The Great War was over. Ahead lay a peace settlement which in its bungling satisfied none of the Great Powers fully, and was eventually to result in World War II.

Among the main terms of the armistice were the following:

1. Germany was to evacuate immediately all occupied territory, Alsace-Lorraine included. All German troops were to withdraw behind the frontiers of 1 August 1914. Allied troops were to enter the territory thus evacuated without hindrance.

2. The left (west) bank of the Rhine was to be evacuated by German military forces. The Mainz, Coblenz, and Cologne bridgeheads were to be handed over to Allied troops. A neutral zone was to be established on the right (east) bank.

3. Vast quantities of matériel were to be surrendered to the Allies.

4. All Allied prisoners were to be repatriated, without immediate Allied reciprocity with regard to German prisoners.

5. All German submarines were to be surrendered; but the Allied blockade would continue.

6. 'Annulment of the treaties of Bucharest and Brest-Litovsk and of the supplementary treaties.'

7. 'Reparation for damage done.' Details included the return of securities or valuables removed from the invaded territories, and 'restitution of the Russian and Rumanian gold yielded to Germany or taken by that power. This gold to be delivered in trust to the Allies until peace is concluded.'

On 1 December Allied occupation forces entered Germany itself, thus initiating a presence which was to last until 1930. By this time the German Army had concocted a number of excuses to shift the blame for defeat away from itself. At first it was said that Germany had asked for an armistice in order to free its civilians from the starvation due to the Allied blockade, and in order to end the endless bloodletting of the battlefield. Later, however, the main emphasis shifted to a sinister tale that betrayal and double-dealing at home had undermined Germany from within – the 'stab-in-the-back' theory.

In truth Germany surrendered and accepted the onerous armistice terms because she had reached the end of her tether. Revolutionary ferment at home would soon rapidly have overcome even those troops at the front who would have been willing to fight on. Probably from the purely military point of view, Germany could have held out until the spring of 1919, for even with American participation the Allies were in no condition to advance indefinitely. Yet everywhere among the Central Powers food and petrol were running out – and if an army travels on its stomach, it also travels on wheels. Thus Germany held out until she could do so no longer. Then she gave in after a tremendous battle of endurance. Ironically, however, it was probably this ability to endure the unendurable, coupled with the absence of actual large-scale fighting and destruction on German soil itself, which fed the legends of Germany's betrayal by others and which shortened her collective memory to allow another world war to break out within a generation.

Victory in Italy

We noted earlier the paradox that the Italian defeat at Caporetto in late 1917 pulled the nation together as no other event throughout the war had done. This was fortunate, for the following spring, the involvement of the rival belligerents on the Western Front made it necessary for each to ask his ally to stage a diversion in and around northern Italy. Germany hoped that, if an Austrian offensive could knock Italy out of the war, Vienna's troops could be brought to bear on the West before the Americans arrived to shore up the enemy. Foch, guessing Austria's intentions, asked Italy to strike first. However, Diaz, the Italian supremo, thought the idea inadvisable; but to mollify the French he sent two Italian divisions to the west.

Meanwhile Austria proceeded with her plans. Conrad was brought to command on the Trentino, and Boroević on the Piave. After a diversion lasting two days, on 15 June 1918 the main Austrian offensive began. Conrad's forces at first made gains, which nonetheless were reversed the

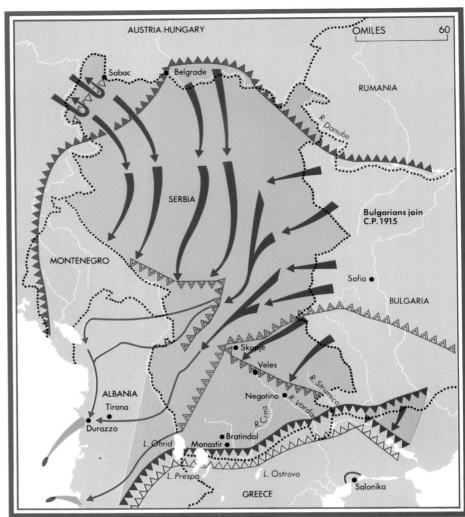

AUSTRIA-HUNGARY

RUMANIA

Sabac • Belgrade

SERBIA

R. Danube

Bulgarians join
C.P. 1915

MONTENEGRO

Sofia •

BULGARIA

Skopje •

Veles •

R. Strumica

ALBANIA

Tirana •

Negotino •

R. Vardar

R. Crna

Durazzo •

L. Ohrid   Monastir •   • Bratindol

L. Prespa   L. Ostrovo

GREECE   Salonika

Abortive Austro-Hungarian
attempts to invade Serbia
September-December 1914.

Successful invasion of Serbia
1915. Serbian retreat and
evacuation to Corfu.

Front lines established after
invasion. Situation of virtual
stalemate. Main actions fought
on these lines:
Salonika offensive 1916;
Sarrail's Spring offensive 1917.

D'Esperey's summer offensive
1918.

Line reached by 30 September.

Line reached by 11 November –
when peace was declared.

next day. Boroević also achieved some successes, but the battle as a whole failed because of difficulties of communications in the region, personality differences between the two Habsburg commanders, and the excellence of the Italian defence. By 24 June Boroević's forces had once more retreated behind the Piave; but Diaz still refused to take Foch's advice and fall upon the tired-out Austrians, for his own armies were in no fit state to do so at present, and he preferred to bide his time until his men were stronger and better equipped and until reserves were in greater supply. In addition, Diaz thought that the war would not be settled before the spring of 1919. Thus he could afford to wait for the propitious moment. Moreover, it was possible that now in desperation the Central Powers would throw their full weight against their weakest link – Italy.

Ludendorff-Spende für Kriegsbeschädigte

Right: Poster appealing for the Ludendorff Fund for War Wounded, which started in May 1918.

Events elsewhere, however, began to change this picture. In September 1918 Franchet d'Esperey took the offensive in Macedonia, and rapidly Bulgaria went under. On 26 September Sofia requested an armistice. Diaz was impressed, and when the major Central Powers, Germany and Austria-Hungary, themselves applied for an armistice on 4 October, the Italian supremo saw clearly that his country had better act swiftly, lest peace be concluded and the lack of a final Italian offensive be held against Rome at the conference table. Furthermore, the Italian Prime Minister, Orlando, now stepped in, urging Diaz by telegram, 'Act at once!'

Despite the dissenting voices of the Treasury Minister, Nitti, and others, the offensive became an increasingly obvious answer as October wore on and Austria-Hungary weakened. Still, the Habsburg commanders were determined to fight on, regardless of what was happening at home, in the hope that their forward positions at the conclusion of an armistice would favourably influence the peace settlement – a hope which proved utterly vain, but which filtered down to the Austrian troops and made their last defence a truly heroic one. At the same time Italian front-line forces, reserves and preparations for battle were still quite inadequate. Political considerations, however, now overrode military ones.

On 24 October the Italians went into action on the Grappa, their superiority in arms counterbalanced by their inferiority in numbers and by the Austrian dexterity in using their ample and deadly supply of machine-guns. A piece of extreme bad luck had also intervened: the sudden flooding of the Piave had delayed a coordinated thrust there, and for a few days the men of the Grappa operation were left on their own. The Austrian counterattack of 27–28 October was particularly bloody, but by the twenty-ninth action on the Grappa had deadlocked, and conditions on the Piave had by now become such as to enable bridges to be thrown across. So far, Italy had lost 24,000 fatalities or casualties; nearly 13,000 more Italians were to fall in the next few days.

On the Piave, after a mediocre start on 26 October, by the twenty-eighth the Italian Eighth Army under Caviglia was plunged into the midst of battle. Now the Austrian lines gave way under successive Italian hammerblows. The Habsburg armies were shattered, while at home efforts at peace moves had been following one upon

another in dizzying succession. On the night of 30–31 October the battle turned into a jumble of encounters in which Italians cut off, outfought, killed or captured series after series of Austrian pockets of resistance. By 3 November the Italians had landed at Trieste. In the evening an armistice was signed near Padua. The Battle of Vittorio Veneto (named for the site of the Austrian headquarters) found Italy triumphant, while Austria's last strength had drained away with the loss of 30,000 dead and wounded and of 500,000 men as prisoners.

A Raemaekers' cartoon of the Kaiser and the Crown Prince in their new role in Holland. They claimed they were visiting the Netherlands for 'an indefinite period'.

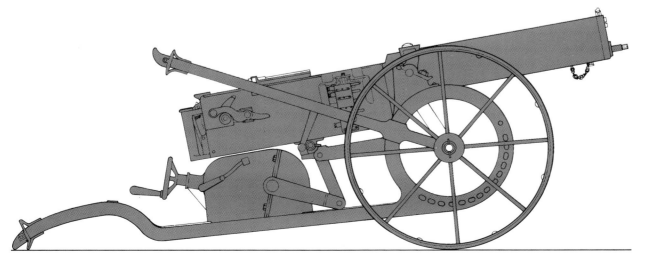

Maxim machine gun on infantry carriage. Crew: 4. Calibre: 7·92mm. Range: 3000 yds.

CHAPTER FIFTEEN
Versailles, The Tragic Peace

With the signing of the November armistice, it might have been thought that peace had come at last to the war-ravaged peoples of Europe and afar. For some, however, peace was not yet to be; indeed, at this very time, revolutionary turbulence was sweeping Germany and Hungary as part of the seismic shock engendered by the Central Powers' defeat while Moscow waited in the wings, gloating that the world revolution was imminent.

However, both the German and the Hungarian revolutions misfired. Their eventual successors were the liberal but in many respects ineffectual Weimar regime in Germany, and the reactionary regency of Miklos Horthy in Hungary, whom the break-up of the Habsburg Empire had left in the unenviable position of being an admiral without a seaport at his disposal. For a time half of Europe trembled on the brink of chaos or shook with fear in anticipation of the effects of the coming new order. Yet European institutions survived; the tidal wave passed. However, to a great degree the whole of the 1918–19 peacemaking process was carried out in the shadow of revolution and the consequent desire of the victors to shield themselves from its effects.

What were these spectres haunting Europe? As the fighting ended, they made themselves manifest. In Germany historians such as Imanuel Geiss have emphasized the paucity of long-term effects of the 'November Revolution', which from start to finish was an extraordinarily confused and hesitant affair. Yet the fears and hopes of large sections of the German people which accompanied the 'winter troubles' were real enough.

It cannot be said that the German breakdown or *Zusammenbruch* was caused by internal upheavals. Germany's collapse stemmed from her own exhaustion and that of her allies, and the strategic implications ensuing from the latter's military defeat. Most of the German people and the organized Left were either quite moderate in their political demands, or sought better social justice without reflecting unduly on the political changes that might be needed. Only in the last weeks of the conflict, when the realization that the war was lost suddenly sank home, did the German people turn against that Bismarckian system with which they had been more or less content as long as it was successful. As for their leaders, they were slow to comprehend the changed popular mood. Richard Watt, historian of the German Revolution of 1918–19, has written that in the end, 'The only people who did not yet understand that time had run out for the German Empire were those

who were directing it.' Geiss points out the additional paradox that 'those who wanted the revolution did not make it, while those who made it did not want it.'

We must look in closer detail at what this meant. On the far Left there was a hard core of radicals and Communists who aimed at the revolutionary overthrow of German society. Yet it appeared that the changes in Germany were being heralded by the Majority Socialists (MSPD), who were already part of the reconstructed German government and who desired only to work for social-democratic change peacefully and within the system. As their leader Friedrich Ebert is said to have told Prince Max of Baden: 'I hate the revolution like sin.' Had the Kaiser abdicated sooner, it is certain that many of these moderates would not have opposed continuance of the monarchy.

In early 1917 the German Socialists had split between a Right-Centre faction including Ebert and Scheidemann and a Left element (USPD) under Hugo Haase. This division greatly weakened the Socialists' effectiveness. The process was exacerbated at the end of 1918 when the ultra-Left element hived off from the USPD and formed the German Communist Party (KPD), led by Karl Liebknecht and one of history's most remarkable women, Rosa Luxemburg – 'the Red Rose', as she was called. Both of these had been active in the affairs of the *Spartakusbund* (Spartacist League), which had been founded earlier in the war in protest against Socialist cooperation in the 'war of imperialisms'. However, even Liebknecht and Luxemburg were prepared to work within the parliamentary system unless and until their larger plans bore fruit, though many of their followers were anarchists and political cranks of a motley variety who thirsted for permanent revolution as an end in itself.

The German 'November Revolution' was sparked off by the mutiny of the fleet at Kiel on 3 November. Thereafter events moved very swiftly under a kind of collective, directionless yet ephemerally powerful momentum. There was no organized plan for revolutionary take-over, which is not surprising considering that until 23 October Liebknecht had been in prison, and his out-and-out supporters numbered only a few hundred men and women in the country as a whole.

Once out of prison, Liebknecht busied himself with taking advantage of the disturbed situation. In Berlin he was acclaimed and was paraded through the streets in a carriage banked with

DER WAHLSTURM FEGT DURCH'S LAND!
BAYRISCH-WEISSBLAU
GEGEN RUSSISCH-ROT!
BAYERISCHE VOLKSPARTEI

WESTERN PACIFIC POSSESSIONS
PRE-WAR GERMAN
POST WAR BRITISH AUSTRALIAN NEW ZEALAND JAPANESE

CHINA
Kiaochow JAPAN Pacific Ocean
INDIA BURMA
SIAM FRENCH INDO CHINA Mariana Islands
Palau Is. Caroline Is. Marshall Islands
Malaya Kaiserwilhelmsland
Equator Nauru Bismark
DUTCH EAST INDIES PAPUA Solomon Is. Archipelago Samoa
New Hebrides
AUSTRALIA
Indian Ocean
NEW ZEALAND

BÚCSÚZTATÓ
HALOTTI ÉNEK AZ OSZTRÁK-MAGYAR MONARCHIA FELETT
IRTA: KARL KRAUS
FORDITOTTA: SZINI GYULA

KULTURA RT. UTK.KINTÉZETE BUDAPEST

KÁROLYI KÖNYVTÁR
„KULTURA" KIADÁSA

little to do with its inception. Nevertheless, by 4 November Kiel was in the hands of 4000 armed men, after which ferment spread to Hamburg, Bremen, Cologne and other cities. Then, on 7 November, the Left-Socialist Bavarian leader, Kurt Eisner, led a mass demonstration in Munich, which ended in an army mutiny at the local barracks. Eisner proclaimed a republic in place of the old Kingdom of Bavaria.

Soon Workers' and Soldiers' Councils gained control in a number of places, and by 9 November dominated Berlin itself. That day the Majority Socialists precipitated a cabinet crisis by resigning from the government while insisting that the Kaiser abdicate. At the same time a virtual general strike was staged as tens of thousands of workers left their jobs and milled about the streets. The unreality of the scene is completed when we recall that in his last hours as German emperor, the Kaiser had hit upon a demented scheme for throwing the army against the people in a civil war. Gröner had to tell him that 'you no longer have an army'. When the Kaiser insisted that the troops had sworn allegiance to himself as their warlord, Hindenburg shrugged and murmured, 'Oath to the colours? Warlord? Today these are only words.'

At 2:00 p.m. on 9 November, Philipp Scheidemann proclaimed a republic in Berlin on the spur of the moment, in order to take the wind out of Liebknecht's sails and to forestall the plans of Ebert. Afterwards Scheidemann nonchalantly returned to his lunch of potato soup.

Next day Ebert formed a new government. In response to popular demand, an 'opening to the left' took place as three Left-Socialists joined their erstwhile Majority Socialist colleagues. Ebert, however, fearful that any further popular turmoil would pave the way for Bolshevism in Germany, quickly concluded a working alliance with Gröner and other militarist elements. Gröner agreed to cooperate at the price he fixed and obtained: the suppression of all agitation under the blanket 'Bolshevist' label. Gröner and Ebert further agreed to get rid of the Left-Socialists from the government as soon as they could. The rest of the story is one of conservative Socialist-army cooperation to put down the German Left, an operation which was very successful.

flowers and hauled along by cheering workers. He decided to call a general strike for 11 November, but events outpaced him and the strike itself occurred spontaneously on the ninth.

Yet it was a series of naval events which actually set the quasi-revolution in motion. On 29 and 30 October a number of sailors defied their superiors and obstructed preparations for the sailing of the German battle fleet from Wilhelmshaven. The Establishment's high-handedness in dealing with the situation caused discontent to spread rapidly, and at the major port of Kiel the mutiny reached its climax. Even so, the inquiry held into the uprising showed that political aims had relatively

Above: The *Freikorps* crushed the Spartacists' Rising in a matter of days.
Above right: The Communists had a short-lived success in Bavaria, establishing a government there under Kurt Eisner. It was soon overthrown by civilian guerrillas such as these, who were ably assisted by soldiers returned from the front.

Karl Liebknecht (right), Spartacist who was exterminated when his coup failed.

Meanwhile the ultra-Left had gone into action, though not quickly enough to prevent the badly shaken middle classes from recovering their composure as they realized that actually little had changed and their interests had suffered only slight damage. On 23 December troop units refused to obey the government's orders to fire on a group of sailor-revolutionaries in Berlin, the Peoples' Naval Division. Now the Left-Socialists quit the government, but in order to prevent the recurrence of a similar spectacle of eroded governmental authority, Gustav Noske, by now the strongman of the regime, organized an auxiliary military force, the *Freikorps* (Free Corps).

At the turn of the year the KPD formally came into being. Although they had voted for the split with the USPD, Liebknecht and Rosa Luxemburg argued in vain against the Communists' plans for a boycott of the forthcoming elections for a National Assembly and for a new uprising in the capital, since the two revolutionaries believed that as yet the Party was too weak for such a stand. Sure enough, when on 6 January the Spartacist Rising began, the *Freikorps* crushed the dissidents in a matter of days, at the same time taking the opportunity to rid themselves of the Communist leaders. On the evening of 15 January a *Freikorps* private smashed in Liebknecht's head with a rifle butt, whereupon 'Spartakus' was shot 'while trying to escape'. A few moments later Rosa Luxemburg met a similar end.

The rest of the story is one of internal German politics and need not concern us. It is sufficient to note that the ill-starred turbulence of the winter of 1918–19 in Germany, as important as it may have seemed at the time and for all the hopes which Lenin placed in it, was a revolution without a future, at least for another generation.

In October 1918 the many minorities of the multi-national Habsburg empire, encouraged by the aims set forth in documents such as the Fourteen Points, took the opportunity to bid for the independence for which they yearned. Their partners in discontent were none other than the haughty Magyars, who somewhat illogically blamed Austria for Hungarian involvement in the Great War.

Despite concessions by Emperor Karl, on 30 October the Hungarian people made their revolution. The new government was headed by Count Mihály Károlyi, who in spite of his high aristocratic connections was a convinced democrat, Anglophile and Germanophobe. One of his earliest tasks was to proclaim a republic in Budapest on 16 November, four days after Austria itself had brought the ancient Habsburg dynasty to an end.

On 29 March 1919 an Allied ultimatum arrived by the hand of Lieutenant Colonel Vyx of the French Military Mission. The Allies demanded the surrender within ten days of large tracts of Hungarian territory, including the second and third largest cities in the country. Vyx implied that Magyar recalcitrance might lead to renewed hostilities on the Entente side.

The Vyx ultimatum proved to be the last straw. The Károlyi government resigned, and the Social Democrats had insufficient strength to rule alone. Now the leading Hungarian Communist, Bela

Communists demonstrate in the streets of Vienna.

Kun, stepped forward and announced that with himself in power, Russia would stand behind him and repel any Allied invasion. This was enough to ensure a Communist-Socialist coalition; as foreign affairs minister, Kun was the real power. On 21 March 1919, he formed a government officially known as the Hungarian Soviet Republic.

By now the Peace Conference was deep in its endeavours in Paris. The establishment of Soviet Hungary rocked the delegates, but in the end it was decided that General Jan Smuts of South Africa should lead a mission to Budapest, presumably to explore the situation. After this the Hungarians were faced with a combined Czech-Rumanian assault 'in the name of' the Allies; and though in fact the Allies had dubious feelings towards this venture, they felt bound to support their recently liberated protégés, and on 7 June they ordered Kun to cease retaliatory hostilities under pain of 'extreme (Allied) measures'. Less than a week later a new Allied ultimatum defined the boundaries to which it demanded that Hungary withdraw forthwith under threat of military intervention. Kun had no choice but to comply.

At home there was now mounting dissatisfaction with the Soviet regime. On 24 June a counter-coup was attempted in Budapest; and though it failed, Kun made a new mistake when on 21 July his troops attacked Rumania because of her 'aggressive . . . defiance of the will of the Entente', as he told Clemenceau ingratiatingly. This coincided with another abortive coup on 20–21 July.

Lack of supplies and poor morale among the troops ensured the failure of Hungary's thrust. As Rumania counter-attacked, Kun resigned on 1 August and went into exile. The lasting legacy of his rule was that the troubled events of 1919 were used throughout the interwar period to justify the policies of the reactionary Horthy regency which was securely established by the following year. Thus the ineffectiveness of Karolyi and the foolish excesses of Kun together killed whatever slim hope there was for Hungarian progressivism in the postwar era.

Despite the widespread material destruction which was the legacy of the Great War, and even though troubles and turmoil still raged in much of Central and Eastern Europe, the peoples of the world breathed a sigh of relief that the war was ended at last. Starvation was widespread in Germany and other parts of the Continent, including Russia. Economists calculated that the conflict had cost Europe eight full years of growth. Yet the Great War was over. Slowly the world gathered itself together, even as it mourned the millions who fell in battle and the countless others whose lives and souls were irreparably scarred by the suffering they had endured or which they had witness. Men grieved for the loss of the Hohenzollerns, the Habsburgs, the Ottomans, and even the Romanovs, while others rejoiced at the fall of these dynasties and the sweeping changes of which this turn of events was a portent.

One thing was certain: Europe would never be the same again. The bloodletting and destruction of four and a half years of war had sapped her strength and mutilated her psyche beyond imagining. At the same time a sobering thought entered many minds. If revolution, even a quasi-revolution only, could occur among the habitually disciplined and orderly Germans, where else could ferment raise its standard?

Even if the German Socialist leaders exaggerated the dangers of revolution internally, they were right in one respect: the Allies feared a German revolution to the point of obsession, especially a Communist uprising, and had one occurred they would have strangled it through occupation. Moscow's own intemperate and provocative language did nothing to assuage the general uneasiness.

Yet among the armies of the field, the guns were silent. The boys – rather, the survivors – were returning home. Parents, wives, brothers, sisters, children, relations, all rejoiced. Whatever lay ahead, surely the worst had to be over? Many leaders were not so sanguine. The fact of demobilization meant that in the democracies, any new conscriptive measures would be awkward in the extreme, indeed politically suicidal. In this way the major Allied coercive instrument began to wither soon after the Armistice itself.

Peace at a Price

As the new year dawned, not all these problems were apparent. Soon, however, most of them were to become manifest. On the stage of world politics the battles had not ceased before arguments over the nature and scope of the peace settlements began in earnest. For example, despite Colonel House's commentary on the Fourteen Points,

Bela Kun, leader of the Hungarian Soviet Republic.

the Allies continued to be chary of this idealistic and imprecise pronouncement, and they had given way only under the threat of a separate American peace with Germany. In any case the House commentary had already served to modify the original Wilsonian document. It was now explained that 'open covenants of peace, openly arrived at' was 'not meant to exclude confidential diplomatic negotiations involving delicate matters'. Regarding Italy's claims, it was now said, contrary to the settlement eventually reached, that Italian *terra irredenta* in the Trentino should be recognized, 'but that the northern part, inhabited by Germans, should be completely autonomous'. Then, in dealing with colonial claims, Wilson now agreed 'to oppose the restoration of the German colonies'. This cleared the way for the mandate system under which these territories were governed by the British and French Empires and by Japan 'in trust for' the League of Nations.

In December 1918, reinforced by his victory in the 'coupon' or 'khaki' election, Lloyd George had set to with a will to obtain British war aims. Early that month he had already agreed with Georges Clemenceau, the French prime minister, on modifications to the Sykes-Picot Agreement of 1916 on the Middle East. Under the new arrangements contemplated, the Holy Land would pass fully into British control, as would the region of Mosul in Mesopotamia. Wilson was already being tactful on the sore point of neutral maritime rights, and now Lloyd George was also successful in securing separate representation at the peace conference for the British dominions.

On 13 December President Wilson arrived in Europe. He was to receive an extraordinary welcome from the masses in several countries. In Italy for a time his portrait was even venerated in homes alongside that of the Virgin Mary. Ordinary folk everywhere hoped that the American president would use his country's material might and his own oft-professed idealism to create a better world. They were to watch in anguish as Wilson was hobbled not only by the force of circumstances, but also by his own obstinacy and the narrowmindedness of an influential group of American senators.

On 18 January 1919 the Peace Conference of Paris opened in plenary session. It was the most important gathering of statesmen since the Congress of Vienna had redrawn the map of Europe just over a century earlier. Twenty-five nations from five continents were represented, including the five main Allied and Associated belligerents: Great Britain, France, Italy, the United States, and Japan. Germany, Austria, Turkey, and the other vanquished states were absent, as was Soviet Russia, which due to its revolutionary nature was a pariah among the nations. Lloyd George advocated a seat for the Russians, and with Wilson's support he attempted to get all sides in the Russian Civil War, which was now raging, to meet and settle matters at a conference under Allied auspices. The French, however, were successful in procuring the abortion of this scheme, referred to as the Prinkipo Proposal.

For various reasons the principal task of the peace conference, the conclusion of terms of settlement with Germany, was somewhat delayed. President Wilson was preoccupied with framing the Covenant of that League of Nations, which he hoped would regulate the postwar world. In addition many of the huge contingent of experts present at the conference showed a disproportionate interest in the formerly subject nationalities of Central and Eastern Europe. Endless committee meetings were spent in hearing their problems – surely a noble and well-meant endeavour, but an imprudent ordering of priorities.

At the end of March the organizational structure of the Peace Conference was much improved, and henceforth the major problems were settled among Lloyd George, Wilson, Clemenceau, and the Italian prime minister, Orlando. These now considered the claims of France, which were chiefly two: that Alsace-Lorraine should be restored with its pre-1790 frontiers, thus including the Saar and its vast mineral resources; and the separation of the Rhineland from the rest of Germany as a buffer state and an insurance against a renewed German invasion of France. Both Wilson and Lloyd George opposed these grasping claims, which if enforced would have created a reverse Alsace-Lorraine psychosis in Germany. A compromise was reached under which the Saar valley would be administered by the League of Nations until 1935, after which its status would be determined by plebiscite (in 1935 the Saar voted by overwhelming majorities to return to Germany). During this interim period, France was to exploit the coal mines of the Saar in compensation for the wanton German destruction of the northern French coalfields. The Rhine buffer idea was shelved subject to three security provisions: an Anglo-American guarantee of immediate military assistance to France in case of unprovoked German aggression (subsequently the treaty embodying this guarantee was not ratified by the United States or Britain, to France's undying chagrin); demilitarization of the west bank of the Rhine and of a zone of fifty kilometres on the east bank; and Allied occupation of the west bank and bridgeheads in zones which would be evacuated in five to fifteen years, or earlier if Germany had met all her treaty obligations. Nevertheless her erstwhile partners never fully appreciated the justifiable apprehensions underlying France's obsession with the need for protection against her more fecund and more economically powerful German neighbour, though the question of French security was to dominate – or rather, haunt – the thinking of Paris throughout the interwar period.

Having been approved in plenary session of the peace conference on 6 May, the following day the draft of the Treaty of Versailles was handed to Count Brockdorff-Rantzau, the German foreign minister. Originally the Allied and Associated Powers had intended the Paris Peace Conference to be a preliminary to a general congress which would include the defeated states. But this idea was shunted aside. Now the Germans were merely asked to present their observations upon the proffered terms.

Germany's most telling argument was that the terms were very severe indeed and in several places contradicted the Fourteen Points. By now

Wilson's arrival in Europe turned into a triumphal procession. Here Wilson and President Poincaré greet the crowd in Paris.

Clemenceau, 'The Tiger', with the soldiers whose victory he hoped to safeguard at the Paris Peace Conference.

Lloyd George discusses terms with Balfour.

Lloyd George arrives at Paris and is greeted by General Wilson and Marshal Foch.

various factors, not least among them the British sense of fair play, had caused the Cabinet to agree with Lloyd George that certain concessions ought to be obtained for Germany. However, these were partly foiled by Clemenceau and, more surprisingly, by Wilson, who maintained exasperatedly that for the British to prevaricate at this stage 'makes me very sick'. Even so, Lloyd George succeeded in obtaining a more just definition of the German-Polish border, as well as the promise of a plebiscite to settle the Upper Silesian dispute. In the matter of reparations, the British Prime Minister was hamstrung by his election promise that Germany would be made to 'pay to the uttermost farthing, and we shall search their pockets for it'. However, he hoped that as emotions died away with time a more reasonable attitude might prevail. Lloyd George and especially Churchill feared that to punish Germany excessively would throw her into the open arms of Russia – the so-called Rapallo complex.

Opposite top: Starvation was widespread throughout Germany in the cruel winter of 1918–19. The continuing Allied blockade of Germany did not make life any easier. **Opposite bottom:** German families suffered disillusionment as well as defeat.

On 16 June Germany was given until the twenty-first (later altered to the twenty-third) to accept the revised version of the Versailles Treaty, failing which an Allied advance into Germany would begin. Under this coercion, on 22 June the German National Assembly at Weimar voted by 237 to 138 in favour of acceptance. Thus Germany, as her communication to the Allies phrased it, agreed 'to sign, under compulsion, a dishonourable peace . . .'.

Versailles: The Lost Peace

The Treaty of Versailles was signed on 28 June 1919, exactly five years after the Sarajevo assassinations, in the *Galerie des Glaces* (Hall of Mirrors) of the Palais de Versailles, where the German Empire had been inaugurated in 1871 in the heady aftermath of Prussia's victory over France. In the middle of the Galerie, the plenipotentiary delegates were gathered round a horseshoe table, in front of which – 'like a guillotine', as Harold Nicolson wrote in his dairy – was the table for the signatures. In addition, the Hall of Mirrors was filled with over a thousand seats for members of delegations and other distinguished guests.

As Wilson and Lloyd George slipped into their seats, Clemenceau glanced to right and left, then signalled for silence. Over an awed hush, the French Prime Minister commanded, '*Faites entrer les Allemands*' (Bring in the Germans).

Through a door at the end of the vast hall emerged the German delegates, Müller and Bell. Their faces were ashen with emotion. After the Germans were seated and Clemenceau had declared the session open, Müller and Bell quickly rose to their feet, anxious to sign and complete the ordeal, only to be motioned to sit down again. After further preliminaries the two Germans at last were led to a small table where, at 12:03 p.m. precisely, they put their signatures to the treaty. As other delegates formed a queue to approach the table and sign, a thunderous salute boomed forth outside, and in the distance the cheering of the Parisian crowd could be heard.

In a surprisingly short period the signing was completed. '*La séance est levée,*' said Clemenceau. According to Nicolson, Müller and Bell were 'conducted like prisoners from the dock, their eyes still fixed upon some distant point of the horizon'. The ceremony was over, the delegates had dispersed. But the story of Versailles had hardly begun. The Treaty of Versailles, 200 pages in length, comprised 440 articles. Its main provisions are summarized below:

Germany was required to surrender Alsace-Lorraine, its borders limited to those in existence in 1870, to France; most of West Prussia and Posen (Poznań) and much of East Silesia and East Prussia to Poland; and part of Upper Silesia (Teschen) to Czechoslovakia. In addition she was to yield Moresnet, Eupen and Malmédy to Belgium and Memel (Klaipeda) to Lithuania. As a result of a plebiscite held in Schleswig, the northern region returned to Denmark and the southern region remained with Germany. On the Baltic Sea, the German city of Danzig was to be created a free city under the League of Nations; although France had wanted Poland to annex Danzig outright, she managed to have the city wrested forcibly from the Reich. Germany was to lose all her colonies, and the Reich 'acknowledges and will respect strictly the independence of Austria', as Article 80 of the treaty forbade a German-Austrian union (*Anschluss*). Plebiscites were to be held to determine the fate of Upper Silesia, as well as Allenstein (Olsztyn) and Marienwerder (Kwidzýn) in East Prussia. (As a result, almost all of the latter two territories remained with Germany, but in the final settlement the smaller and richer part of Upper Silesia passed to Poland.) These changes caused Germany to lose about 13·5 per cent of its territory and economic potential, and about 10 per cent of its population.

The Versailles Treaty contained many other provisions. Germany was forbidden to fortify a large section of the Rhine. The Allied occupation of the Rhineland was to proceed as described earlier. The German army was to consist of not more than 100,000 officers and men, the navy of not more than 15,000. There was to be no German air force. The General Staff as such was abolished, and no staff college was to be maintained. Conscription was forbidden.

The most controversial part of the treaty concerned Article 231, the so-called war guilt clause. This stated that:

The Allied and Associated Governments affirm and Germany accepts the responsibility of Germany and her allies for causing all the loss and damage to which the Allied and Associated Governments and their nationals have been subjected as a consequence of the war imposed on them by the aggression of Germany and her allies.

As we saw in the first chapter, Germany alone could hardly be held uniquely responsible for the war. Nevertheless, as a result of this clause, Germany was to pay 20,000 million gold marks (£1,000 million) in instalments by 1 May 1921 as reparations, subject to a final assessment by a specially established Reparations Commission which at first set a total bill of £6,600 million (33 billion dollars), an impractical sum which was later substantially reduced and then abandoned altogether in 1932. In addition to numerous other levies, Germany was to pay for the armies occupying the Rhineland.

Article 227 of the treaty castigated the former German Emperor 'for a supreme offence against international morality and the sanctity of treaties'. A tribunal was to try the Kaiser for his alleged crimes, but this idea was thwarted since the neutral Dutch declined to revoke the asylum which Wilhelm II had sought in their land.

Such was the Treaty of Versailles, a treaty which satisfied few men except the rulers of the succession states of Central-East Europe. Otherwise the settlement was too harsh for the British government, but too soft for the French. Versailles was not Utopian enough for Wilson, yet too Utopian for some cynics. The Germans rejected the entire concept of a *diktat* (dictated peace), which underlay the peace conference.

As Lloyd George well knew, Versailles was also at least partly counter-productive. A portion of German reparations would have to be paid for by exports which would compete with British trade.

The settlement also contained many other flaws. On the other hand, had the positions been reversed and had the Germans emerged as victors, in view of her far-reaching war aims and the settlement of 1918 at Brest-Litovsk, Germany might have imposed an even harsher peace.

Though Versailles was the main treaty of peace, several other settlements remained to be concluded. These were the Treaties of St Germain-en-Laye with Austria, signed on 10 September 1919; of Neuilly with Bulgaria (signed 27 November); of Trianon with Hungary (4 June 1920); and of Sèvres (10 August 1920), and subsequently of Lausanne with Turkey. The first three of these were essentially concerned with the winding up of the Habsburgs' affairs and the tidying of the borders of southeastern Europe.

Under the terms of the Treaty of St Germain, the ex-Emperor Karl was not arraigned as a war criminal. However, Austria was reduced from a sprawling multinational empire to a rump state in which nearly a third of its six and a half million citizens lived in Vienna, a splendid but now obsolete imperial capital. Austria also had to pay reparations and demobilize her troops. The new state suffered the amputation of the South Tyrol (Alto Adige) in favour of Italy; and Austria received the Burgenland from Hungary and retained Klagenfurt by plebiscite in 1920.

The eastern treaties greatly favoured the cause of national self-determination, and even more than at Versailles, this principle was carried out at the expense of the former ruling states. The Treaty of Trianon reduced the Hungarian Crown Lands of St Stephen (István) to a tiny land-locked state, very approximately coincidental with the ethnic Magyar homeland, but leaving a huge Hungarian minority in the now-Rumanian region of Transylvania. In addition, Hungary had to sacrifice Croatia, Slavonia, and the Voivodina to the new Yugoslav state which formed around a core of Serbia and then Montenegro. Austria was similarly required to yield Bosnia and Herzegovina to the Kingdom of the Serbs, Croats, and Slovenes, as Yugoslavia was known at first.

In the north Slovakia was taken from Hungary to join the ex-Austrian lands of Bohemia and Moravia, which together with Sub-Carpathian Ukraine (Ruthenia) formed the new republic of Czechoslovakia. In many ways, Czechoslovakia in the period between the world wars proved to be the most democratic state east of the Rhine; but from its birth it was bedeviled by huge minorities, the foremost of which was a Sudeten German population of over three million, as well as smaller but substantial numbers of Magyars, Poles and others. Thus, from the start Czechoslovakia was burdened with a certain artificiality best summed up in Rohan Butler's description of the state as 'an ominous miniature of the defunct Habsburg monarchy'.

Rumania, once only the ancient lands of Wallachia and Moldavia, now reaped the harvest of her adherence to the Allied cause. In addition, to Transylvania, Bucharest added to her territory part of the Banat (the rest went to Yugoslavia), the Bukovina, and ex-Russian Bessarabia.

At Neuilly, Bulgaria paid the penalty of defeat in her failure to regain the Dobrudja and in her loss to Greece of the Thracian 'window on the Aegean'. Sofia was also required to make minor cessions to Yugoslavia.

In the case of Poland, besides her enormous gains from Germany and Austria, including a corridor to the Baltic Sea which separated East Prussia from the rest of the Reich, by 1920–21 she had incorporated Eastern Galicia, Vilna, and other lands into a state grossly inflated beyond the boundaries of ethnic Poland. Poland's inordinate ambition was encouraged by Allied fears that otherwise the Poles could not be persuaded to stand as an eastern bulwark against Bolshevism. The victors were also influenced by Polish propaganda concerning their country's historical role of 'bastion against Asia', in this case meaning Russia. Moreover the French, with their traditional ties with Poland and their wish to see the new states of Eastern Europe linked to Paris in a *cordon sanitaire* between Germany and Russia, repeatedly advocated a Poland which was 'large and strong, very strong' (grande et forte, très forte).

Despite numerous injustices, however, national self-determination was applied to a considerable extent in the postwar settlements. The proof of this is that the borders of 1919 were left substantially unchanged after the Second World War. The fact was that however the borders of Central and Eastern Europe might be drawn, the tangle of nationalities cheek-by-jowl was such that a just yet viable settlement would have been impossible in many cases. In certain instances, as with the Magyars of Transylvania or the Sudeten Germans, massive transfers of population with appropriate compensation might have been a solution. (In 1945 the Germans of Czechoslovakia were simply expelled; in time history sanctifies the most iniquitous acts.) As it was, large minorities were left dotted about the eastern half of Europe; and though these peoples were supposed to be protected by the succession states' statutory obligations to the League, in practice the minority treaties proved of little value.

The settlement outside Europe was in many cases even more unjust. Nationalist voices such as

Prince Feisal, who led the Arabian Commission to the Peace Conference. T. E. Lawrence, one of his advisers, is on the right. Their demands for Arab independence were ignored.

Ho Chi Minh, who pleaded for the independence of Vietnam from the French, went unheeded. For Britain and France, the colonial powers *par excellence*, self-determination was largely disregarded wherever it conflicted with their own ambitions. Yet in Eastern Europe and elsewhere the peacemakers were frequently confronted with accomplished facts. For instance, prior to the break-up of the Habsburg Empire, the Czechs and South Slavs had declared their independence; it would have been difficult indeed to dislodge these nations from territories which they claimed as their homelands. Moreover, the harsh and punitive nature of the various armistices created irreversible situations to which the peacemakers could only nod approval.

The greatest criticism which can be levelled at the several peace treaties is that ethnic self-determination was applied selectively and as if it were a panacea of itself. The result was that states such as Austria were separated from their natural markets. Indeed, the prosperity of Danubian Europe as a whole was endangered by chauvinist restrictions on trade and movement of goods. Perhaps most ominously of all, in spite of its losses Germany was left as the one large and powerful state between a psychologically exhausted France and an outcast Russia. The Reich was bordered on the south and east by a patchwork of small and economically unsound units. The situation was one which German dynamism was bound to exploit sooner or later, given the factors of Britain's desire to play the balancing role in continental disputes, and to avoid commitments in Eastern Europe in particular; America's aloofness; France's prostration; and Italy's revanchist bitterness at the paucity of her wartime gains. Soon British and French differences of interpretation over the postwar settlements came to the fore, the latter nation insisting time and again on the juridical rigidity of the treaties in situations which the British would have preferred to handle flexibly. As for Italy, the Fiume question, where both Italy and Yugoslavia claimed a chiefly Italian-speaking region the festering sore which had caused Orlando to walk out of the

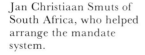

Jan Christiaan Smuts of South Africa, who helped arrange the mandate system.

Paris Peace Conference in April 1919, remained unsettled until the Fascists under d'Annunzio acquired much of the region a few years later, when Italy had already given up her claims to Dalmatia as a whole.

In Africa, meanwhile, the Italians were fobbed off with Jubaland, which the British ceded in 1924, and an arid concession from the French on the borders of Libya. In the Far East, despite the cession of former German territory which she seized in 1914, Japan was enraged that her request for affirmation of the principle of racial equality had been denied. In succeeding years the defeated powers were able to exploit these dissensions among the former Allies to great advantage.

Yet the most severe of all the peace treaties was that concluded with Turkey at Sèvres, but not implemented. Turkey was required to yield all her Arab territories and her suzerainty over both Egypt and Cyprus. In addition, she was to cede Thrace, Crete, and most of the Aegean Islands to Greece, as well as the Dodecanese Islands and Kastellorizo to Italy. A special Greek-controlled regime was to be created at Smyrna (now Izmir), which after five years might apply for incorporation into Greece itself. However, the nationalist Turks under Mustapha Kemal (later known as Ataturk) refused to accept the settlement and drove the Greeks from Smyrna. Furthermore, the French concluded a new and separate treaty with Turkey, the Franklin-Bouillon Agreement. Finally a relatively mild settlement was reached at Lausanne on 24 July 1923, whereby Turkey regained sovereignty over part of eastern Thrace, Smyrna, Kurdistan, and Turkish Armenia. The Allies had long since been saved from embarrassment over their wartime promise of Constantinople to Russia by the fact that in 1917 the Bolsheviks had denounced secret treaties and renounced territorial gains as the result of war (the territorial expansion of the Soviet Union after the Second World War gives this pronouncement a hollow ring). In 1924 the Entente finally returned the Zone of the Straits to Turkish control, but it was agreed in a separate Lausanne Straits Convention that demilitarized zones would be created around the Bosporus and the Dardanelles and in an area in Thrace bordering on Greece and Bulgaria.

The League of Nations

Meanwhile, on 19 March 1920, the most signal defeat for the Wilsonian concept of the postwar world had taken place. That day the American Senate failed to ratify the Versailles Treaty because of the isolationist opposition of Senator Henry Cabot Lodge and his coterie to the League of Nations Covenant, which was incorporated as Part I of each of the treaties of peace. Thus the League began its existence without America – indeed, the United States never joined, though the other notable absentees, Germany and Russia, were admitted several years later.

A product of the idealism of Wilson, Smuts, and others, the League was intended as a world organization to secure and maintain permanent peace and justice. In the international anarchy of sovereign states, these hopes were at best extremely optimistic and at worst wildly impractical.

The basic document of the League was its Covenant. This provided for the reduction and control of armaments and of their private manufacture (sometimes referred to as the 'merchants of death' complex) and for the registration with and publication of all future treaties by the League Secretariat. Other articles dealt with the League's duty of supervision over the mandated ex-German or ex-Turkish colonies. Although in practice this turned out to be a largely hypothetical governance, the League mandate system was a compromise which Smuts of South Africa had arranged in order that the British dominions and Japan in particular might consent to the Covenant.

The main organs of the League included the Assembly of all its members, each with one vote, and the Council, initially to be composed of five permanent representatives of the great powers (Britain, France, Italy, Japan; and the United States, if it had joined) and four representatives of the smaller powers, these seats to be elected by the Assembly on a short-term basis.

The League was also to have a Secretariat; and one of the Council's tasks was to be provision for a Permanent Court of International Justice which might act as a recommending body in the referral of international disputes.

As part of their drive for security, the French had strongly urged that the League be given extensive and permanent powers of law enforcement, with a general staff to direct the settlement of such issues as might arise. However, Wilson realized that the result would appear to Americans as a supranational permanent military alliance, an idea which was a generation too early for the people of the United States to accept.

Members of the League were required to pledge themselves to renounce war with a fellow member state. If disputes arose which were insoluble by routine methods, League members would submit them for investigation and recommendation, or alternatively for arbitration, by the Council of the League.

The most important part of the Covenant dealt with collective security. Article 10 stated:

'The Members of the League undertake to respect and preserve as against external aggression the territorial integrity and existing political independence of all Members of the League. In case of any such aggression or *in case of any threat or danger of such aggression* the Council shall advise upon the means by which this obligation shall be fulfilled.'

The notion of collective action was reiterated in the succeeding article:

'Any war *or threat of war, whether immediately affecting any of the Members of the League or not,* is hereby declared a matter of concern to the *whole* League . . .' (author's italics)

The League came into operation on 16 January 1920, when the necessary number of states had ratified the Treaty of Versailles. It proved a poor creature which, despite the hopes which so many had placed in it, was unable to prevent the slide into war in succeeding years.

As a final note on the problems of the postwar order, one might cite two particular bones of contention among the Allies themselves. The first was the question of war debts, especially the vast sums owed to the United States. The attitude of the European victors was that until the spring of 1918, they had paid for the war – for America's war as well, as they thought – in lives, while the United States had paid only in dollars. The American position was immortalized by President Calvin Coolidge, who rasped, 'They hired the money, didn't they?' Few European countries paid their war debts even when reduced considerably by the United States, which resulted in American bitterness toward their former Allies which was to prove costly to them in 1939–40. The second was the issue of Anglo-French rivalry in the Middle East and beyond, and the general bittersweet nature of the London–Paris partnership of convenience. If the more innocent among the masses thought that peace might bring an end at least to their major headaches, the immediate future, and above all the succeeding two decades, were to show the utter hopelessness of this assumption.

The Great War was the most destructive conflict which the world had yet seen. Its toll of lives was so vast as to defy imagination. Civilian deaths, apart from the influenza pandemic, amounted to at least 9,000,000, though some writers have set the figure at more than 12.6 million. Military loss of life is calculated at over 8,000,000, broken down as follows:

Germany	1,770,000 to 2,000,000
Russia	1,700,000
France	1,360,000
Austria-Hungary	1,100,000 to 1,200,000
Great Britain	760,000*
Italy	460,000 to 650,000
Turkey	325,000 to 375,000
British Empire	250,000*
United States	110,000 to 126,000

* Total 1,010,000.

If we include figures for wounded, prisoners and missing, total military casualties were about 37,500,000 – over 22,000,000 for the Allies, over 15,000,000 for the Central Powers.

It has been estimated that the total economic cost of the war was £75,077,000,000 (over $375 billion), of which the Allied governments spent £7,852,000,000 and the Central Powers £13,476,000. The price paid in physical devastation was greatest on French territory: 1,875 square miles of forest destroyed, along with 8,000 square miles of agricultural land and about a quarter of a million buildings.

These are cold statistics, and the reader may not sense from them the disillusionment that percolated downwards as ordinary people realized slowly the horrendous price which they had paid for a reordering of the world's affairs which was proving unsatisfactory at best. Plenty of men and organizations were waiting on the sidelines to harness and exploit this sentiment. The heirs to this fathomless disappointment, this harvest of broken dreams, were Fascism and Communism; pacifism and nihilism; anarchism, fatalism, escapism or sheer apathy. No one can understand how the world drifted into World War II almost in spite of itself without remembering the dejected legacy of World War I.

The Legacy of World War I

I have given orders to my Death Units to exterminate without mercy or pity men, women and children belonging to the Polish-speaking race. It is only in this manner that we can acquire the vital territory which we need. After all, who remembers today the extermination of the Armenians?

Adolf Hitler, 22 August 1939

Index

254

255

Acknowledgements

The introduction to this book first appeared as an original article in Purnell's *History of the First World War*, © 1969 BPC Publishing Limited.

The publishers would like to thank John Batchelor for the armament illustrations, and are also grateful to the following individuals and organizations for their kind permission to reproduce the pictures which appear on the pages shown:

Bapty: page 20, 44 (top left), 97, 116 (top left), 124 (top right), 141 (top), 149 (bottom), 244 (top).
Bundesarchiv: page 183 (top), 235 (top centre), 236, 242 (top right).
Hultons/Radio Times Picture Library: page 178 (bottom).
Robert Hunt Picture Library: page 14 (top left, top centre, top right, bottom), 15 (left, right), 16, 17, 18 (left, right), 19 (bottom), 21 (top, bottom), 22/3, 24/5, 26, 27, 28, 29, 30, 32 (top, left, right), 33, 34 (bottom right), 35 (top right, bottom left, right), 36 (top, bottom), 37, 39 (bottom right), 40 (top, bottom), 41, 44 (top right), 44/5, 46/7 (top), 46 (bottom), 48 (top, bottom), 49 (top, bottom), 50/1, 52 (bottom), 54/5, 54 (bottom),

55 (bottom), 56, 62/3 (top centre, bottom), 65 (top left, right, bottom left, right), 66 (bottom), 68 (top, bottom), 69 (top, bottom), 70, 72/3, 74/5, 79 (bottom), 80 (left, centre, right), 81, 82/3, 84/5, 84 (bottom), 85 (bottom), 91 (top right), 92 (top, bottom), 93, 96, 98 (bottom), 99 (top, bottom), 100, 101, 103, 104/5, 106 (top), 106/7 (top, bottom), 107 (top, bottom), 108, 109 (top right, bottom), 110/11, 112, 113 (top, bottom), 115 (bottom), 116 (bottom left), 117 (top right, bottom), 118 (top), 118/9, 122/3 (top, bottom), 124 (top left), 124/5, 125 (top), 126 (top right), 128 (top left, right, bottom), 129, 132 (bottom), 133 (top), 135, 136, 137 (top, bottom), 140, 143 (top, bottom), 144

(top, bottom), 145 (top, bottom), 146 (top left), 153 (top), 154, 156 (top), 157 (top left, right, bottom), 158/9 (top), 161, 165 (top, bottom right), 166 (top, bottom), 167 (top left, right), 168/9, 169, 172 (top, bottom left), 173, 174, 175, 176, 177 (top left, bottom), 178 (top left, right), 179, 180 (top, bottom), 181 (top), 182 (top), 184/5 (top), 184 (bottom), 187 (top, bottom left, centre), 192 (top, bottom), 193 (top, bottom left, right), 194 (top left), 194/5 (bottom), 195 (top right), 196 (top, bottom), 197 (top, bottom), 200 (bottom), 201 (top left, right, bottom), 203 (top left, bottom left), 204 (top, centre), 205 (top, bottom), 206/7, 207, 208 (top left, right), 210/11, 211, 213 (top, bottom), 216/17, 225 (top), 228 (bottom), 232 (bottom), 235 (top left, bottom), 237, 240 (top, bottom), 242 (top left), 243 (top), 244 (bottom), 245 (top), 247, 248 (bottom).
Imperial War Museum: page 4/5, 19 (top), 34/5 (top), 34 (bottom right), 35 (top left, centre right), 38/9, 38 (bottom), 39 (centre, bottom left), 47 (bottom), 57 (left, right), 58/9, 60, 61, 62 (top left), 63 (top centre, right), 66 (top), 76, 77, 78 (top, bottom), 79 (top), 80 (bottom right), 86/7 (top, bottom), 88/9 (top), 88 (centre left, right), 89 (top, bottom), 90/1, 91 (left, bottom), 94/5, 98 (top), 102 (top), 109 (top left), 114, 115 (top), 117

(top left), 120/121, 126 (top left, centre), 126/127, 127 (top left, right), 130/131, 132 (top, centre), 133 (bottom), 134, 139 (top, bottom), 141 (bottom), 142, 146 (top right), 146/7, 147, 148 (top, bottom), 149 (top, bottom right), 150, 150/1, 151 (top, centre, bottom), 152, 153 (bottom), 155 (top, centre, bottom), 156 (bottom), 158/9 (top), 159, 160 (top, bottom), 162/3, 163, 164/5, 165 (bottom left, middle), 170/1, 172 (bottom right), 177 (top right), 181 (bottom), 182/3, 184/5 (bottom), 186, 187 (bottom right), 188, 189 (top, centre, bottom), 190 (top left, right), 191 (top left, right, bottom), 194 (top right), 195 (top left), 198, 199 (top, bottom), 200/1, 202 (top centre, bottom), 203 (bottom right), 204 (bottom), 208 (bottom), 209, 212, 214, 218/9, 220, 222 (top, bottom), 223, 224 (top, bottom), 225 (bottom), 226, 226/7, 227 (top right), 228 (top left, right), 229 (top left, right, bottom), 230/1, 231, 232, 232/3 (top, bottom), 234 (top left, right), 235 (top right), 241 (top, bottom), 243 (bottom), 245 (bottom centre), 248 (top), Cover.
Paul Popper: page 67, 102 (bottom), 242 (bottom).
Search: page 6
U.S. Army: page 252/3
U.S. National Archives: page 202 (top left), 202/3, 206 (top, bottom), 214/5, 227 (top left), 238, 245 (top), 250.